Investing in Commercial Mortgage-Backed Securities

Frank J. Fabozzi, Ph.D., CFA
Editor

Published by Frank J. Fabozzi Associates

© 2001 By Frank J. Fabozzi Associates
New Hope, Pennsylvania

This publication is designed to provide accurate and authoritative information in regard to the subject matter covered. It is sold with the understanding that the publisher is not engaged in rendering legal, accounting, or other professional services.

ISBN: 1-883249-88-0

Printed in the United States of America

Table of Contents

Contributing Authors

Steve Banerjee	Prudential Securities Inc.
Steven Berkley	Lehman Brothers Inc.
Patrick Corcoran	J.P. Morgan Securities Inc.
Ed Daingerfield	Nomura Securities International, Inc.
Mark Feldman	Bear Stearns & Co.
Lang Gibson	First Union Securities, Inc.
Alex Golbin	Lehman Brothers Inc.
Rich Gordon	First Union Securities, Inc.
C.H. Ted Hong	Beyondbond, Inc.
David P. Jacob	Nomura Securities International, Inc.
Brian P. Lancaster	Bear Stearns & Co. Inc.
Philip O. Obazee	First Union Securities, Inc.
Jignesh Patel	Beyondbond, Inc.
Lisa Pendergast	Prudential Securities Inc.
Joshua Phillips	Nomura Securities International, Inc.
Anthony B. Sanders	The Ohio State University
V.S. Srinivasan	Bear Stearns & Co.
Weisi Tan	Prudential Securities Inc.
Dale Westhoff	Bear Stearns & Co.
Michael Youngblood	Banc of America Securities LLC

Chapter 1

Introduction to Commercial Mortgage-Backed Securities

Brian P. Lancaster
Managing Director
Bear Stearns & Co. Inc.

W hile CMBS existed as early as the late 1980s and 1990 mostly in the form of private placements, it was the Resolution Trust Corporation (RTC) that in 1991 and 1992 jumpstarted the market from a sleepy backwater to a respectable bond sector. Commercial mortgage-backed securities (CMBS) are securitizations of mortgage loans backed by commercial real estate. Investors were interested in the new sector's generous spreads and prepayment protection while issuers were looking for new financing outlets. But it was really the RTC that created models or templates for future transactions. It was the volume of RTC issuance and the attractive pricing of their deals that increased investor awareness, stimulated demand and provided pricing benchmarks. However, as RTC issuance faded in the ensuing years, the market continued to grow as Wall Street conduits, led by the now defunct Capital Company of America, stepped in to fill the void left by traditional bank and portfolio lenders.

By 1998, annual issuance had grown by 37% per year to hit $80 billion. Currently about $300 billion of CMBS are outstanding (see Exhibit 1) or about 25% of U.S. commercial real estate debt. The U.S. CMBS market is almost the same size as the non-agency market and about 40% of the size of the ABS market (see Exhibit 1). However, 1998 was far more than an issuance watershed. In late August 1998, a default in Russia triggered a bond market panic that stifled trading in nearly all U.S. bond sectors. With fewer and more leveraged investors than other sectors, the CMBS market was hit harder than most. Liquidity almost completely dried up and one of the few key leveraged investors in the critical subordinate sector, CRIIMI Mae, filed for bankruptcy protection.

Which leaves us where we are today — a market in transition. The dislocations of 1998 shook out a number of weaker leveraged players, sobered up all participants to the risks of the sector and created opportunity for newer ones. While trading and spreads in higher rated tranches, such as triple-As, have tightened, they still remain about 40% greater than their average spread in the previous year. In the lower rated sectors, such as double-Bs, spreads still remain close

1

to their historic wides although new funds are being set up each month to invest in the sector. With real estate prices in most areas still appreciating and spreads still wide, opportunities abound for the savvy investor. This chapter is designed to provide an introduction to the opportunities in the triple-A CMBS sector. The appendix to this chapter provides summaries of the various rating agencies' approach to the CMBS rating process.

WHAT ARE COMMERCIAL MORTGAGE-BACKED SECURITIES?

Commercial mortgage-backed securities are securitizations of mortgage loans backed by commercial real estate. These securities are typically structured as sequential-pay bonds and receive credit ratings from AAA through the lower credit grades (AA through B-/CCC/Not Rated). Sequential pay simply means that after each tranche is paid off, starting with the highest rated tranche, the next lower rated tranche begins to receive principal and so forth in sequential order until all tranches in the deal are paid off (see Exhibit 2). Unlike the sequential-pay structure in the residential mortgage security market, CMBS sequential-pay structures often have only a 5-year and a 10-year tranche due to the maturities of the underlying loans. Due to the need to protect outstanding higher rated tranches, most subordinate tranches have average lives of 10 years or greater.

Exhibit 1: CMBS versus Other Securitized Markets

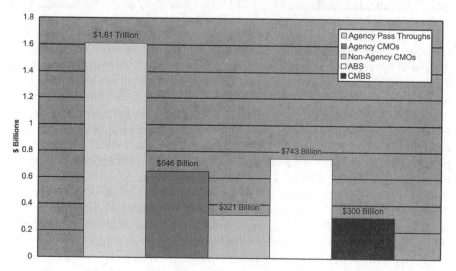

Source: Bear Stearns, *Inside MBS & ABS*

Exhibit 2: CMBS Paydown and Loan Schedule

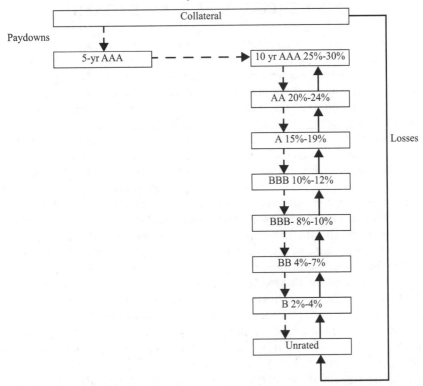

At issuance, about 70% to 75% of the deal's securities typically receive a AAA rating. AAA rated securities represent the bondholders' first claim on receipt of principal and interest from the underlying collateral. The remaining 25% to 30% of the deal consists of lower rated subordinate tranches which credit enhance higher rated tranches. In contrast, residential mortgage security subordination levels range between 4% and 5%. Thus if a loss occurs on the underlying collateral, the lowest rated or unrated tranche's principal is "hit" or reduced by the amount of the loss. If the loss is greater than the unrated tranche then the next higher rated tranche's principal is reduced and so forth (see Exhibit 2).

A common misconception in the market is that AAA tranches of CMBS deals with higher percentages of subordination are "better." On the contrary, at issuance higher subordination levels are a sign of lower credit quality collateral since the rating agencies require greater subordination to make up for any deficiencies in the collateral. This as we shall see has negative implications for the stability of the cash flows.

THE CHARACTERISTICS OF
COMMERCIAL REAL ESTATE LOANS

The loans that serve as CMBS collateral commonly are secured by commercial real estate such as apartment buildings, shopping or strip malls, warehouse facilities, etc. Unlike most residential mortgage loans, these loans often do not provide recourse to the borrower[1] nor any form of guarantee. Lenders and investors look to the collateral, not the borrower, for ultimate repayment. Thus analysis of the cash flows generated by the underlying properties as well as their value is critical. Residential mortgage securities also typically consist of thousands of small loans versus hundreds for commercial mortgage securities.[2] The larger number of loans allows for greater diversification. Also, unlike most residential loans, commercial mortgage loans typically have excellent call protection and average life stability. Commercial mortgage loans may or may not amortize but most do, typically over a 20- to 30-year period.[3] However, they usually balloon after 10 or 15 years and must be paid in full. Amortization of principal helps to reduce risk as it reduces the loan to value ratio of the property over time and increases the borrower's equity in the property assuming stable or increased property values.

Because of the balloon feature of most commercial loans as well as the lack of borrower recourse, refinancing of the loan at the balloon date is critical. A rise in interest rates, which significantly increases the debt servicing requirements of a floating-rate loan or the refinancing requirements for a fixed-rate balloon loan, could significantly alter its economics increasing the risk of default. More commonly, terms may be renegotiated between the lender, here represented by the special servicer,[4] and the borrower, which could result in an extension of the loan term and the average life of the commercial mortgage security.

Of course the loan could also be paid down at or before the balloon date whereby the deal would "deleverage" (i.e., the ratio of the subordinates to the senior tranches could increase). This can result in an upgrade of some of the remaining tranches in the deal. Declining interest rate and rising commercial property price environments, such as those experienced between 1990 and 1999, can result in the deleveraging and upgrading of CMBS deals. Falling property prices and rising rates may have the opposite effect.

---

[1] Lack of borrower recourse is common in the U.S. but not in other countries, such as Japan where borrower recourse is typical. Commercial loans are sometimes cross collateralized to mitigate the risk of borrower default. Cross collateralization means that if a borrower defaults on one property it is effectively treated as a default on all properties.

[2] Residential mortgage loan sizes often range from $100,000 to $400,000 per loan whereas commercial mortgage loans are usually ten times as large or greater.

[3] Agency commercial loans may amortize over a 40-year period but this is atypical. A number of commercial loans also have only an interest only period followed by a balloon date but these are less common.

[4] The master servicer typically handles routine administrative tasks while the special servicer usually handles workouts and delinquencies. Special servicers often invest in the lower rated tranches of CMBS so their interests are typically aligned with those of the investor.

ANALYZING AND VALUING CMBS: WHAT TO LOOK FOR

Given the relative youth of the CMBS market, newer investors approach the market with a variety of different perspectives and backgrounds. Some are "bond people" with backgrounds in corporate bonds or residential MBS; others are "real estate people." The following section provides a basic framework which investors with either background may use when analyzing CMBS transactions. All deals require some subjective assessment, but using the following methodology should be an effective approach to compare and contrast various CMBS transactions and to make relative value decisions regarding specific bonds.

Credit Indicators: DSCR and LTV

Two of the most important indicators of the credit quality of the collateral backing a CMBS deal are the debt service coverage ratio (DSCR) and the loan to value ratio (LTV). The primary indicator of the credit quality (default and loss risk) of a commercial mortgage is the loan's debt service coverage ratio (DSCR). The DSCR is considered most important because it is more precise than LTV. The DSCR is based on current debt service and current net operating income. The LTV is viewed as less reliable as the value of the property will change significantly depending on the capitalization rate assumed (the discounting term for the cash flows generated by the property).

The debt service coverage ratio which equals "net operating income" divided by "mortgage payment" quantifies how much cash flow a property is generating versus required loan payments. As the DSCR rises, default risk declines. Investors look at the DSCR to assess how much of a downturn a borrower can withstand and still be able to make loan payments.

It is important to consider not only the weighted average DSCR but also the dispersion or range of DSCRs for the loans in a pool. Thus investors should ask what is the weighted average DSCR as well as the range of DSCRs for a deal. Acceptable levels of DSCRs vary depending on the property type, loan type, rating level and credit enhancement features. However, most conduit transactions' weighted average DSCRs fall in the range of 1.35 and 1.45. The percent of loans in a deal with DSCRs below 1.25× should raise a red flag since these are loans with greater default risk. If the percent is under "10%" this would generally be considered acceptable. Under 5% would be "good." (Exhibit 3 summarizes a number of quality indicators for CMBS deals.) It is important for the AAA holder to consider the DSCRs as defaults will likely translate into prepayments at par.[5] A triple-A rating addresses timely payment of interest and ultimate repayment of principal. It does not address the issue of prepayments due to liquidations.

---

[5] Legally borrowers are supposed to pay yield maintenance and/or other prepayment penalties on default, however there is rarely sufficient cash left over to do so.

Exhibit 3: A Quick Guide to CMBS Quality

Average DSCR		Good	Fair	Poor	
		1.45	1.45-1.35	1.35	

% of Deal with DSCRs below 1.25		Good	Fair	Poor	
		Under 5%	10%	>10%	

Average LTV	Very Good	Good	Fair	Poor
	<65%	65%	75%	>75%

% of Deal with LTVs >75%	Excellent	Very Good	Good	Fair
	<5%	6%-10%	11%-15%	>16%-20%

Prepayment Protections	Excellent	Very Good	Good	Fair
	Treasury Defeasance - Lock-out	Yield Maintenance	Prepayment Penalty Points	

Geographic Concentration	Acceptable	High
	<40% in one State	40% or greater in one State

Property Type Concentration	Acceptable	High
	<40% in one Property Type	40% or greater in one Property Type

This exhibit is designed to serve as a rough guide to quality in the CMBS market. There are of course, exceptions to these basic indicators. As such each deal should be analyzed on its own merits.

The loan to value ratio (LTV) is used in conjunction with the DSCR to determine how much a property is leveraged. A common way of calculating property value is to apply a capitalization rate to projected net operating income (NOI).[6] The problem is what capitalization rate to use. This potential subjective element can diminish the effectiveness of the LTV as an indicator of the credit quality of a commercial property.

Here too the investor should ask what is the weighted average LTV and the range of LTVs for a deal. Most conduit transaction weighted average LTVs fall in the range of 65% to 73%. The percent of loans in a deal with LTVs greater than 75% should be considered because these loans have greater default risk due to higher leverage. The lower the percent the better. Under 15% is good, under 10% is very good and under 5% is exceptional. The percent of a deal with LTVs greater than 75% is probably more important than the weighted average LTV.[7,8]

---

[6] Net operating income (NOI) equals the gross revenues of a property less cash expenses. i.e., does not include non-cash expenses such as depreciation.

[7] Credit lease deals can skew the above mentioned percentages because most credit lease deals are done with high LTVs and 1.00× to 1.10× DSCRs because they are more corporate credit deals than real estate deals. Credit lease deals could be removed from the pool analysis to arrive at more standardized numbers. For a useful analysis of credit tenant leases see, Moody's Investor Service special report, October 2, 1998, *CMBS: Moody's Approach to Rating Credit Tenant lease (CTL) Backed Transactions.*

[8] Shorter amortization schedules can also skew the LTVs since a higher LTV loan which rapidly amortizes causing the LTV to fall may be just as good or better than a lower LTV loan which slowly amortizes or does not amortize at all.

Exhibit 4: Default Rate*

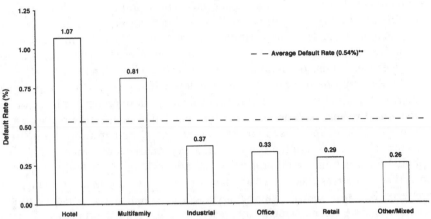

* Default rate equals number of defaults by type divided by the number of loans by type.
** Average default rates equals number of total defaults divided by number of total loans.

Source: Fitch

Property Location and Types

A dispersion of properties geographically is desirable in securitizations since changes in real estate values tend to be primarily influenced by local economies. Geographic diversification can reduce credit risk and is recognized by the rating agencies as doing so. A concentration of 40% or higher in any single state is generally considered a significant concentration.

The investor should consider the diversity of property types backing the loans in a CMBS deal. Diversification by property type is desirable in securitizations. There is no ideal percentage mix by property type, however a concentration greater than 40% to 50% is considered a large concentration. While there are several characteristics of commercial mortgage loans that are common to all property types, there are also a tremendous number of issues that are specific to different property types. Default rates for several property types are shown in Exhibit 4.

Good quality commercial real estate meets two standards: many different tenants can use the property, and the property can be leased or managed by many different operators. These characteristics reduce the risk that a mortgage loan ultimately depends on a single tenant or landlord.

Multifamily loans are generally considered to be most desirable because their short-term leases allow revenues to rise with expenses. Multifamily properties have strong historic credit experience, limited leasing risk, relatively transparent financial reporting and represent a large market-about 34.5% of total outstanding commercial real estate loans (see Exhibit 5). In addition, the universe of potential new tenants is larger than for other property types. However, the short-term nature of the leases also make multifamily loans susceptible to economic downturns. Multifamily properties also tend to have higher LTVs than other types. Fitch IBCA in a recent study found multifamily loans had the second highest default rate of various loan types (see Exhibit 4). Financing for multifamily properties tends to be widely available and highly competitive as Freddie Mac and Fannie Mae compete for loans along with conduits and portfolio lenders. Freddie Mac, Fannie Mae and the Federal Home Loan banks also have a mandate to purchase CMBS tranches backed by high concentrations of multifamily loans (usually 35% or greater).

Retail properties range from regional malls to community strip centers. The critical qualitative consideration in evaluating these properties is the quality of the tenant roster combined with the fundamental aspects of the real estate and the relationship of the lease rents to market rent. Whether a retail property is "anchored" (e.g., a shopping center with a supermarket) or "unanchored" is an important distinction. Retail properties that are anchored have traditionally been perceived to be less risky. A strong anchor can be a stabilizing influence on a property. Retail properties can be adversely affected by the presence of such retailers as dry cleaners, which may present hazardous waste problems.

A wide range of office property types exist, with different considerations for each. A common view is to differentiate properties within a central business district versus suburban office properties. For both, an assessment of quality centers on tenancy and location. An analysis of lease structures and roll over risk and the relationship of the lease rents to market rents is essential.

Office properties have longer-term leases than other property types — which can provide steady cash flow, but pose substantial risks at lease expiration. The cost of attracting new tenants can be high as offices, lobbies etc. must be tailored to the needs of new occupants. For example, given the increasing technology needs of financial institutions expenses can be high to reoutfit buildings to accommodate new wiring schemes, air conditioning systems, power systems etc. Office loans are often large — most loans are under $10 million, but many exceed $100 million, which creates "lumpy" pools diminishing diversification.

Exhibit 5: Breakdown of CMBS Issued in 1998 and 1999 by Property Type

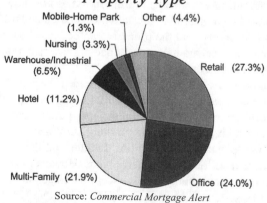

Source: *Commercial Mortgage Alert*

Exhibit 6: Commercial Delinquency Rates by Property Types (1998)

Property Type	Delinquency Rate	Yearly Change	4th Quarter Change
Apartment	0.21	−0.14	−0.01
Retail	0.49	−0.39	−0.17
Office Buildings	0.72	−0.51	−0.06
Industrial	0.28	−0.26	−0.03
Hotels	0.78	−0.17	0.66
Other Commercial	0.21	−0.04	−0.24
Commercial, Total	0.48	−0.42	−0.09

Source: American Council of Life Insurance

Major tenants are critical to an office property. Longer-term leases defer rollover risk and also offer some protection against inflation with partial passthroughs[9] of expenses and consumer price index rent escalators in many cases.

Industrial properties have strong historic credit experience and short leases, but require underwriting expertise for specialized uses. Concerns with industrial properties are potential limitations on alternative uses for the property should the tenant decide to vacate and environmental problems. Many lenders stick to warehouses and distribution facilities. A qualitative review of industrial property focuses on site characteristics including clearance heights, column spacing, number of bays and bay depths, divisibility, truck turning radius and overall functionality and accessibility. Of equal importance is the property's access to the local labor pool, proximity to supply sources and customers, and accessibility to major highways, rail lines and airports. A thorough analysis of lease structure and roll over risk and the relationship of lease rent to market rent is important.

Hospitality properties require a separate underwriting discipline. Many investors contend that these are as much operating businesses as they are commercial real estate. The market distinguishes between limited service properties which can be subject to stiff competition and low barriers to entry and luxury or destination properties which may possess unique attributes. One obvious risk: the leases last for 24 hours. Occupancy rates in certain locations can be volatile and highly dependent on the vagaries of the economy and consumer travel budgets, a discretionary expenditure.

Health care and related properties are also largely operating businesses and are subject to regulations (and, often, price controls). Some CMBS include a small exposure to health care, although the trend is to exclude this property type. Special purpose properties are introduced reluctantly. Properties such as cold-storage facilities or car washes may be highly creditworthy, but even given excellent credit, educating the market presents a substantial barrier. Other property types include self-storage facilities and theaters. Current delinquency rates by property types are shown in Exhibit 6.

---

[9] Passthroughs are expenses, such as real estate taxes, utilities, insurance, upkeep of common areas, which are passed through to the tenant.

Loan Size/Concentration

Within the universe of CMBS, the underlying loans have some obvious differences: balances can vary from under $1 million to over $500 million. While smaller loans typically allow for greater diversification of collateral in a CMBS deal and hence a reduction in the credit risk of an overall transaction,[10] it is more difficult for an investor to analyze the credit quality of many small loans. Here the investor has to rely more on the rating agencies and diversification as well as updates of loan level information provided by the servicer and third party information sources, such as Conquest.[11] A deal consisting of a few larger loans on the other hand allows the investor to analyze the properties more readily and thoroughly in a cost-effective manner.

Different investors continue to favor different deal types. Large loan deals tend to be purchased by "buy and hold" accounts such as insurance companies and pension funds which have real estate expertise and typically are not actively traded. On the other hand, smaller loan conduit deal investors tend to consist of more total return, "mark to market" accounts. As such liquidity is generally better. While each deal must be analyzed individually, in general large loan deals can be analyzed more easily since only a few loans have to be scrutinized in great detail. However, while conduit deals have the significant benefit of diversification, it is more difficult to analyze the real estate individually. While one can argue the merits of each type of deal, we expect the market to favor more diversified conduit deals in the immediate future given the market's ongoing liquidity concerns.

The investor should ask what percent of the collateral pool is represented by the largest loan. In the past the rule of thumb used to be that the rating agencies liked to see that no single loan exceeded 5% of the pool. However, we are now beginning to see this "rule of thumb" broken more frequently with the advent of "hybrid" or "fusion" deals. These are deals that combine smaller "conduit style" loans with large or "mega" loans. Unless an investor can become comfortable with the credit of the particular property backing the largest loan, it is generally desirable not to have too large an exposure to any single property. The investor should also determine what percent of the collateral pool the three largest loans make up — and then the 10 largest loans.

The rating agencies also note that even if no loan makes up more than 5% of a pool, the pool may still be concentrated. For example, a pool consisting of 20 or 30 loans with each accounting for less than 5% of the pool could still be highly concentrated. Concentration is important because it is sometimes difficult for the rating agencies to predict which commercial loans will default and why. For example, a major competitor could move in next to a property or a major tenant could leave. With greater diversity, deterioration in any one cash flow will have less impact on the overall deal.

Consider credit support (subordination) of 28%. This would protect against a 70% frequency of default and 40% loss severity.[12] If there are 100 loans each

---

[10] This is recognized by the major rating agencies that give a "credit" for sufficient diversification.

[11] Conquest, an on-line service, currently provides loan level data on most commercial mortgage securities.

making up 1% of the pool, it is highly unlikely that 70 separate loans will each experience a 1% default rate to achieve the 70% default rate. However, if there are 20 or 30 loans that make up 3% or 4% of a pool, it would be more likely for these 20 or 30 loans to experience a 1% default rate.

Loan Types

Coupon rates of commercial loans may be either fixed or floating. Commercial loans with floating coupons of course can be more risky as the debt service coverage ratio will change along with interest rates, improving as rates fall, deteriorating as rates rise. Medium and long-term commercial mortgage loans (5+ years) are generally fixed rate. Short-term loans or interim financing may have an adjustable rate. About 86% of CMBS issued since 1996 have fixed-rate coupons with the balance floating-rate coupons.

Fixed-rate loans are typically level pay, amortizing on a 20-year to 30-year schedule. Most loan terms are 7 to 10 years. Unamortized principal is payable as a "balloon balance" at the loan's due date. The need to finance balloon payments introduces refinancing risk (sometimes called "balloon extension risk").

Loan Underwriting Standards

The investor should always consider (1) who underwrote a particular CMBS transaction and (2) who originated the underlying loans. Some conduits originate the mortgages directly, while others use brokers to originate. In both cases, the issuer most of the time "re-underwrites" the loans to assure quality control.[13] Some deals have collateral contributed from multiple originators (four to five); other deals have collateral from only a few originators (one to three); neither one is necessarily better or worse. It depends most importantly on the quality of the originator and the underwriting process.

Loan underwriting standards vary substantially between lenders and it is important to have a "feel" for which issuers have a good name in the market and which ones don't. One of the easiest ways to distinguish among underwriters is to talk to the rating agencies and ask them specific questions regarding the conduits.In addition, one can usually examine the historic credit quality of underwriters' deals for high and/or rising delinquency rates, defaults or special servicing.

All real estate lenders balance two basic underwriting decisions: loan proceeds and coupon rates. Proceeds-driven lenders tend to offer maximum loan proceeds, while charging relatively high interest rates. These lenders contend that extra rate more than compensates for additional credit risk. Rating agencies generally require higher subordination levels to support AAA ratings — sometimes over 31%. Coupon-driven lenders tend to offer a minimum loan coupon while providing more modest levels of loan proceeds. These lenders put a premium on

---

[12] Loss severity is the percent of a mortgage that is lost after a loan is liquidated.

[13] Some issuers such as Fannie Mae do not reunderwrite the loan but rather delegate the underwriting and servicing to a third party, hence the Fannie Mae delegated underwriting and servicing program (DUS).

minimizing credit exposure, and contend that borrowers who choose lower rates and proceeds are more likely to repay their loans. Rating agencies respond with lower subordination levels to support AAA ratings — sometimes under 25%.

Prepayment Terms/Call Protection

Call or prepayment protection is the key structural component of a CMBS transaction as call protection is the primary reason investors buy CMBS. Most commercial mortgage loans have several forms of call protection. Many are "locked out" for the first two to five years, after which there is a "yield maintenance period" which continues up until several months before maturity. This short period at the end of the loan lasting a few months is called the free period since there is usually no prepayment penalty. These and other principal types of call protection in the CMBS market are described below.

Lockout

Prepayment lockouts explicitly prohibit prepayments for a specified period of time. As such it provides complete protection against voluntary or optional prepayments. Lock-outs usually only cover the first few years of a loan and are often used in combination with other forms of prepayment protection.

Defeasance

One of the best types of call protection is defeasance. The borrower must purchase a portfolio of Treasuries or Treasury equivalents, which replicates future cash flows of the mortgage to defease future payments. The cost to borrowers is similar to the cost of yield premiums discounted by Treasuries flat. Investors see no change in their bond payments (i.e., it is as if the mortgages were locked out for the entire term). Thus unlike yield maintenance agreements there is no issue of how to allocate prepayment penalty proceeds among various tranches in the deal.

The replacement of mortgages with Treasuries or other high quality securities[14] also improves the credit quality of the deal possibly leading to upgrades. Also the investor is not required to pay additional taxes since no prepayment penalties are distributed. Commercial mortgages are typically locked out for 3-4 years after which time the borrower can then defease the loan.

Yield Maintenance Agreement

The yield maintenance penalty is designed to compensate the lender for the early retirement of principal. If prevailing interest rates are lower than when the loan was originated, prepayment will cause the investor to reinvest at a lower rate and lose interest income. The yield maintenance penalty calculates the present value of this lost income, and imposes this amount as a prepayment disincentive to the borrower and protection to the investor. If current interest rates are higher than when the loan was originated, there is generally no penalty and the investor is not

---

[14] Fannie Mae allows borrowers to defease FNMA DUS MBS with FNMA debentures.

worse off because he can reinvest at higher rates. In many cases, the yield maintenance penalty equals the present value of the future cash flows of the commercial loan discounted by the yield of the Treasury with an average life equal to the remaining term of the commercial loan. In this case yield maintenance is truly a prepayment penalty since the lender or investor receives more than the present value of the lost income.

One of the most important issues concerning yield maintenance is the allocation of proceeds to the various tranches in a commercial mortgage deal. Depending on the formula or methodology all tranches may not be made whole. The simplest way to understand this is to realize that the average yield of all of the bonds in a CMBS deal is unlikely to be the same as the coupon on the loan that is being prepaid. The shape of the Treasury yield curve typically changes so that short and long bond yields as well as the yields of the underlying loans will all be different after origination when prepayments occur requiring different levels of compensation. Since the yield maintenance penalty is designed to generate sufficient cash flow to compensate for the foregone interest of the prepaid loan, not the foregone average yield of all the bonds in a deal, the proceeds of the penalty may be more or less than necessary to compensate all bondholders.

There are a number of methods that try to distribute the penalty in the most equitable fashion, but most favor one bond class or another under various circumstances. The three most common ones are the principal allocation method, the base interest fraction method and bond side yield maintenance.[15]

Prepayment Penalty Points

The least common type of call protection, the prepayment penalty points method is often expressed as a percentage of the mortgage balance. Unlike the yield maintenance penalty, it is unrelated to prevailing interest rates, and is expressed as a fixed percentage of the prepaid balance. There are many variations in the magnitude and schedule of prepayment penalty points. Typically, the prepayment penalty points decline with loan age, and goes to zero after a certain point. A common type of percentage premium is the 5-4-3-2-1-% each year for five years after the loan lock-out ends. Prepayment penalty points are generally regarded as a weak form of prepayment protection, due to their short time frame and the fact that the amount of the penalty is usually much less than if it were calculated using most yield maintenance methods. However, they may be superior in rising rate environments. For example, the prepayment penalty resulting from yield maintenance could be zero if rates rise high enough, whereas it would still be significant if the penalty were calculated as a percentage of the mortgage balance.

---

[15] Principal allocation percentage method considered the simplest method, allocates the yield maintenance penalty in proportion to the amount of prepayment principal that each bond receives. These methods are explained in Da Cheng, Adrian R. Cooper, and Jason Huang, "Understanding Prepayments in CMBS Deals," Chapter 8 in Frank J. Fabozzi and David P. Jacob (eds.), *The Handbook of Commercial Mortgage-Backed Securities* (New Hope, PA: Frank J. Fabozzi Associates, 2000).

Lockout and defeasance are the most desirable form of call protection; yield maintenance is slightly less desirable; percent penalties are generally the least desirable form of call protection. Investors should get a breakdown of the collateral pool by type of call protection and take note as to how large the average open prepay window is (the period between the expiration of call protection and loan maturity).

The simplest way to get a quick sense for how call protected a deal is, is to look at yield tables that show prepay speeds of 0 CPR to 100 CPR applying the speeds on a loan level basis after any lockout, defeasance, or yield maintenance period expires. How the average life of the bond changes will give a good indication of how well protected the collateral of a pool is. As a general rule, a change in average life of less than one half year when speeds range from 0 CPR to 100 CPR would indicate "decent" call protection.

Call protection provided by commercial mortgages varies widely. In older CMBS pools, the underlying loans may include all sorts of call protection. In newer transactions, a given pool's call protection tends to be more consistent. Prepayment terms may include combinations of lock-outs, penalties, or Treasury defeasance.

Finally the investor should be aware that in a strong real estate market and falling rate environment, loans with anything but lockouts and defeasance might be prepaid even with very large prepayment penalties. There are a number of reasons for this. The prepayment penalty is tax deductible for the borrower which reduces its "sting". The penalty may be financed such that the loan payments on the new borrowed amount even including the penalty may be lower than the original payments. Finally and most importantly if the borrower, often a real estate developer, can cash out a significant amount of equity from a property through refinancing he will do so regardless of the penalty.

Imagine the case where a developer pays $5 million for a property and borrows $3 million to finance it. Several years later rents rise, rates fall, the property's value increases to $8 million and the prepayment penalty is $500,000. If the borrower can get a new loan for $5 million, he can pay off the old loan ($3 million), finance the penalty ($500,000) and take out $1.5 million which would give him a 75% return on his equity investment. In addition, he can get a tax deduction for $500,000. He can then take the $1.5 million, borrow more money, develop another property and start all over again. If rates have fallen enough, the increase in his monthly loan payments may easily be supported by higher rents. For example if rates fell from 8.5% to 6%, annual interest payments on the old mortgage would be $255,000 ($3,000,000 × 8.5%) versus $300,000 ($5,000,000 × 6%) on the new larger loan.

HOW CMBS TRADE

Because of their excellent prepayment protection and sensitivity to credit risk, highest quality investment grade CMBS (AAAs through As) tend to trade more like corporate bonds than residential MBS. In general they tend to be more sensitive to changes in swap levels (which tend to reflect A/AA rated corporates) and credit spreads than interest rate levels. Most Wall Street firms, conduits and many investors in the sector use swaps to hedge their positions. The relationship between swap levels and CMBS spreads is apparent in Exhibit 7 and discussed further in Chapter 13. The practice of pricing AAA CMBS versus swaps first began with several issues during the bond market panic between August and November of 1998, due to the difficulty in pricing deals over Treasuries. Today all new issue tranches, as well as those trading in the secondary markets rated from AAA down to A, are quoted versus the equivalent average life interpolated swap.

However, investment grade CMBS tend to widen more than non-callable corporate bonds as their price increases over par. The reason is investor concern over a default-induced prepayment. Unlike a regular prepayment, which is either forbidden due to lock out or compensated for in the case of prepayment penalties, yield maintenance or Treasury defeasance, the CMBS investor usually receives his cash back at par without compensation if the prepayment was caused by a default (assuming the cash is available). For example, in early May 1999, a high quality 10-year AAA CMBS (one with low subordination at origination) would trade 2 bps wider if it had a 103 "handle"[16] than if it had a par "handle." The spread would widen by about another 2 bps/point until a 105 "handle" after which the spread would widen by about 3 bps per point.

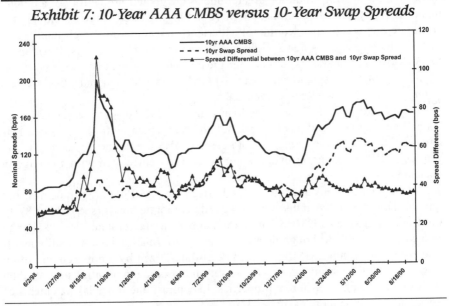

Exhibit 7: 10-Year AAA CMBS versus 10-Year Swap Spreads

[16] For real estate participants that are new to the bond market, "handle" refers to that part of a bond's price that is valued in points. For example, a bond priced at 102:16 would have a 102 "handle." A bond priced at 100:12 would have a "par handle."

Exhibit 8: 10-Year AAA CMBS versus 10-Year A Corporates and 10-Year Swaps

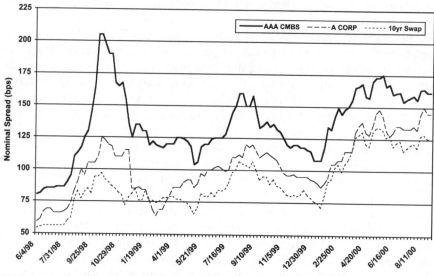

For lower quality triple As (ones with higher subordination levels at origination), the widening would be greater due to the greater probability of a default induced prepayment. In contrast, single A and higher rated 10 year non-callable corporate bonds typically would not experience widening until their handles hit 110 in which case the spread might widen one or two basis points. Residential MBS (RMBS) of course experience far greater widening than CMBS. For example in early May, the spread between a par GNMA passthrough and a GNMA pass through with a 103 handle was about 28 bps.

In addition, CMBS average lives can extend if the borrower cannot make his balloon payment and has to work out an arrangement with the servicer. It is important to note however that in both cases CMBS are not nearly as negatively convex as RMBS as either event is not necessarily correlated with a change in interest rates.

Because of this average life and price risk, CMBS tend to trade at wider spreads than same rated and same average life corporate bonds (see Exhibit 8). In addition, the nature of CMBS collateral can pose a greater analytical challenge than corporate debt. Although detailed property information is now readily available[17] because conduit CMBS tend to be collateralized by a hundred and often more property loans, investors have to rely more on agency ratings rather than analyzing in detail the different properties. In contrast, the financial statements of corporations can be more easily analyzed.

---

[17] For example, Charter Research's Conquest allows investors to look at the loan level detail in each deal.

Although the multiple loans of CMBS deals can pose a greater analytical challenge, they can offer the advantage over corporates of "slow motion" credit deterioration. The large number of loans in a deal often offers the investor the time to act if one or two start to become delinquent. With corporate bonds event risk can suddenly trigger a rating downgrade. In addition, the paydown of individual loans can result in the deleveraging of a deal so that subordination increases and a tranche is upgraded.

Spread differences between corporate bullet bonds and CMBS can also arise due to the presence of amortizing loans in a CMBS. The market currently tends to calculate spreads in both the CMBS and corporate bond markets on the same basis (the difference between the yield of the security and the yield of the nearest equivalent average life Treasury benchmark). However, while calculation of the spread of the bullet corporate versus one point on the Treasury curve is reasonable since the bulk of the corporate bond's cash flow occurs on the bullet date, amortizing CMBS cash flows are spread out along the Treasury curve. Calculating their spread to one point on the Treasury curve can be misleading. Because some of the cash flows occur after the average life of the CMBS bond and some before, these cash flows should be compared with corresponding equivalent maturity Treasury cash flows. The best method to compare bullet and amortizing security spreads is to compare their cash flow spread or Z spread.[18] Thus, it may be important to compare the cash flow spread (or zero volatility OAS) of CMBS and corporate bonds, particularly in a steep yield curve environment.

CMBS also tend to trade differently than corporates for a number of technical reasons. For example, while liquidity was limited in other bond markets between August and December 1998, the situation was exacerbated in the CMBS market by two factors.

First, unlike corporates, CMBS dealers warehouse collateral originated by their conduits. A CMBS dealer can be exposed to a billion dollars or more of commercial mortgages for 3 to 6 months which have to be warehoused until there is sufficient size to do a securitization. If spreads begin to widen, this collateral can represent a significant exposure to the sector. In the fall, many dealers already had substantial exposure to the sector when investors had to liquidate securities. In contrast, corporate dealers are not long collateral. They are more able to provide liquidity in a crunch. New issuance in the corporate market is underwritten on an agency basis, not as a principal. Today, this is less of a problem in the CMBS market as dealers more carefully manage their loan inventories through faster and smaller deal issuance. This keeps the gestation period and inventory for deals at lower levels thereby enabling dealers to provide more liquidity to the market.

Second, short-term leverage hampered some substantial investors in both investment grade and non-investment grade CMBS. Highly leveraged hedge

---

[18] Also called the zero-volatility option-adjusted spread (OAS). This cash flow spread is that spread which when added to all of the Treasury spot rates corresponding to the cash flows of the CMBS, discount the CMBS cash flows back to the present value of the CMBS.

funds played a significant role in the AAA CMBS sector, while mortgage REITs, also leveraged players, had an even more dominant role in the non-investment grade sector. In fact, most mortgage REITS used repo debt to lever their holdings, effectively lending long and borrowing short. As spreads widened, margin calls pulled these positions apart. The below investment grade market spiraled downward, as falling values and margin calls reinforced each other. Less leveraged sectors were not as susceptible. This situation while still present in CMBS, is gradually improving as newer, less leveraged investors enter both the investment and non-investment grade CMBS sectors.

Within the CMBS sector, similarly rated CMBS with similar average life can trade at spreads as different as 20 bps. As shown in Exhibit 9, 10-year AAA bonds traded as tight as 110 bps (Bear Stearns 1999-C1 A2s) to as wide as 130 bps (Commercial Mortgage Asset Trust 1999-C1 A3s). For example, AAA bonds that at issue have lower subordination because of the strong credit quality of the collateral, such as bank names,[19] trade between 5 bps and 20 bps tighter than other names. The reason for this is the concern of a default-induced prepayment. The rating agencies AAA rating certifies only an expectation that the investor in the AAA will get his money back not when. Therefore the market is more concerned about a default-induced prepayment if the collateral is of such low quality that high subordination levels are required.

Liquidity concerns can also cause spread tiering. Given the experiences of many last fall, liquidity concerns are still understandably paramount in the minds of many. For example, 10-year AAA tranches of Nomura (Capital Company of America-CMAT 1999-C1 A3) at this writing trade 10 to 20 bps wider than other paper because of the firm's exit from the CMBS market and market concerns that there will be less support for secondary trading activity in the paper. These concerns have increasingly lead to joint issuer deals to reassure investors that several firms will make markets in a deal after it is issued.

Exhibit 9: Selected Triple-A CMBS Bonds

Deal	Offer (4/26/99)	% Subordination at Orig/Now	Coupon	WAL/ Window	Bid/Offer
BSCMS 1999-C1 A2	110/Cur	22.5/22.535	6.02	9.63(5/08-2/09)	2 bps
MSC 1999-WF1 A2	111/Cur	23.0/23.035	6.21	9.31(4/08-9/08)	2 bps
CHASE 1998-1 A2	114/Cur	27.0/27.245	6.56	8.81(12/06-5/08)	3 bps
JPMC 1998-C6 A3	120/Cur	29.0/29.389	6.61	8.65(7/07-1/08)	3 bps
DLJCM 1998-CF1 A1B	120/Cur	29.5/29.816	6.59	8.89(2/08-2/08)	3 bps
MSC 1998-XL1 A3	125/Cur	27.5/27.718	6.48	8.73(4/07-5/08)	4 bps
MCFI 1998-MC3 A2	124/Cur	30.5/31.09	6.34	9.03(9/07-7/08)	4 bps
GSMS 1998-C1 A2	128/Cur	30.5/30.65	6.62	9.09(7/07-10/08)	4 bps
CMAT 1999-C1 A3	130/Cur	28.5/28.5	6.56	9.88(7/08-9/10)	5 bps

[19] Bank names currently tend to trade tighter than many conduit names because there is a perception that banks have more of a "credit culture" than conduits.

While liquidity is critical and bonds with tighter bid/offer spreads tend to trade at tighter offer spreads, this certainly doesn't explain all of the extra spread the market currently demands for certain bonds. For example, the difference between the bid/offer spread of MSC 1999-WF1A2s (2 bps) and that of GSMS 1998-C1A2s (4 bps) is only 2 bps, yet the latter is offered 17 bps wider. Clearly liquidity alone as represented by bid/offer spreads does not explain the large spread differentials.

How well a "name" trades and has traded versus other "names," currently seems to be as important or more important than fundamental value. For example, the current market "wisdom" is that bank issues should trade better than many issues generated by Wall Street conduits or some investment banks, on the theory that commercial banks have more of a "credit culture."

While we would argue and agree that 10 year AAAs backed by high quality collateral should trade tighter than AAAs backed by lower quality collateral due to cash flow uncertainty this is not always the case in the market. While Bear Stearns, BSCMS 1999 C1 A2s justifiably trade tighter than Chase and First Union due to the high quality of the collateral (see Exhibit 9), bank deals do tend to trade tighter than investment bank conduit deals. For example, Chase and First Union AAA bonds tend to trade at the tight end of the spectrum while those at the wide end are all investment bank deals, with Nomura's trading the widest.

However whether all bank deals are of better quality is questionable. For example, 1.04% of NLFC 98-1, a deal originated by NationsBank, is either 30 or 60 days delinquent, an additional 0.29% is 90 days or more delinquent and 2.73% of the deal is being specially serviced. Using the "percent subordination at origination" as an objective indicator of the credit quality of the underlying collateral, Chase 1998-1 A2 and JPMC 1998-C6 A3 had about the same or greater subordination at origination as compared with DLJCM 1998-CF1 A1Bs and MSC 1998 XL1 A3s (see Exhibit 9). Yet they trade as much as 11 bps tighter. Even the window of MSC 1998-XL1 A3s is about the same as the bank deals and the DLJ tranche has a bullet window, which is narrower. For investors willing to break out of the herd mentality and look through the name and to the fundamental credit quality of a deal, there is significant value to be found.

WHO SHOULD INVEST IN TRIPLE-A CMBS

A wide variety of investors should consider investing in CMBS including corporate bond buyers, insurance companies, pension funds, and state funds, money managers versus an index, as well as banks. CMBS offer significantly greater spread than lower rated corporate bonds yet can have excellent call protection and average life stability. In addition, they can help diversify portfolio risk. While insurance companies and banks were initially the largest investors in higher rated CMBS, money managers are becoming increasingly important. And with the entry of the Lehman CMBS index into its Aggregate index we expect more pension funds and state funds to increase their current investments as well. Finally,

U.S. CMBS can offer non-U.S. investors significant opportunity. Commercial loan capitalization rates in the U.S are typically higher than those in Europe. As such U.S. CMBS may offer better rates of return than those available in Europe.

ERISA Eligibility

ERISA is the Employee Retirement Income Security Act of 1974, the federal law that regulates private-sector employee benefit plans, including pension plans. Various funds may be subject to ERISA or to parallel provisions in Section 4975 of the Internal Revenue Code, including:

- any employee benefit plan or other retirement plan or arrangement, including individual retirement accounts and annuities, Keogh plans, and collective investment funds;
- insurance company separate accounts and (in some cases) insurance company general accounts in which such plans, accounts or arrangements are invested; and
- any entity the assets of which include assets of such a plan.

Persons with discretionary authority over such plans and accounts should carefully review with their legal advisors whether the purchase and holding of Commercial Mortgage Pass-Through Certificates is permitted under ERISA, the Internal Revenue Code and applicable guidelines. In general ERISA imposes certain restrictions and may prohibit certain transactions between employee benefit plans and "parties-in-interest" which may include the service providers in a securitization. Generally, these prohibited transaction rules may apply to the purchase of CMBS and to the operation of the asset pool backing such Commercial Mortgage Pass-Through Certificates.

Certain employee benefit plans, such as governmental and church plans, may not be subject to ERISA restrictions. State and local government plans, however, may be subject to similar restrictions under applicable State laws.

Exemptions granted by the U.S. Department of Labor permit ERISA plans to purchase certain certificates and relieve the operation of the underlying asset pool from application of the prohibited transaction rules of ERISA. The principal exemption applicable to the Commercial Mortgage Pass-Through Certificates is the Underwriter Exemption, which makes ERISA-eligible the seniormost Certificates of a series of Commercial Mortgage Pass-Through Certificates as long as certain conditions are met, including that these Certificates are rated in one of the three highest rating categories by a rating agency.

Subordinate classes of Certificates generally are not ERISA-eligible. Insurance company general accounts, however, may be permitted to purchase subordinate Certificates. Under an amendment to ERISA adopted in 1996, after the Supreme Court's Harris Trust decision, insurance company general accounts are generally exempt from ERISA's plan asset and prohibited transaction rules pending issuance of final regulations by the U.S. Department of Labor. Regulations regarding the application of ERISA to insurance company general accounts have been proposed but are not yet final. Insurance company general accounts may be permitted to purchase subordinate Commercial Mortgage Pass-Through Certificates if they meet the requirements of Prohibited Transaction Class Exemption 95-60. Insurance companies should review these requirements with their legal advisors.

SMMEA Eligibility

A mortgage-backed security is SMMEA eligible if it qualifies as a "mortgage related security" under the Secondary Mortgage Market Enhancement Act of 1984 (as amended by Section 347 of the Riegle Community Development and Regulatory Act of 1994 "SMMEA"). SMMEA amends several federal banking laws and securities laws with respect to mortgage related securities to, among other things, (1) relax the margin requirements previously imposed by the Securities Exchange Act of 1934, (2) remove restrictions on investment in private mortgage-backed securities by federally-chartered depository institutions, savings and loan associations and credit unions previously subject to regulatory limitations and (3) preempt state legal investment laws and blue sky laws which previously limited investment in private mortgage-backed securities by state-chartered financial institutions and required registration under the various state securities laws.

The 1994 Amendment to SMMEA, which became effective on December 31, 1996, added securities backed by mortgages secured by commercial structures to the definition of securities subject to SMMEA eligibility. In order to qualify as a mortgage related security, the security must be rated in one of the two highest rating categories by at least one nationally recognized credit-rating agency (i.e., Fitch, Moody's, or S&P) and the mortgage loans backing the security must meet certain criteria.

In general, (1) the related mortgage note (or similar instrument) must be secured by a first lien on (A) a single parcel of real estate, in the case of property on which is located residential structure or (B) one or more parcels of real estate, in the case of property on which is located multifamily or commercial structures and (2) the mortgage loan must be originated by an institution supervised and examined by federal or state authority or by a mortgage lender approved by the secretary of the Department of Housing and Urban Development (HUD). The staff of the Division of Market Regulation of the Securities and Exchange Commission (SEC) has issued several no-action letters discussing the requirements a mortgage-backed security must meet in order to be considered SMMEA eligible.

THE LEHMAN CMBS INDEX: IMPACT ON THE MARKET

The introduction of the Lehman CMBS index on January 1, 1999 should benefit the CMBS market. The index provides a measurable benchmark against which all industry participants may be judged and may impose greater discipline on portfolio lenders. To the extent that both CMBS investors and portfolio lenders are benched against the index, this creates greater efficiency and transparency between these two major groups of lenders.

To the extent market participants can short the index to hedge positions, this will help reduce risk for conduits warehousing loans. Lehman Bros. swap group is reportedly working on developing a swap based on their new index. While there is the risk that many market participants will all want to go one way (i.e. shorting the index), Lehman Bros. noted that they have seen two way interest. Some investors who do not have the manpower to analyze each individual CMBS sector may want to go long with respect to it in order to beat the Lehman Aggregate Fixed Income Index.

Lehman Brothers will also include part of the CMBS index in their Aggregate index on July 1, 1999. This should be a plus as it will bring in a number of investors that have not invested in CMBS before but need to be weighted in the sector. We expect that this could bring in another $3 billion to $5 billion of new money primarily from pension funds which often use the aggregate index as a performance measure. Initially, CMBS will make up only about 1% of the Aggregate Index, however given the long average maturities of CMBS this percentage should grow significantly over time.

The Lehman CMBS Index: Description

The Lehman CMBS index actually consists of three independent indices: a CMBS investment grade index which includes CMBS classes rated Baa3 or higher,[20] a CMBS high yield index which includes classes rated Ba1 or lower and NR classes as well as private certificates; and a CMBS IO index which includes all ratings and private certificates. A combination of all three indices comprises the commercial whole loan index. The size and number of classes in each index are shown in Exhibit 10.

To be included in the indices, classes must be denominated in U.S. dollars, have an average life of at least one year, be from a deal with an original size of at least $500 million and a current deal balance of at least $300 million. Conduit, fusion and large loan deals are included while agency deals, floaters and residual classes are excluded. All certificates must be fixed, capped WAC or WAC bonds.

Month to date index returns calculated using Lehman's models consist of price return, coupon return, paydown return, and prepayment premium return and will be calculated weekly and at month end. Pricing will occur on Friday at 3:00 PM using a pricing speed of 0. If the market begins pricing deals with a speed then that speed will be used.

---

[20] Moody's will be the primary rating agency. If the bonds are unrated by Moody's, Lehman will look first to Standard and Poor's, and then Fitch. Private certificates are excluded.

*Exhibit 10: Lehman Bros. CMBS Index**

Rating	Number of Classes	Market Value ($ mm)	% of Total
Investment Grade			
AAA	158	$53,405	79.8%
AA	63	$4,094	6.1%
A	66	$4,182	6.2%
BBB	117	$5,269	7.9%
Total	404	$66,949	100.0%
High Yield			
BB	134	$3,188	67.8%
B	119	$1,199	25.5%
NR	79	$315	6.7%
Total	332	$4,702	100.0%
I/O Classes			
Total	90	$4,421	100>%

SUMMARY

The CMBS market is currently in transition. The dislocations caused by spread widening last year while unsettling to some have set the market up for what we believe will be a favorable year. The market is young and growing pains are to be expected. New investors continue to enter the sector searching for the investment opportunities brought about by the dislocations, the ability to diversify their bond portfolios or because CMBS are now a part of the Lehman Aggregate index. Whatever the reason, we hope this chapter will serve as a useful point of entry and framework to discover the opportunities in the AAA sector.

APPENDIX

GENERAL OVERVIEW OF RATING AGENCY APPROACHES

Fitch's Approach to Rating
Commercial Mortgage Securities

Commercial mortgage-backed securities (CMBS) enable an issuer to aggregate cash flow from numerous loans secured by diverse commercial properties, structure the priority of payments, and sell bonds with ratings that match investor risk tolerance. The formation of a rating is a statistical analysis of credit risk. Subordination of various tranches or classes is the most common and often the only form of credit enhancement.

CMBS can be composed of either new loans originated for the purpose of securitization (conduits) or seasoned loans from an existing portfolio. Generally CMBS pooled transactions range from $500 million to $1.5 billion.

Fitch's credit analysis includes a reunderwriting of real estate assets and stressing of loan terms to refinance constants. The rating incorporates a review of the quantitative aspects of the collateral, as well as an assessment of the financial and legal structure of the CMBS transaction. This report outlines Fitch's methodology for rating transactions backed by pools of performing commercial mortgages. It also summarizes data requirements, the due diligence process, and the legal and structural issues considered in a transaction.

Fitch's Model Overview

Fitch's performing loan model is predicated on research indicating that debt service coverage ratios (DSCRs) are the best indicators of loan default and that a loan with a high DSCR is less likely to default than a loan with a DSCR below 1.00 times ($\times$). Fitch begins its modeling analysis by calculating DSCRs assuming an "A" stress environment. Also, Loan to Value (LTV) is calculated by dividing the Fitch Net Cash Flow (NCF) by the stressed capitalization rate. The default probability and loss severity assumptions based on the DSCR and LTV for each loan are adjusted based on certain property and loan features to determine credit enhancement based on individual loan characteristics. Next, the composition of the pool is analyzed to identify any concentration risks. Finally, the transaction structure is evaluated and incorporated into the ratings. The results are further adjusted to reflect various stresses from "AAA" to "B." The final credit enhancement levels for a transaction equal the sum of the loan-by-loan expected loss plus or minus adjustments (add-ons) for particular asset characteristics, pool concentration issues, and deal structure requirements.[21] A sample credit enhancement is shown below:

---

[21] This section is excepted from Fitch's 9/18/98 report, *Performing Loan Securitization*, and incorporates updated information to reflect the recent merger between Fitch and Duff and Phelps.

Moody's Approach to Rating
Commercial Mortgage Securities[22]

For most structured transactions, Moody's seeks to ensure that the credit support protects bond holders from levels of default frequency and loss severity consistent with a given rating. Moody's approach to establishing the credit support level for commercial real estate is by necessity, somewhat more qualitative than for other structured finance assets. Only a limited amount of dependable long-term performance data is available, and the data that is available is seldom on point with the facts of the transaction being rated.

To demonstrate the order of magnitude of commercial real estate (CRE) credit support, a pool of seasoned life insurance company quality loans might require a 25% credit support to receive a Aa rating. This would protect an investor from a scenario in which 50% of the loans defaulted and in which the defaulting loans lost 50% of their value. In contrast, an Resolution Trust Co. (RTC) commercial real estate pool may require credit support as high as 45% to achieve a Aa rating, which would protect an investor from default rates as high as 90% combined with 50% losses on the defaulting loans.

Moody's approach to developing credit support for a pool is to first assign a credit support level consistent with the highest requested rating to each property in the pool and then to take the weighted-average credit support of all the properties and adjust it for portfolio factors. The credit support that we assign to each loan is a function of Moody's assessment of the probability of default and severity of loss for a given property. Loans with high debt service coverages and low LTVs require little credit support, as some is already built into the loan in the form of borrower's equity.

Moody's also adjusts credit support to reflect our opinion of the relative quality of a given asset within its class, with the closest scrutiny given to individual assets and to smaller pools. Among our concerns are:

- Location,
- Creditworthiness of tenants.
- Terms of the tenants in occupancy,
- Physical condition.

As part of the review process, Moody's verifies physical condition through inspection reports, site visits, and engineering studies.

Default Frequency
The key factor in Moody's assessment of potential frequency of default is the debt service coverage (DSC) of a loan. Loans with debt service coverage ratios below 1.00 are expected to have a high frequency of default, as borrowers cannot be expected to fund losses indefinitely.

---

[22] This section was contributed by Moody's Investor Services.

Loans with debt service coverage ratios above 1.00 have a lower likelihood of default because they have a built-in excess cash flow buffer available which would have to erode before the borrower would experience losses and consider defaulting. For example, a property with a 1.20 DSC should be able to withstand a decline in gross income of 10% before hitting break-even, assuming that its expenses are 40% of income.

Loss Severity

The key determinant of severity of loss is the potential for decline in the value of the property securing a given loan. Moody's studied data from most of the major US markets since 1980, which helped us determine how far rents can fall and vacancies can rise in order to establish potential severity ceilings. With this data, we've created sample proformas that we use to size the resulting declines in net income and value from the peak of the market to the trough.

However, a mitigating factor in our assessment of potential severity is the current LTV ratio of a given loan, because part of any potential decline can be absorbed by built-in overcollateralization.

Another mitigating factor is our assessment of the strength of a specific market and its potential for declines. In most cases, we are not using the full potential peak-to-trough decline as a severity adjustment, giving some credit for the substantial declines that have already taken place. We generally do not lower the severity adjustment to minimal levels, however, because we like to have protection against false bottoms and other unforeseen circumstances.

The Role of NOI

The net operating income (NOI) of a property is what drives debt service coverage and LTV; therefore, we are extremely sensitive to the quality of the NOI that the issuer/underwriter supplies for a transaction. The optimal situation is to have audited historic NOIs for each property in a pool, together with a mark-to-market scenario that indicates the NOIs potential for rising or falling in the near term.

These data are not always available for each transaction that Moody's rates, and we make conservative assumptions when it is missing. When the transaction involves a single property or a small pool, we give each income statement additional scrutiny and make additional deductions for items such as vacancy, management fees, and capital expenditures. We place little or no reliance on "annualized" or projected income estimates.

The Risk Continuum

Moody's views on credit support are shaped by our opinions on the inherent risk of each asset class. We believe that the stability of asset values of the major property types, ranked in order from best to worst, is as follows: regional malls, multifamily, anchored community retail, industrial, office, and hotel.

Standard and Poor's Rating Process for CMBS Transactions[23]

Standard & Poor's rating process begins when an issuer, or an investment banker representing the issuer requests our analysis of the credit quality of a single commercial mortgage or a pool of commercial mortgages. For a first time issuer this usually entails a meeting to discuss S&P's criteria and overall analytical approach. After the initial meetings, Standard & Poor's will perform a preliminary analysis of the collateral to determine the indicative credit support requirements. If the issuer accepts these indicative levels, after a formal engagement, Standard & Poor's begins the official rating process.

Standard & Poor's breaks down CMBS transactions into two major categories-property specific and pool transactions.

1. The property specific analysis is used for the following transactions:

• single-loan backed by a single asset;
• single-loan backed by multiple assets,
• multiple properties with multiple loans to a single-borrower,
• or small pools of less than 50 borrowers.

The property specific transaction is an in-depth analysis of the asset/assets and all of the related engineering, appraisal, and environmental reports. Among the major considerations are the asset's construction quality, location, tenancy, lease structures, historical performance, market position, current and anticipated competition, lien status, and overall loan structure. A very important aspect of this analysis is S&P's evaluation of the borrower/sponsor and its management capabilities based on an in-depth meeting with the corporate and on-site management teams and visit to the assets. Even more important are the legal considerations regarding the borrowing entity and the overall deal structure, the absence or presence of bankruptcy-remote borrowing entities, the borrowers and its affiliates credit history, the borrower's ability to incur additional debt and the form of additional debt that can be incurred.

2. A pool analysis consists of a combination of asset-specific analysis and some statistical sampling. This approach is applied to pools that consist of loans to 50 or more separate, unaffiliated borrowers. Fusion transactions are analyzed differently i.e; the large loans are analyzed and credit support is determined based on property specific standards, the conduit loans are analyzed using the combination pool treatment, and credit tenant leases are analyzed based on the credit tenant approach. The credit support requirements for each component are derived separately, weighted, then pooled to determine the ultimate transaction credit support.

S&P's evaluation of a CMBS transaction can be divided into three major areas: (1) the real estate analysis and (2) pooling and credit support determina-

---

[23] This section was contributed by Standard & Poor's.

tion, and (3) the legal and financial analysis of the transaction. It is the integration of the results of these analyses that will determine the ultimate credit support requirements and the final ratings for the transaction.

S&P begins with the evaluation of the underlying real estate. S&P reviews the due diligence file that is provided by the issuer. Our analysts visit the assets, evaluate the tenancy, and re-underwrite the property cash flows to incorporate adjustments to reflect market and economic expectations. S&P typically visits 60% of the pool, but the number of assets that are visited will depend on property types, geographic concentration, loan skewness, borrower concentration, and the number of loans in the pool. S&P also will sample and re-underwrite additional loans and property types to arrive at a true representative sample of the pool in order to extrapolate the results to the rest of the unseen assets.

Cash flow adjustments typically include marking rents down to market, increasing vacancy assumptions, increasing expenses to reflect a normalized level, as well as deducting the expenses related to future tenant rollover and leasing costs, and ongoing capital expenditure requirements. These adjustments (haircuts) are made to the property's in-place, current cash flow to derive an S&P stabilized cash flow and the resulting debt service coverage ratio (DSCR). S&P then applies a capitalization rate to this adjusted cash flow to determine an appropriate value for the property and the resulting LTV for the loan. S&P's analysts also read the related environmental, engineering, and appraisal reports as part of the real estate evaluation of the assets. S&P views the "bricks and mortars approach" as the foundation of any analysis of CMBS pools, since it is important to ensure that the properties can maintain their ability to generate cash flow throughout the life of the transaction.

The cash flows resulting from this loan-by-loan analysis are stressed at each rating category and aggregated to determine the credit support required for the overall pool. The absence of special hazard coverage, such as earthquake and windstorm insurance requirements and unresolved environmental issues can result in increased credit support requirements.

Overlaying the real estate analysis are the legal and financial issues that govern the transaction structure, and these issues play a critical role in determining the final credit support levels for the transaction. This analysis focuses on the strengths and weaknesses of the deal; the structure of the borrowing entities, the representations and warranties provided by the mortgage sellers, and the legal opinions governing the transfer (true sale) of the assets from the seller to the depositor. Other issues that are considered include the flow of funds within the transaction and any additional liquidity that may be required to prevent an interruption of payments to the bondholders, priority of payments to the rated tranches, the Servicing and Trustee roles, including their required Rankings and ratings, and the ratings of the providers of hazard insurance coverage.

Chapter 2

The Commercial Mortgage-Backed Securities Deal

Anthony B. Sanders, Ph.D.
Professor of Finance and Galbreath Distinguished Scholar
The Ohio State University

T he purpose of this chapter is to provide a broad overview of the CMBS market from the point of view of a sample CMBS deal.

THE CMBS DEAL

A CMBS is formed when an issuer deposits commercial loans into a trust. The issuer then creates securities in the form of classes of bonds backed by the commercial loans. As payments on the commercial loans (and any lump-sum repayment of principal) arc received,. they are distributed (passed through) to the bondholders according to the rules governing the distribution of proceeds.

Bond Passthrough Rates

An example of a recent CMBS deal can be used to highlight the distribution of cash flows to the bondholders and the rules governing the distribution. The GMAC 1999-C3 deal, underwritten jointly by Deutsche Bank and Goldman Sachs, is summarized in Exhibit 1. The balance of the bonds as of the cutoff date (9/10/99) is $1,152,022,048. The gross weighted-average coupon (WACg) is 7.90% and the net weighted-average coupon (WACn) is 7.79%. The weighted-average maturity (WAM) is 117 months

The bonds are sequential-pay. The passthrough rate for class A-l-a is 6.97% and fixed. The passthrough rates for classes A-l-b, A-2, B, C, G, H, J, K, L, M, and N are equal to the lesser of the fixed passthrough rate and net WAC of the mortgage pool. For example, the A-1-b bondholders will receive the lesser of the fixed passthrough rate (7.27%) and the net WAC (7.79%). Passthrough rates for classes D, E, and F are equal to the WAC of the mortgage pool.

Class X is an interest-only class. Class X receives the excess of the net WAC received from tile pool over the weighted-average passthrough rate paid to the sequential-pay bonds. Class X's notional balance equals the outstanding balance of the sequential-pay bonds.

Exhibit 1: Bonds for GMAC 1999-C3 deal

Bond	Moody Rating	Fitch Rating	Original Amount	Subordination Original	Coupon	Coupon Type
A-1-a	Aaa	AAA	$50,000,000	0.2700	0.0697	Fixed
A-1-b	Aaa	AAA	$190,976,000	0.2700	0.0727	Fixed
A-2	Aaa	AAA	$600,000,000	0.2700	0.0718	Fixed
B	Aa2	AA	$51,840,000	0.2250	0.0754	Fixed
C	A2	A	$57,601,000	0.1750	0.0779	Fixed
D	A3	A−	$20,160,000	0.1575	0.0779	WAC-0b
E	Baa2	BBB	$37,440,000	0.1250	0.0779	WAC-0b
F	Baa3	BBB−	$23,040,000	0.1050	0.0779	WAC-0b
G	NA	NA	$57,601,000	0.0550	0.0697	Fixed
H	NA	NA	$8,640,000	0.0475	0.0697	Fixed
J	NA	NA	$11,520,000	0.0375	0.0697	Fixed
K	NA	NA	$14,400,000	0.0250	0.0697	Fixed
L	NA	NA	$11,520,000	0.0150	0.0697	Fixed
M	NA	NA	$5,760,000	0.0100	0.0697	Fixed
N	NA	NA	$11,524,048	0.0000	0.0697	Fixed
X	NA	NA	$1,152,022,048n	NA	0.0053	WAC/IO
R	NA	NA	$0r	NA	0	

Source: Charter Research.

CMBS Ratings and Subordination Levels

The rating agencies play a critical role in the CMBS market. The role of the rating agency is to provide a third-party opinion on the quality of each bond in the structure (as well as the necessary level of credit enhancement to achieve a desired rating level). The rating agency examines critical characteristics of the underlying pool of loans such as the *debt service coverage ratio* (DSCR) and the *loan-to-value ratio* (LTV). If the target ratios at the asset level are below a certain level, the credit rating of the bond is reduced. Subordination can be used at the structure level to improve the rating of the bond. For example, suppose that a certain class of property requires a DSCR of 1.50× to qualify for an A rating; if the actual DSCR is only 1.25×, additional subordination can be added at the deal level to bring the rating to an A rating.

The credit ratings for the bonds in the GMAC 1999-C3 deal are presented in Exhibit 1. Fitch rated the first three bonds (A-1-a, A-1-b, and A-2) AAA Moody's rated the same bond classes as Aaa. The B through F bonds have progressively lower ratings. The subordination level decline with the bond ratings: 27% subordination for the AAA bond down to 10.5% for the BBB− bond. The subordination levels continue to drop for the C bond (17.5%) through the N bond (0%).

Prioritization of Payments

The highest-rated bonds are paid-off first in the CMBS structure. Any return of principal caused by amortization, prepayment, or default is used to repay the highest-rated tranche first and then the lower-rated bonds. Any interest received on outstanding principal is paid to all tranches. However, it is important to note that many deals vary from this simplistic prioritization assumption.

For example, consider the GMAC 1999-C3 deal. The bonds that are rated AAA by Fitch (classes A-1-a, A-1-b, and A-2) are the Senior Certificates. Classes B through M are organized in a simple sequential structure. Principal and interest are distributed first to the class B and last to the class N. Unfortunately, the Senior Certificates are not as simple in their prioritization.

The loans underlying the GMAC 1999-C3 are divided into two groups. Group 2 consists of the multifamily loans and Group 1 consists of the remaining loans (retail, office, warehouse, and so on). In terms of making distributions to the Senior Certificates, 61% of Group 1's distribution amount is transferred to Group 2's distribution amount. Group 1's distribution amount is used to pay:

1. Interest on bond classes A-1-a, A-1-b, and the portion of interest on the Class X on components A-1-a and A-1-b pro rata, and
2. Principal to the Class A-1-a and A-1-b in that order.

Loan Group 2's distribution amount is used to pay:

1. Interest on Class A-2 and the portion of interest on the Class X components from A-2 to N pro rata, and
2. Principal to the Class A-2;

In the event where the balances of all the subordinated classes (Class B through Class M) have been reduced to zero because of the allocation of losses, the principal and interest will be distributed on a pro rata basis to Classes A-1-a, A-1-b, and A-2.

Loan default adds an additional twist to the structuring. Any losses that arise from loan defaults will be charged against the principal balance of the lowest rated CMBS bond tranche that is outstanding (also known as the *first loss piece*). For the GMAC 1999-C3 deal, losses are allocated in reverse sequential order from Class N through Class B. After Class B is retired, classes A-1-a, A-1-b, and A-2 bear losses on a pro-rata basis. As a consequence, a localized market decline (such as a rapid decline in the Boston real estate market) can lead to the sudden termination of a bond tranche. Hence, issuers seek strategies that will minimize the likelihood of a "microburst" of defaults.

As long as there is no delinquency, the CMBS are well behaved. Unfortunately, delinquency triggers intervention by the servicer (whose role will be discussed later in the chapter). In the event of a delinquency, there may be insufficient cash to make all scheduled payments. In this case, the servicer is supposed to advance both principal and interest. The principal and interest continue to be advanced by the servicer as long as these amounts are recoverable.

Call Protection

In the residential MBS market, the vast majority of mortgages have no prepayment penalties. In the CMBS market, the vast majority of mortgages have some form of prepayment penalty that can impact the longevity and yield of a bond. Call protection can be made at both the loan level and in the CMBS structure. At the loan level, there exist several forms of call protection: prepayment lockout, yield maintenance, defeasance, and prepayment penalties.

Prepayment lockout is where the borrower is contractually prohibited from prepaying the loan during the lockout period. The lockout is the most stringent form of call protection since it removes the option for the borrower to prepay before the end of the lockout period. The prepayment lockout is commonly used in newer CMBS deals.

Under *yield maintenance,* the borrower is required to pay a "make whole" penalty to the lender if the loan is prepaid. The penalty is calculated as the difference between the present value of the loan's remaining cash flows at the time of prepayment and principal prepayment. Yield maintenance was a common form of call protection in older CMBS deals but it is less common in newer deals.

Defeasance is calculated in the same manner as yield maintenance. However, instead of passing the loan repayment and any penalty through to the investor, the borrower invests that cash in U.S. Treasury securities (strips/bills) to fulfill the remaining cash flow structure of the loan. The Treasuries replace the building as collateral for the loan. The expected cash flows for that loan remain intact through to the final maturity date. Like yield maintenance, it was more popular with older CMBS deals and is less common in newer deals.

With *prepayment penalties,* the borrower must pay a fixed percentage of the unpaid balance of the loan as a prepayment penalty if the borrower wishes to refinance. The penalty usually declines as the loan ages (e.g., starting with 5% of the outstanding principal in the first year, 4% in the second year, etc., until the penalty evaporates).

Exhibits 2 and 3 examine the largest 20 loans underlying the GMAC 1999-C3 deal. In terms of call protection, each of the loans is locked-out. The average lockout has about 114 months remaining. Hence, the loans underling this CMBS deal have just less than 10 years of prepayment protection.

In addition to call protection at the loan level, call protection is available in structural form as well. Since CMBS bond structures are sequential-pay, lower-rated tranches cannot pay down until the higher-rated tranches are retired. This is the exact opposite of default where principal losses hit the lowest-rated tranches first.

Timing of Principal Repayment

Unlike residential mortgages that are fully amortized over a long time period (say, 30 years), commercial loans underlying CMBS deals are often *balloon loans*. Balloon loans require substantial principal payment on the final maturity date although the loan is fully amortized over a longer period of time. For example, a loan can be fully amortized over 30 years but require a full repayment of outstanding principal after the tenth year. The purpose of a balloon loan is to keep the periodic loan payment of interest and principal as low as possible.

Exhibit 2: The 20 Largest Loans Underlying the GMAC 1999-C3 Deal

	Name	Location, MSA	Category	Loan Amount
1	Biltmore Fashion	Phoenix, Arizona	Retail	$80,000,000
2	Prime Outlets	Niagara Falls, New York	Retail	$62,835,426
3	Equity Inns	Various	Hotel	$46,511,317
4	One Colorado	Pasadena, California	Retail	$42,628,093
5	Comerica Bank	San Jose, California	Office	$33,640,510
6	120 Monument	Indianapolis, Indiana	Office	$28,955,362
7	125 Maiden	New York, New York	Office	$28,500,000
8	Texas Development	Houston, Texas	Apartment	$26,926,701
9	Sherman Plaza	Van Nuys, California	Office	$25,984,904
10	Alliance TP	Various	Apartment	$24,888,157
11	Bush Tower	New York, New York	Office	$23,000,000
12	County Line	Jackson, Mississippi	Retail	$20,990,264
13	Sherwood Lakes	Schererville, Indiana	Apartment	$20,162,442
14	Laurel Portfolio	Various	Apartment	$17,950,331
15	Sweet Paper	Various	Warehouse	$17,420,000
16	Sheraton Portsmouth	Portsmouth, New Hampshire	Hotel	$15,949,087
17	Trinity Commons	Fort Worth, Texas	Retail	$15,242,981
18	Village Square	Indianapolis, Indiana	Apartment	$14,993,950
19	Golden Books	Fayetteville, North Carolina	Warehouse	$14,493,350
20	Air Touch	Dublin, Ohio	Office	$13,992,523

Source: Charter Research.

Exhibit 3: Loan Characteristics for the 20 Largest Loans Underlying the GMAC 1999-C3 Deal

	Name	Coupon	Maturity	Current Occupancy	DSCR	LTV	Prepay Lockout
1	Biltmore Fashion	7.68%	07/01/09	96.00%	1.43	60.40%	114
2	Prime Outlets	7.60%	05/01/09	96.00%	1.36	72.70%	109
3	Equity Inns	8.37%	07/01/09	NA	1.90	49.50%	114
4	One Colorado	8.29%	07/01/09	91.00%	1.25	72.30%	114
5	Comerica Bank	7.55%	05/01/08	99.00%	1.43	65.20%	32
6	120 Monument	8.09%	06/01/09	100.00%	1.23	74.40%	113
7	125 Maiden	8.12%	09/01/09	97.00%	1.31	73.80%	116
8	Texas Development	7.44%	05/01/09	NA	1.34	72.00%	114
9	Sherman Plaza	7.68%	08/01/09	95.00%	1.24	68.40%	115
10	Alliance TP	7.32%	08/01/09	NA	1.19	86.40%	112
11	Bush Tower	7.99%	08/01/09	97.00%	1.27	46.00%	115
12	County Line	7.91%	08/01/09	98.00%	1.39	84.00%	115
13	Sherwood Lakes	6.99%	02/01/08	94.00%	1.32	76.70%	94
14	Laurel Portfolio	7.37%	05/01/09	NA	1.22	73.60%	112
15	Sweet Paper	8.26%	06/01/09	NA	1.25	71.40%	113
16	Sheraton Portsmouth	8.53%	05/01/09	71.00%	1.28	72.50%	116
17	Trinity Commons	7.93%	08/01/09	97.00%	1.44	68.80%	115
18	Village Square	7.80%	10/01/07	97.00%	1.28	79.30%	93
19	Golden Books	8.50%	08/01/09	100.00%	1.69	67.40%	119
20	Air Touch	7.98%	08/01/09	100.00%	1.20	77.70%	117

Notes: A * in the Prepay Lockout column denotes that yield maintenance is used in conjunction with Prepay Lockout.

Source: Charter Research.

Balloon loans pose potential problems for investors due to the large, lump-sum payment that must be refinanced. If there is a change in the quality of the underlying asset (e.g., a decline in the real estate market, increased competition leading to a decline in lease rates, etc.), there is a danger that the loan will not be refinanced; this can result in default. In order to prevent this type of loan failure at the balloon date from occurring, there are two types of loan provisions: the internal tail and the external tail.

The *internal tail* requires the borrower to provide evidence that an effort is underway to refinance the loan prior to the balloon date (say, 1 year prior to the balloon date). The lender would require that the borrower obtain a refinancing commitment before the balloon date (say, 6 months prior to the balloon date). With an *external tail,* the maturity date of the CMBS deal is set to be longer than that of the underlying loans. This allows the borrower more time to arrange refinancing while avoiding default on the bond obligations. The servicer advances any missing interest and scheduled principal in this buffer period.

THE UNDERLYING LOAN PORTFOLIO

There are two sources of risk relating to the underlying loan portfolio. The first risk is prepayment risk and the second risk is default/delinquency risk.

Diversification

A factor that is often considered when analyzing the risk of a CMBS deal is the diversification of the underlying loans across space. The reasoning for what is termed "spatial diversification" is that the default risk of the underlying pool of loans is lessened if the loans are made on properties in different regions of the country. Rather than have the entire portfolio of loans being subject to an idiosyncratic risk factor (e.g., the decline in oil prices and the collapse of the Houston real estate market), the portfolio can spread its risks across numerous economies. Thus, a collapse of the Houston real estate market (which may lead to higher defaults on commercial loans) will be less of a concern if the commercial property markets in Chicago, Kansas City, New York, and Seattle remain strong.

The strategy of spatial diversification can be seen in Exhibit 4. Approximately 22% of the loans underlying the GMAC 1999-C3 are on properties in California, 14% on properties in Texas, and 11% on properties in New York. The remaining loans are spread out among other states such as New Hampshire, Missouri, Illinois, and Mississippi. Thus, the GMAC 1999-C3 deal has achieved a significant degree of spatial diversification. Although a 22% concentration factor for California is still quite large, it is considerably less than a 100% concentration-factor (which is often referred to as a "pure play" strategy). Furthermore, California, Texas, and New York represent the states where most of the commercial loans are being originated.

Exhibit 4: Aggregate Loan Amounts by State for GMAC 1999-C3 Deal

State	Loan Amount	No. of Loans	% of Pool
California	$257,522,410	33	22.35%
Texas	$162,355,125	26	14.09%
New York	$130,070,471	7	11.29%
Arizona	$99,942,794	5	8.68%
Indiana	$68,623,516	5	5.96%
Ohio	$44,982,528	5	3.90%
Mississippi	$23,067,864	2	2.00%
New Jersey	$22,983,973	5	2.00%
Other	$342,473,371	50	29.73%
Total	$1,152,022,052	138	100.00%

Source: Charter Research.

Exhibit 5: Aggregate Loan Amounts by Property Type for GMAC 1999-C3 Deal

Property Type	Loan Amount	No. of Loans	% of Pool
Apartment	$259,779,802	39	22.55%
Office	$322,053,844	36	27.96%
Retail	$350,683,062	34	30.44%
Warehouse	$99,126,075	15	8.60%
Hotel	$105,832,139	8	9.19%
Other	$14,547,130	6	1.26%
Total	$1,152,022,052	138	100.00%

Source: Charter Research.

In addition to spatial diversification, CMBS pools can be diversified across property types. Rating agencies tend to give lower levels of credit-enhancement to deals that contain diversification across property types since a pool that is diversified across residential, office, industrial, and retail will likely avoid the potential of a national glut in one of the sectors (such as the retail market).

The degree of property type diversification can be seen in Exhibit 5. Approximately 90% of the loans are on retail, apartments, and office properties with retail having the largest percentage (30.44%). As a consequence, the GMAC 1999-C3 deals have reduced the risk of default by not being heavily concentrated in only one of the property groups.

The loan characteristics of the pool underlying the GMAC 1999-C3 pools are presented in Exhibit 6. The hotel properties are viewed as being the most risky given that they have the highest coupon (8.50%), the highest DSCR (1.65×), and the lowest LTV (58.93%). The apartment properties are viewed as the safest risk with the lowest coupon (7.62%), the lowest DSCR (1.29×), and the highest LTV (76.51%). As can be seen in Exhibits 5 and 6, 90% of the underlying loans are in the three least-risky property types: apartment, office, and retail.

Exhibit 6: Characteristics for Loans Underlying the GMAC 1999-C3 Deal by Property Type

Property Type	Coupon	Due	Current Occupancy	DSCR	LTV	Prepay Lockout
Apartment	7.62%	06/29/09	92.92%	1.29	76.51%	113
Office	7.79%	04/03/09	96.17%	1.33	67.84%	107
Retail	7.95%	09/19/09	95.21%	1.36	69.77%	116
Warehouse	8.13%	06/27/09	99.56%	1.42	68.28%	115
Hotel	8.50%	12/31/08	75.18%	1.65	58.93%	109
Other	7.83%	05/13/09	95.11%	1.54	67.00%	113

Source: Charter Research.

Cross-Collateralization

Diversification of the underlying collateral is one way of reducing default risk. Another way to reduce default risk is to use cross-collateralization. *Cross-collateralization* means that the properties that serve as collateral for the individual loans are pledged against each loan. Thus, the cash flows on several properties can be used to make loan payments on a property which has insufficient funds to make a loan payment. This "pooling" mechanism reduces the risk of default. To add some additional enforcement penalties to the cross-collateralization mechanism, the lender can use cross-default which allows the lender to call each loan within the pool, when any one defaults.

Loan Analysis

There are several products available that provide analysis of the underlying collateral for CMBS deals. An example of a package that allows for the analysis of the CMBS deal and the underlying collateral is Conquest, an on-line service provided by Charter Research in Boston. Conquest provides for a detailed examination of each loan in the underlying portfolio. In addition to simply describing the loan data (DSCR, LTV, loan maturity, prepayment lock type, etc.), Conquest provides default risk (delinquency) analysis as well. Using vendors such as Torto Wheaton, Conquest forecasts the growth in net operating income and value for each property in the underlying portfolio.

Torto Wheaton, for example, provides 10-year forecasts of net operating income and value by geographic area (MSA) property type (office, industrial, retail, and apartments). These forecasts are updated quarterly. Torto Wheaton provides five scenarios ranging from best to worst cases. Given these five scenarios, the user is able to examine the future path of debt service coverage and loan to value for each loan in the pool. Thus, the user is able to examine default and extension risk tendencies on a loan-by-loan basis. This information is aggregated to the deal level so that changes in the riskiness for each of the underlying loans is reflected in the cash flows for each tranche at the deal level.

Stress Testing at the Loan Level

Stress testing the collateral in a CMBS deal is important from both the underwriter and investor perspective. By allowing the forecasts on net operating income and value to be varied over time, underwriters and investors can better understand the default risk and extension risk likelihoods and how these in turn impact CMBS cash flows.

For CMBS markets, stress tests must be performed in a manner that is consistent with modern portfolio theory. While diversification across property type and economic region reduces the default risk of the underlying loan pool, the effects of diversification are negated if the stress test ignores the covariance between the properties. For example, there should be some degree of common variance across all properties (reflecting general economic conditions). Furthermore, there should be some degree of common variance across property type and economic regions.

The Torto Wheaton approach of generating five forecast paths by property type and geographic location permits the construction of a distribution of future outcomes for property value and net operating income growth for the loan pool. Based on Torto Wheaton forecasts, the user can determine the degree to which the portfolio is diversified (by reducing the variance of the distribution of future outcomes). An index of diversification can be created that allows users to compare the degree of diversification across different CMBS deals. Thus, stress testing the underlying properties can be measured in the aggregate by how much the diversification index is changed.

In addition to being able to create a diversification index, the user can construct a default risk/extension risk index as well. As the underlying loans are stressed, a distribution of outcomes in terms of default and extension risk can be obtained. This would allow users to compare CMBS deals not only for the diversification of the underlying loan portfolio, but compare CMBS deals for sensitivity to the stress test.

Historical Aspect on Loan Performance

While a detailed analysis of loan performance models is beyond the scope of this chapter, it is important to recognize that CMBS deals are not free of prepayment, default, and delinquencies. In Exhibit 7, the historical default and prepayment information for deals with a cutoff date in 1994 (from the Conquest database) are presented. As one can see, there is a wide range in terms of the ratio of performing loans to original loans in the pool. The KPAC 1994-M1 deal has the lowest performing loan ratio of 11.48%. On the other hand, the DLJ 1994-MF 11 has a performing loan ratio of 98.72%. The average performing loan ratio is 46.34% for the 13 deals from 1994.

It should be noted that the average performing loan ratio of 46.34% could be explained, in part, by underlying loan maturity. On average, 20.58% on the loans underlying deals from 1994 matured. Mortgage prepayments account for approximately 30.33% of the original loans terminating. Foreclosures, defaults, and real estate owned (REO) comprise only 2.50% of the 13 deals from 1994. Interestingly, the DLJ CMBS deals have a very high performance loan ratio (90% and 98%) with few loan maturities and prepayments (and no defaults or foreclosures).

Exhibit 7: Historical Default and Prepayment for CMBS Deals with Cutoff Dates in 1994

Deal	Loans	Performing	Matured	Prepaid	Bankrupt	Fore.	REO*
ASC 1994-C3	40	21	3	13	0	3	0
ASC 1994-MD1	9	7	1	1	0	0	0
ASFS 1993-2	30	19	4	5	1	1	0
ASFS 1994-C2	39	6	26	7	0	0	0
CLAC 1994-1	89	37	33	19	0	0	0
CSFB 1994-CFB1	63	21	8	34	0	0	0
DLJ 1993-MF 17	42	38	0	4	0	0	0
DLJ 1994-MF 11	78	77	0	1	0	0	0
KPAC 1994-M1	61	7	13	41	0	0	0
MCFI 1994-MC1	44	9	9	26	0	0	0
MLMI 1994-M1	80	32	28	20	0	0	0
SASC 1994-C1	185	67	51	53	0	0	14
SASC 1995-C1	142	30	21	71	0	5	15

Source: Charter Research.

Exhibit 8: Percentage Disposition of Loans Underlying 1994 CMBS Deals

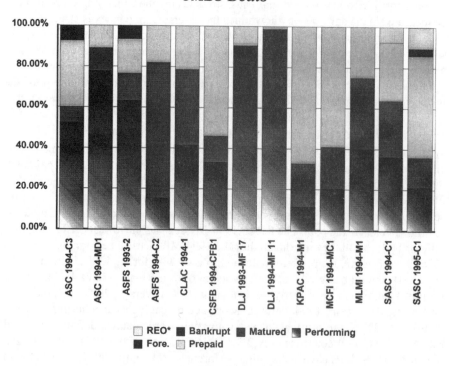

Source: Charter Research

Despite the historical performance of these deals, analysts must be careful about projecting these results for current deals. Prepayment lockouts, which are more popular now than they were in 1994, will be more effective in determining prepayments than simple yield maintenance provisions. Also, longer-term mortgage loans will extend the duration of the underlying loan pool (keeping the performance loan ratio higher for a longer period of time). Finally, improvements in underwriting and the investor's ability to understand the underlying collateral should improve default and foreclosure risk over time.

CREATING A CMBS MODEL

As mentioned before, there are a number of CMBS models available in the marketplace. Whether someone chooses one of the "one size fits all" models or designs a customized model tailored to specific needs, there are several key features that should be in a CMBS model.

1. An econometric model of historical loan performance using logit or proportional hazards model. This permits a better understanding of property and loan attributes that predict default and prepayment.
2. If default does occur, empirical estimates of loss severity by property type and state are needed.
3. Database of actual *NOI and Value volatility* by property type and geographic location (see the discussion of Torto Wheaton earlier in this chapter). This step permits the construction of default risk indicators.
4. Monte carlo simulation of interest rates and NOI paths to estimate foreclosure frequency and prepayment risk.
5. Finally, the deal structure (and waterfalls) should interface cleanly with loan-by-loan simulations.

A CMBS model with these features should be able to capture the critical elements of pricing, risk and return.

THE ROLE OF THE SERVICER

The servicer on a CMBS deal plays an important role. The servicer collects monthly loan payments, keeps records relating to payments, maintains escrow accounts, monitors the condition of underlying properties, prepares reports for trustee and transfers collected funds to trustee for payment.

There are three types of servicers: the subservicer, the master servicer and the special servicer. The *subservicer* is typically loan originator in a conduit deal who has decided to sell the loan but retain the servicing. The subservicer will then send all payments and property information to the *master servicer*. The master servicer oversees the deal and makes sure the servicing agreements are maintained. In addition, the master servicer must facilitate the timely payment of interest and principal. When a loan goes into default, the master servicer has the responsibility to provide for servicing advances.

Unlike the subservicer and the master servicer, the *special servicer* enters the picture when a loan becomes more than 60 days past due. Often, the special servicer is empowered to extend the loan, restructure the loan and foreclose on the loan (and sell the property). This critical role is of great importance to the subordinated tranche owners because the timing of the loss can significantly impact the loss severity, which in turn can greatly impact subordinated returns. Thus, first-loss investors usually want to either control the appointment of the special servicer or perform the role themselves. This creates a potential moral hazard problem since the special servicer may act in their own self-interest and potentially at the expense of the other tranche holders.

Chapter 3

Floating-Rate Commercial Mortgage-Backed Securities

Patrick Corcoran, Ph.D.
Vice President
J.P. Morgan Securities Inc.

Joshua Phillips*
Vice President
Nomura Securities International, Inc.

T his chapter examines the growing market for floating-rate CMBS. It compares their features to the better known fixed-rate market, surveys some recent deals, summarizes rating agency approaches, and offers opinions about future direction and relative value.

BORROWER PREFERENCES FOR FLOATING-RATE FINANCE

A borrower preference for floating-rate financing rather than traditional fixed-rate debt can arise for several reasons. First, a borrower may be in the process of renovating or repositioning a property. Since improvements are expected in both cash flow and the certainty of the cash flow stream, the borrower does not desire to lock in long-term financing terms that fail to fully reflect the property's anticipated improvement. Hence, the borrower opts for a short-term financing.

A second broad motive for short-term financing comes from acquisitions. Acquisition activity as of this writing is being fueled by consolidation in the REIT sector, where the securities valuation of many entities continue at discounts to the value of properties owned. Short-run borrowing needs of property acquirers are not well met by traditional 10-year fixed-rate commercial mortgages, featuring strong prohibitions against prepayment.

A final motive for short-term financing arises from the judgment that long-term financing is at the time of this writing too expensive. A sharp increase

---

* Mr. Phillips was an associate at J.P. Morgan Securities when this chapter was written.

in borrowing rates in 1999-2000 has led to an increase in floating-rate loans secured by both transitional and completely stabilized properties.

A Credit Perspective: Transitional Property versus Stabilized Property Financing

Thus, depending on borrower motive, floating-rate CMBS deals can include loans on either fully stabilized properties or transitional properties. However, floating-rate deals often differ from traditional fixed-rate deals because of their typical emphasis on transitional property loan collateral.

Transitional properties involving renovation or repositioning can be thought of as containing two elements. First, there is a stabilized property component represented by value corresponding to in-place cash flows. Second, there is an improvement component, which may arise in several different ways. First, changing market conditions within the broad property type or alternatively at the local market level may warrant a repositioning of the property. In a strong rental market, a typical indicator is leases that are well below market rents. Depending on the details, such repositioning will involve improved marketing or management, new "concepts," alternative ideas about site plans or tenancy, local market studies, and so on, in addition to actual physical renovations. Second, rising demand for space in the local market may highlight the benefit of a renovation or expansion of the facility. Here, the most obvious costs relate to physical expansion or improvement in the property.

In either case, the improvement component's value added is the difference between the total costs of the investment and the higher value realized in the repositioned or expanded property. In some ways, this value-added paradigm resembles that for new construction activity. However, repositioning or expanding existing properties with in-place cash flows should generally be considered as a lower risk than stand-alone construction projects.

Property improvements or renovations are subject to a different risk/return dynamic over the property market cycle. This can be seen in Exhibit 1. The solid line shows our proprietary "Credit Drift" for office property exposure. It is designed to measure the attractiveness of office property exposure taken in fixed-rate commercial mortgages. Notice that the Credit Drift measure turned positive in 1993, indicating that commercial mortgage exposure had turned attractive, following the real estate debacle of the early 1990s. Essentially, this turning point was supported by two distinct developments. First, in the property rental market, rents stopped falling and vacancies peaked at elevated levels and began to decline. Second, property prices had fallen to about 50% of replacement cost levels. The latter development was particularly striking. Since the difference between property prices and new development costs represents the gross profit margin to the developer, the large negative margin pointed to an absence of development activity for some time to come.

Exhibit 1: Credit Drift Scores for Stabilized Property and Repositioning/Improvement Activity (Downtown Office)

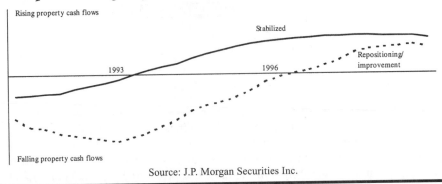

Source: J.P. Morgan Securities Inc.

Both of these factors were very positive for intermediate-term commercial mortgage exposure to stabilized properties. However, deeply discounted property prices were not positive for repositioning or additions to existing properties. After all, one could buy a property with "embedded" improvements at 50% of new development costs. So it made no sense to buy an older property and undertake new improvements at 100% of cost. A positive backdrop for renovation /repositioning activity had to await a substantial recovery of property prices several years later.

Exhibit 1 also shows an experimental measure designed to signal the attractiveness of shorter-term exposure to repositioning/improvement activity. This measure only turned positive several years later. Any particular transitional property will represent a mix of the stabilized property and pure improvement components, depending on their relative importance in the project. Since the mix can vary widely, so do the risk characteristics.

The environment as of this writing provides a contrast with 1993. Property prices have returned to a positive margin above new development costs. In addition, while rents and property cash flows are growing somewhat more slowly than in earlier years as a result of ample new construction, cash flows remain steady. Thus, the Credit Drift reading (Exhibit 1) corresponding to loan exposure in stabilized office properties remains healthy. Moreover, the transitional index, measuring the attractiveness of repositioning/improvement activity, is currently looking almost as strong as the index for stabilized properties (Exhibit 1).

In summary, transitional properties represent a combination of stabilized property exposure and exposure to repositioning and improvement activity. Since stabilized properties and any renovation component represent different risk exposures, our rating methodology offers the potential for evaluating a wide range of different risk profiles. Second, the wider range in signals for repositioning activity (Exhibit 1) highlights greater risk in transitional properties than in stabilized properties. However, in our view, the negative performance in the early 1990s downturn in real estate (Exhibit 1) overstates this additional risk in the more stable modern CMBS market.

Exhibit 2: National Credit Drift for Transitional versus Stabilized Properties

	Stabilized	Repositioning
Office	1.9	2.2
Suburban Office	2.0	1.5
Retail	4.0	5.0
Apartment	5.8	1.9
Industrial	3.8	2.8

Source: J.P. Morgan Securities Inc.

Exhibit 2 shows the Credit Drift readings for both stabilized properties and repositioning activity. In these indices, scores of 1-3 correspond to rising property cash flows, 4-6 to stable cash flows and 7-9 to falling cash flows. Strong readings point to an overweight of the indicated property type. They must also be balanced against the higher risk of repositioning activity. In apartment, industrial and suburban office loans, repositioning activity posts stronger scores than stabilized properties. In the downtown office sector, where scores are very strong, repositioning activity is only slightly less bullish than stabilized properties. In the case of retail properties, the repositioning index is somewhat behind a roughly neutral reading for stabilized properties.

Overall, the improving pattern in the repositioning index (Exhibit 1) evident in downtown office properties is also mirrored in the other property types. The property market in early 2000 is generally much more favorable to such activity than was the case as recently as 1994-1995.

FIXED AND FLOATING-RATE CMBS: RATING AGENCY APPROACHES

In looking at the early RTC CMBS deals, the rating agencies observed that floating-rate deals had higher default probabilities, other things equal, than comparable fixed-rate deals. They worried that interest rate spikes could increase the likelihood of term defaults. As a result, they encouraged borrowers to buy caps protecting them from rate spikes.

As a result of their default analysis, the rating agencies underwrite floating-rate deals more stringently than fixed-rate deals through the use of so-called "loan constants." The loan constants, which are different for the various property types, are designed to mimic the impact of a stress scenario in which floating rates spike or property income drops sharply. The constant is the sum of an assumed interest rate and amortization rate. Calculations of debt service coverage ratios (DSCR) look at the ability of net property cash flow (as underwritten by the agencies) to cover the assumed debt service, as measured by the loan constant. Typically, the rating agency DSCR is the most important input into the credit enhancement models that determine bond tranching.

Exhibit 3: Fixed versus Floating-Rate Rating Agency Underwriting Analysis

Appraised property value	= $140
Loan face amount	= $100
Issuer underwritten cash flow	$11.50
Rating agency underwritten cash flow	$11.00

Fixed-rate underwriting
Rating agency loan constant = 9.75%

$$\text{Agency DSCR} = \frac{\$11}{(0.0975)(\$100)} = 1.1282\times$$

Floating-rate underwriting
Rating agency loan constant = 11.50%

$$\text{Agency DSCR} = \frac{\$11}{(0.1150)(\$100)} = 0.9565\times$$

Source: J.P. Morgan Securities Inc.

Suppose for a particular fixed-rate loan, the loan constant is 9.75% (see Exhibit 3). For the same face loan amount, the loan constant in a floating-rate loan might be 11.50%. If rating agency underwritten cash flow were equal to 11.0% of the loan's face amount, the calculated DSCR for the floater would be 0.9565× (see Exhibit 3). However, for the fixed-rate loan, the DSCR would be 1.1282×. This simple calculation illustrates the most important reason why subordination levels for floating-rate CMBS are substantially above fixed-rate conduit paper.

If the borrower chooses to buy an interest rate cap (covering both the loan's term and any extension options), the borrower's situation improves somewhat. In this case, the rating agency takes the debt service to be equal to the capped interest rate plus assumed amortization. However, the agencies will not allow caps to reduce the loan constant below that used in fixed-rate deals.

COMPARING LOAN COLLATERAL IN FIXED AND FLOATING RATE DEALS

Loan Count and Average Loan Balance

Exhibit 4 shows some basic features of four floating-rate deals issued in the second half of 1999. The most obvious aspect, relative to fixed-rate conduit CMBS, is the relatively small number of loans and the relatively large loan size. There is an immediate implication for investors. Similar to fixed-rate large loan deals, the analysis must focus squarely on specific credit and loan collateral characteristics. This is true in analyzing both prepayment and credit loss scenarios. Unlike a conduit deal of 150-200 loans with average loan balance of $5 million, little comfort can be derived from statistical analysis and the law of large numbers. From the rating agency perspective, this means that significantly less credit is given for diversification benefits compared to those typically present in a fixed-rate conduit deal.

Within the four floating-rate deals, there is also substantial variation in average loan size. The DLJ 1999 FL-1 is most similar to conduit specifications with an average loan balance of $12.5 million. Although the GMAC 1999 FL-1 has a similar average loan size to the DLJ deal, it actually consists of a $130 million investment-grade large loan and 29 conduit loans averaging about $8-9 million per loan. By contrast, the COMM 2000 FL-1 and CDC 1999 FL-1 deals are large loan deals. Both of these deals have average loan balances around $50 million (Exhibit 4). Moreover, the COMM 2000 FL-1 deal has about three-quarters of its loan collateral in the form of loan participations. In each of these instances, notes junior to those included in the Trust are held outside the Trust. Finally, lumpiness in the floating-rate deals also shows up in the relatively high percentage of the deals accounted for by the top five and top ten loans (Exhibit 4), as well as in the uneven distribution of loan balances by property type.

Exhibit 4: Recent Floating-Rate Deals

Overview	GMAC 1999 FL-1	DLJ 1999 STF-1	COMM 2000 FL-1	CDC 1999 FL-1	1999 Conduit Average
Deal Size	$374.16	$428.53	$1,002.88	$549.14	$912.40
	11/16/99	11/30/99	1/26/00	12/16/99	
No. of loans	30	35	19	11	201
No. of prop	58	35	37	39	221
Avg Loan size (MM)	$12.5	$12.2	$52.8	$49.9	$4.5
Hard Lockboxes	2%	38%	68%	95%	N/A
Top 5 loan %	70%	53%	60%	70%	
Top 10 loan %	86%	79%	90%	96%	33.4%
Property Types	Conduit Only				
Office	48	22	33	33	18.9
Retail	5	10	19	22	25.9
Multifamily	30	41	4	6	31.0
Industrial	5	0	0	4	8.8
Hotel	0	27	11	34	8.9
Other	12	0	32	0	6.5
Rating Agencies					
Moody's	X	X	X	X	
S&P	X		X		
Fitch	X			X	
Duff					
Issuer					
DSCR	1.35	1.16	2.13	1.47	1.42
LTV	68.3%	69.2%	52.0%	57.7%	69.6%

Source: J.P. Morgan Securities Inc.

Exhibit 5: Rating Agency Analysis of Recent Floating-Rate Deals

Moody's	GMAC 1999 FL-1	DLJ 1999 STF-1	COMM 2000 FL-1	CDC 1999 FL-1
DSCR Whole Loans	1.09(conduit only)	1.22	1.19	1.18
LTV (%) Whole Loans	93.8%(conduit only)	89.9%	84.9%	87.0%
DSCR Inv Grade loans	1.64			
LTV (%) Inv Grade Loans	64.2%			
DSCR Participation			1.52	
LTV (%) Participation			66.4%	
WA Gross Margin (bps)	260	311	220	332
WAM (wo extensions)	22	20	28	29
WAM (w/ max extension)	26	37	38	36
Adjustment to Cash Flow	(Conduit Only)			
In Place Cash flow	−3.5%	17.1%	−7.4%	−7.1%
Stabilized Cash flow		−18.4%	N/A	−22.2%
Herfindel Score	26	15	10	8
AAA subordination Levels	44.5%	50.0%	30.25/45.3%*	47.0%
Stabilized/transitional	Largely stabilized	Largely not stabilized	Largely stabilized	Largely not stabilized

* The 45% level is the subordination level had the junior interests in the participation's been included in the trust.

Source: J.P. Morgan Securities Inc., Moody's Investors Services

Stabilized and Repositioned Properties

The fall 1998 crisis caused several investment banks to finance substantial inventories of loans, many involving turnaround properties, as floating-rate deals. Examples included several large balance sheet floaters by Lehman Brothers and CSFB. Despite the volatile capital markets environment, however, these early floater deals issued in late 1998 and early 1999, were supported by strong real estate credit fundamentals — as highlighted in Exhibits 1 and 2. As credit spreads tightened between the end of 1998 and late 1999, the deals paid down fairly quickly and performed strongly.

These earlier floating-rate deals are not examined in this chapter because they are not indicative of more recent floater deals that began to emerge in the second half of 1999. On average, the latter floaters have less of an improvement/ turnaround component than earlier floaters. Nonetheless, the variation in underlying property collateral can be substantial.

At one end of the spectrum is largely stabilized property collateral. According to Moody's presale report, the properties underlying COMM 2000 FL-1 were "virtually . . . all stabilized." Consistent with the largely stabilized loans/ properties are low rating agency subordination levels and a relatively light rating agency haircut to stabilized cash flow (see Exhibit 5).

The relatively low subordination levels for AAAs in COMM 2000 FL-1 benefit substantially from the use of the Note A/Note B loan structure. The participation structure effectively takes what would otherwise have been junior loan principal outside the Trust and leaves the amount of AAA bonds approximately unchanged, thereby reducing subordination. If the junior Note B interests are counted as additional credit support to the AAA bond classes, total subordination (both within and outside the Trust) is 45.3%. This compares with a 30.0% within-the-trust credit support level. However, the higher 45.3% credit support number highlights the fact that rating agency credit support levels have been within a very tight band, even though loan collateral has varied rather widely.

An example of a deal with largely stabilized properties but some transitional properties is GMAC 1999 FL-1. According to the Fitch presale report, about 71.5% of the properties were considered "stable," meaning that the properties have relevant historical operating history that the rating agency used as the basis of its underwriting, parallel to the approach taken in fixed-rate conduit deals. The rating agency considered the remaining 28.5% of the properties as having "low cash flow volatility." This category includes properties that are nearing the end of a successful repositioning strategy. Such properties are often fairly far along in a "lease-up" period and showing material improvement between trailing 12-month and current annualized revenue numbers. The preponderance of stabilized and "low volatility" properties in the GMAC 1999 FL-1 deal also shows up in a relatively modest cash flow haircut (Exhibit 5).

Somewhat further along the spectrum is the DLJ 1999 STF-1 deal. This deal appears to correspond largely to properties in the lease-up phase. This means that various improvements to properties have already been made and that what remains is for the properties to work their way through lease-up (i.e., getting from occupancies near pre-improvement levels to new "stabilized" occupancy and rent levels in the improved property). One way this shows up is in a substantial difference between underwritten net cash flow and DSCR and underwriter projections of "stabilized" cash flow and DSCR. In the case of DLJ 1999 STF-1, projected stabilized net cash flow is about 45% higher than current underwritten cash flow. This clearly represents a substantial improvement component.

Notice that the rating agency treatment of DLJ 1999 STF-1 haircuts stabilized net property cash flow by 18.4% (Exhibit 5) while actually giving a positive adjustment to in-place cash flow. By contrast, the COMM 2000 FL-1 deal, where the properties are largely stabilized, receives a modest 7.4% haircut (Exhibit 5).

The CDC 1999 FL-1deal, like the DLJ deal, contains properties that have been recently renovated or re-tenanted. In addition, some properties are currently undergoing renovation or other repositioning of the property. In this deal, Moody's identified a larger number of properties in non-stabilized condition than Fitch IBCA. In addition, Fitch IBCA put most of the transition properties in its "low volatility" bucket. According to Moodys, as a result of those properties still undergoing repositioning, four loans representing 24% of the pool balance include future funding obligations subject to various criteria. The aggregate amount of this subordinate financing totals to about $31 million, compared to collateral pool balances of about $600 million. For one large retail loan, advances of up to $10.5 million may be made, and principal repayment of these balances (if extended) will be made *pari passu* with the loan included in the Trust.

According to Moody's presale report, the CDC deal features underwritten net cash flows, once the properties become completely stabilized, that are about 24% larger than in-place cash flows. This is a smaller increase than the DLJ deal, but it also features future renovation and property repositioning (with additional lending and structural complexities) rather than pure lease-up risk.

Low Leverage versus High or Low Leverage

In early floating-rate deals in late 1998 and early 1999, leverage was unquestionably higher than that of typical fixed-rate conduit deals. For example, in SASCO 1999-C3, Moody's stressed LTV was 122% while the Fitch IBCA stressed debt service coverage ratio was 0.65×. These levels compare with typical 1999 fixed-rate conduit marks of 88% (LTV) and 1.15× (DSCR).

In the floating-rate deals examined in this chapter, however, it is not so clear that leverage is indeed higher. Of course, since fixed-rate deals involve purely stabilized properties, we can only compare floating-rate deals with largely stabilized properties to fixed-rate conduit deals. Let's use the GMAC 1999 FL-1 as an example, since it involves largely stabilized properties.

Exhibit 6 shows that this deal's leverage is only slightly above the average for 1999 fixed-rate conduit deals. Following our earlier discussion of rating agency underwriting approaches, we approximate loan constants to roughly calculate the Fitch stressed DSCR on a fixed-pool basis. In addition, we show the Moody's stressed LTV measure. Both rating agency measures show only slightly higher leverage than average fixed-rate conduit deals in 1999.

Call Protection

In fixed-rate conduit CMBS deals, call protection consists of lock-out, defeasance, and yield maintenance charges which either forbid or strongly discourage prepayment. By contrast, floating-rate loan collateral generally has much weaker call protection.

Exhibit 6: Leverage in GMAC 1999-FL1

	Floating-rate	Fixed-rate equivalent	1999 fixed-rate conduit average
Fitch Stressed DSCR			
Large loan	1.19×	1.40×	
Conduit loans	0.92×	1.08×	1.15×
Total	1.01×	1.17×	
Moody's Stressed LTV	93.8%		88.0%

Source: J.P. Morgan Securities Inc., Fitch-IBCA, Moody's Investor Services

Exhibit 7: Call Protection in Recent Floating-Rate Deals

	GMAC 1999 FL-1	DLJ 1999 STF-1	COMM 2000 FL-1	CDC 1999 FL-1
Yield Protection on Loans	• 35% of the loans have no call protection • 65% of the loans lockout • 1 to 15 months.	• All loans with lockout • Average lockout term 1.29 years • Lockout terms range from 1 to 1.67 years	• Lockout in year one • Afterwards fixed penalties	• Yield maintenance based on "LIBOR flat"
Stabilized/ transitional	Largely stabilized	Largely not stabilized	Largely stabilized	Largely not stabilized

Source: J.P. Morgan Securities Inc.

Floating-rate loans are typically in the 2- to 5-year maturity range. Call protection is a less important issue than in traditional 10-year fixed-rate mortgages. If a borrower prepays to take advantage of lower borrowing costs, investors in the fixed-rate loan are missing a component of the interest income stream for a much longer period and the present value of the missing cash flow is commensurately higher. In the floating-rate loan, resets in the floating interest rate remove one of several possible reasons that borrower financing costs could fall, thereby creating incentives to prepay the loan. The relative absence of call protection in floating-rate CMBS is similar to other floating-rate product, such as credit card or auto loan paper. In floating-rate CMBS, moreover, weak call protection meets the need for flexibility in seeking long-term takeout financing, repositioning a renovated property, or financing a portfolio acquisition short-term.

Since lock-out is necessary in selling a deal's IO on favorable terms, some lock-out may be negotiated with the borrower, but extension options are also common. Following the pattern in the fixed-rate market, loan terms are more likely to be customized with larger loans and borrowers.

In addition, there may naturally tend to be a trade-off in floating-rate deals between call protection and credit characteristics. For example, a borrower who uses a floating-rate loan to temporarily fund the acquisition of fully stabilized properties is much more likely to want complete flexibility and, depending on his short term plans, may be reluctant to accept lock-out. For example, in the case of the GMAC 1999 FL-1 deal with its generally stabilized or near-stabilized properties, call protection varied widely (Exhibit 7). 35% of the loans were without call protection while the remaining loans used lock-out (rather than prepayment premiums) ranging from 1 month to 15 months.

The GMAC deal is also unusual in combining a very large investment-grade loan with conduit collateral. The large loan is about one-third of the entire pool. In this situation, the rating agencies would be reluctant to assign bond sizing levels that gave "full credit" to the investment-grade loan without having confidence that it would be around for a while. This means that it would be difficult to do such a deal without having significant call protection on the large loan. In the large loan, lock-out is 15 months on a 24-month term. In essence, the heterogeneous character of the loan collateral in the GMAC deal forces the strong call protection on the large loan.

Another deal with mostly stabilized properties is the COMM 2000 FL-1 transaction. Here again, there was substantial variation among the loans (Exhibit 7). Call protected loans generally had a year of lock-out combined with decreasing fixed penalties over the next two years.

On the other hand, if properties are just beginning "lease up" after improvements have been finished, the borrower will want to wait until the end of this phase before considering permanent financing. In the DLJ 1999 STF-1 deal, where the properties appeared to be generally in the early "lease-up" phase, a year or so of lock-out was uniformly afforded on 2-year loans. Since the loans are very unlikely to be prepaid in the middle of the lease-up period, both the ease of obtaining the lock-out and the value of the protection are very different from the case where the property collateral is entirely stabilized.

The CDC1999 FL-1 deal affords an example of more flexible call protection in a deal with many non-stabilized properties. The approach used here was a modified form of yield maintenance using "Libor flat" (Exhibit 7) to discount the loan's floating-rate cash flow stream. The theory here is similar to using "Treasury flat" in fixed-rate yield maintenance. Clearly, no loan ever improves in quality to the point that the Treasury rate is the correct discount rate for the remaining cash flows. However, since improvements in property and loan quality are correlated with higher likelihood to prepay, Treasury flat helps to deal with the adverse selection problem. (See discussion below on this issue.) The same can be said for Libor flat. Libor-based rates are roughly equivalent to the credit of an AA-rated bank. Thus, the Libor flat discount rate is not as tough a hurdle as Treasury flat for fixed-rate loans.

Clearly, loan collateral in floating rate deals can vary greatly. As emphasized in our discussion of credit earlier, the mix of risk characteristics between stabilized properties and improvements are very different as well. The rating agencies underwrite the in-place cash flow for stabilized properties in floaters in the same way as for fixed-rate deals. However, they are much tougher on cash flows that are attributed to property improvements during lease-up. In a lease-up phase that is well along and appears to be moving ahead successfully, the agency may give credit for in-place cash flows but no credit for vacant space.

Extension Options

Like call protection, extension options can also be related to whether the collateral is stabilized or transitional loans/properties. In general, the demand for extension options by borrowers is likely to be greater with transition properties than fully stabilized properties. As shown in Exhibit 8, it is the deals with largely stabilized property collateral (GMAC 1999FL-1 and COMM2000FL-1) that exhibit the lower shares of loans with extension options. The other two deals with more transitional property loans have the larger shares of loans with extension options.

Exhibit 8: Extension Provisions in Recent Floating-Rate Deals

	GMAC 1999 FL-1	DLJ 1999 STF-1	COMM 2000 FL-1	CDC 1999 FL-1
Percent of loans with extension options	28.8%	100.0%	43.5%	60.7%
Extension terms	Average 11.3 months	All loans with options Range 6-12 months Four loans with second extension option	Average 24.1 month option	All loans 12 month option

Source: J.P. Morgan Securities Inc.

BONDS AND STRUCTURING ISSUES IN FLOATING-RATE CMBS

In looking at structural questions in floating-rate CMBS, the issues can be broadly divided into two categories. First, floating-rate deals are lumpy deals with much larger average loan size than fixed-rate conduits and far fewer loans. Since 1998, the market has been wary of lumpiness in fixed-rate deals. In response to this development, there have been a variety of structural innovations such as Note A/ Note B structures to reduce the lumpiness of larger loans in fixed-rate conduit and fusion deals. Since floating-rate deals are lumpy, lumpiness has been an issue just as it has in fixed-rate deals.

Second, the weaker call protection in floating-rate deals brings out the so-called "adverse selection" problem. This describes the tendency for improving loan credits and properties to have a higher probability of prepayment while deteriorating loans are more likely to extend at the balloon date. As compared with fixed-rate deals, this issue assumes larger importance in the floating-rate market both because of weaker call protection and widespread extension options. In an extreme scenario, when rapid early prepays combine with a high percentage of extensions, the loan coupon payments could be inadequate to pay the interest on the lower rated bonds, thereby hurting B-piece returns in such scenarios.

To provide a greater comfort level for subordinate bond buyers, recent deals have varied the bond structure from strict senior/subordinated sequential pay. As a practical matter, in the current market environment, this involves negotiations with B-piece investors and a balancing act with the rating agencies, who allow more favorable allocations of higher-rated bonds in the presence of a strict sequential pay structure. However, if a better reception by B-piece investors can be secured through a partial tilt to a pro-rata allocation of non-default related prepayments, proceeds from the deal may possibly be increased despite fewer highly rated bonds being allocated in the structure.

For example, the 1999 CDC deal allowed lower-rated bonds to share on a pro-rata basis in unscheduled principal payments not related to default (Exhibit

9). In the case of defaults, recoveries of principal are returned on the normal sequential senior/sub basis. Similarly, the DLJ 1999 STF-1 deal pays on a pro-rata scheme (Exhibit 9). Interestingly, both these deals are ones with a greater share of transition properties rather than largely stabilized collateral.

In our view, demand by B-piece buyers for pro-rata structuring of non-default prepays is likely to be larger the larger the "window" in which adverse selection can operate. This window includes both periods that are freely open to call and also extension period options. Moreover, adverse selection seems likely to play out most forcefully in extension options when the collateral corresponds largely to non-stabilized properties. In these deals, the greater uncertainty surrounding the success of the turnaround activity, compared to risks on stabilized properties, suggests greater scope for adverse selection to operate.

Exhibit 9: Structural Provisions in Recent Floating-Rate Deals

	GMAC 1999 FL-1	DLJ 1999 STF-1	COMM 2000 FL-1	CDC 1999 FL-1
Overall Structure	Sequential	Pro-Rata	Sequential; several loans are participations	Pro-Rata Contingent on a rule-set that once violated permanently reverts to sequential-pay
Scheduled Principal	sequential	Pro-rata if current balance is greater than .325 of original After the factor reaches .325 the deal is sequential	Sequential	Modified sequential
Unscheduled Principal			Paid pro-rata between senior interests and junior interests (outside the trust) before an event of default	
Prepayment premiums	No prepay premiums Lockout only Exit fees ranging from 1-4%	No prepay premiums lockout only	All to the IO	Allocated between the IO and a "remainder" class
Other Unique Features			72% of the loans are participation loans Junior interest held outside the trust.	

Source: J.P. Morgan Securities Inc.

In cases where borrowers owning stabilized properties are reluctant to agree to lock-out, this by itself may raise the demand by B-piece buyers for pro-rata sharing of prepay principal returns. In addition, specific deal features can also play a role. As discussed above in the GMAC deal, for example, rating agency issues essentially forced strong call protection on the large loan in the deal. When the latter feature is combined with the largely stabilized collateral, the likely result is to reduce pressure from B-piece buyers for pro-rata sharing arrangements. And, in fact, we find the deal is sequential (Exhibit 9).

The COMM 2000 FL-1 deal allows junior Note B loan interests outside the Trust to share in non-default unscheduled principal paydowns (Exhibit 9). Once these arrangements had been negotiated at the loan level, they were not subject to change as a result of discussions with potential B-piece buyers. In addition, if the junior interests had been included within the Trust in a conventional CMBS structure, the importance of B-pieces in the CMBS structure would have been far larger.

In terms of mechanics, pro rata allocation rules can be based upon loan pool statistics or, alternatively, they can operate at the individual loan level, reflecting rating agency concerns about particular loans. An example of a pool-based rule can be seen in the DLJ 1999 STF-1 deal (Exhibit 8). If the aggregate loan balance in the deal falls below 32.5%, principal allocations revert to straight sequential pay.

In summary, pro rata principal allocation rules help B-piece buyers deal with the adverse selection problem. From the perspective of the AAA investors, compensation for the departure from strict sequential pay comes in the form of both higher subordination levels and reduced prepayment risk.

CONCLUSION AND RELATIVE VALUE IN FLOATING-RATE CMBS

AAA subordination in the floating-rate deals examined in this chapter falls within a tight 44% to 50% range, even though the collateral ranges from largely stabilized to largely transitional. This compares with AAA subordination levels in the mid-twenties in typical fixed-rate conduit deals. As discussed above, this higher subordination represents a rating agency response to (1) lower loan count, (2) weaker diversification, as well as (3) more stringent underwriting by the Agencies for floaters.

Loan collateral in late 1999 floaters has moved much closer to fixed-rate conduit collateral than was the case in earlier 1998-1999 floaters. We expect this process to continue to evolve. In particular, we expect to see some floating-rate deals with larger loan counts, better diversification, and closer conformity in general to fully stabilized fixed-rate conduit collateral.

Historically, defaults came "early and often" in 1970s and 1980s vintage loans as well as the RTC CMBS deals (including floaters) in the early 1990s. By contrast, the non-RTC CMBS market, which began in 1993-1994, has been marked by an absence of early term defaults and stellar loan performance in general. In our view, rating agency underwriting of floating-rate loans is conservative. Thus, even in deals that move closer to fixed-rate collateral in loan count and diversifcation, subordination levels should remain significantly higher than those on fixed-rate deals. From a credit standpoint, in our opinion, this points to good relative value in AAA paper backed by stabilized properties.

Since collateral varies widely within floating-rate deals, there is a need for careful analysis of transitional property collateral. While loans backed by transitional properties are somewhat higher risk than stabilized property collateral, the additional risk is mitigated by the strong performance of property rental markets in the modern real estate markets since 1993. Credit Drift scores for repositioning activity can be used with scores for stabilized property markets to assess opportunities in transitional properties. Attention must also be paid to the fine points of repositioning plans and improvements.

As shown in Exhibit 10, pricing of AAA floating-rate securities examined have been quite close to fixed-rate 5-year AAA CMBS, on a swap-adjusted basis. (Note this is a plain vanilla swap and not a "balanced guaranteed" or true asset swap.) Pricing of the fixed-rate AAAs is as of Friday the week the floating rate deals priced. The GMAC 1999 FL-1 and COMM 2000 FL-1, the two deals with largely stabilized property collateral, both priced slightly tighter in spread than the fixed-rate AAAs, on a swap-adjusted basis. On the other hand, the two deals with transitional property collateral, DLJ 1999 STF-1 and CDC 1999 FL-1, priced wider in swap-adjusted spread than the fixed-rate paper. While these differentials in swap-adjusted spread are in the "right direction," the differentials look small, in our opinion, compared to differences in collateral.

Another indication that floating-rate deals with transitional collateral are not always "efficiently" priced can be seen in the SASCO 1999-C3 deal, also shown in Exhibit 10. Even though this deal priced in October 1999, it is similar to earlier higher-leverage floaters with highly transitional collateral. Despite this, it priced at a swap-adjusted spread tight to generic 5-year fixed-rate AAA paper.

Exhibit 10: Pricing of Floating-Rate AAA bonds

	GMAC 1999 FL-1	DLJ 1999 STF-1	COMM 2000 FL-1	CDC 1999 FL-1	SASCO 1999-C3
AAA Libor spread (bps)	+36	+40	+30	+45	+40
AAA Average life (years)	1.52	1.50	2.10	1.98	1.58
Pricing date	11/16/99	11/30/99	1/26/00	12/16/99	10/20/99
2yr AAA credit card Libor spread (bps)	+14	+14	+10	+12	+17
5yr AAA CMBS fixed-rate spread minus swap spread (not balanced guaranteed, bps)	+39	+34.5	+32	+27.5	+43

Source: J.P. Morgan Securities Inc., *Commercial Mortgage Alert*

Exhibit 11: 3-Year Credit Cards: Floating-Rate versus Fixed-Rate-Swap Spread

(5 day moving averages in bps)

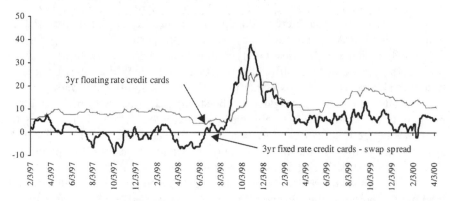

The long position in 5-year fixed-rate AAA CMBS and short a plain vanilla swap is not of course a true floating-rate exposure. A true floating-rate exposure would require an asset swap linked to the 5-year fixed-rate CMBS. While such "balanced guaranteed" swaps have been written on 10-year fixed-rate AAA CMBS, they have not been written on 5-year paper. The obvious reason is that the five-year fixed-rate bond occupies a more vulnerable position to default-related prepays in the deal structure.

Thus, with rough parity in swap-adjusted spread between fixed- and floating-rate AAAs (Exhibit 10), floating-rate investors would generally opt for the AAA floater. At rough spread parity, the fixed-rate AAA CMBS looks expensive relative to AAA floating-rate bonds, in our opinion. In part, this pricing may reflect the less lumpy, more diversified collateral in fixed-rate conduit pools, pointing to reduced volatility in bond cash flows.

The pricing configuration for fixed and floating-rate AAA CMBS bears some resemblance to pricing in AAA credit card paper. Exhibit 11 compares spreads on 3-year floaters to swap-adjusted fixed-rate spreads. Over the 1997-2000 interval, floating-rate credit card paper has persistently looked a few basis points cheap to fixed-rate paper. Since the floating-rate side of the credit card market is better developed than in CMBS, the result seems to reflect demand-supply dynamics of investors and issuers in fixed and floating-rate debt and less than complete integration in pricing.

Chapter 4

Multifamily Project Securities

Ed Daingerfield
Managing Director
Nomura Securities International, Inc.

P rojects are mortgages on multifamily homes that are insured by the Federal
Housing Administration (FHA) under various federal programs of the National
Housing Act of 1934, as amended. For more than 65 years, one of the primary
goals the U.S. government has set for the FHA is to enhance the nation's supply of
multifamily housing. Several FHA programs have evolved to provide federal insurance for the construction financing and permanent mortgage financing on many types
of multifamily residences (including rental apartments, condominiums and cooperatives), on nursing homes, residential facilities for the elderly, hospitals and on other
health care units. In addition, the FHA has long-established insurance programs used
for refinancing mortgages on these types of properties and/or rehabilitating them.

FHA AND GNMA PROJECTS:
TWO PRIMARY STRUCTURES OF PROJECT SECURITIES

Projects most commonly trade in two forms: either as FHA-insured passthrough
participations or as Ginnie Mae securities. Regardless of form, all projects are
guaranteed by the United States government through the Department of Housing
and Urban Development (HUD) and the FHA insurance funds. Projects may only
be originated by mortgage lenders in good standing with the FHA and HUD, and
all projects are first created as *FHA-insured multifamily loans*. However, FHA-
insured whole loans may only be purchased by FHA-approved lenders, and so the
secondary market for projects in whole loan form is relatively small. More common are *FHA Participation Certificates (PCs) or FHA pools*. FHA PCs are created whenever an FHA-insured project loan is used to collateralize a passthrough
security issued by an approved mortgage banker. FHA pools are simply a collection of FHA-insured projects aggregated together.

    GNMA project passthrough securities are created when a mortgage
banker originates an FHA-insured multifamily loan but then selects the additional
guarantee and standardization provided by GNMA securities. This is analogous to
the single-family market, where the FHA or VA insures mortgages that are then
issued as GNMA passthroughs. The credit backing of all FHA and GNMA projects
derives from the FHA insurance fund, and so projects issued in both GNMA and
FHA form enjoy the full faith and credit backing of the U.S. government.

Exhibit 1: Primary Differences between GNMA and FHA Projects

GNMA	FHA
If default:	If default:
- 100% of principal paid upon default	- 99% of principal upon default
- Full and timely payment of P & I	- Ultimate payment of P & I
	less one month interest
44-day payment delay	54-day payment delay
Securities wired through depository	Physical delivery of certificates
Denominations of ≥ 25,000	Standard piece limit: 3 – 4 per pool
Delivery of GNMA Prospectus	Delivery of participation and servicing
Supplement available	agreement is recommended
Pool data on Bloomberg	Pool data not on any central database
Supplemental data available	Supplemental data available
on GNMA's web site	on the FHA's web site

Differences Between FHA and GNMA Projects

There are several important differences between projects issued in FHA-insured form and projects issued as GNMA securities, and as a result GNMA project securities command a price premium over FHA projects (see Exhibit 1). Like single-family GNMA securities, GNMA projects pay principal and interest with a 44-day delay, while FHA projects pay with a 54-day delay. In the event of default, GNMA project passthrough securities incorporate the same standardized procedures as single-family GNMA passthroughs: full and timely reimbursement of principal and interest is guaranteed in the event of default, and claims for GNMA insurance are paid out in cash, in a timely manner.

In contrast, in the event of default, procedures are not standardized with FHA project securities: investors may have to rely on specific information written into the servicing agreement to determine the exact default proceedings. Also, although FHA projects do insure full payment of principal and interest, the FHA takes a 1% administrative fee when a project defaults and is assigned to HUD, and so the investor receives only 99% of principal in default. In addition, the FHA does not guarantee timely payment of principal and interest. Investors may have to wait several months in the event an FHA-insured project defaults, although interest does continue to accrue during this time (with the exception of a one-month grace period for which no interest is paid, although no interest is lost on a GNMA project). Finally, although all projects issued in GNMA form pay cash in the event of default, claims on some FHA project defaults are paid in cash, while others are paid in FHA debentures, which are federal agency debt issues of the FHA. Many FHA projects are designated either "cash pay" or "debenture pay" at origination, while others are designated cash or debenture pay at the time of default at the option of either the mortgagee or HUD. FHA projects designated "cash pay" pay default claims in cash, while those designated "debenture pay" may pay default claims either in FHA debentures with a 20-year maturity or in cash, at the option of HUD. Given all these differences it is no surprise that FHA projects trade cheaper than GNMA projects, nor that the spread differential between GNMA and FHA projects widens or tightens in response to market factors.

GNMA and FHA Trends in Originations

Whether projects are issued in FHA form or in GNMA form is a function of the rates at which either can be sold in the secondary market, as well as the costs to issue and insure either form of project. GNMA projects are more expensive to issue than FHAs, given the increased costs of GNMA's wrap. However, this cost difference has varied widely in recent years, as GNMA has adjusted its costs. Consequently, at various points in time new issuance in projects shifts back and forth between predominately FHA to predominately GNMA originations. Prior to 1981, the majority of all projects were issued as FHA passthrough certificates, or in FHA pools. With the advent of the coinsurance program (see below) in 1983, issuance shifted and most projects were issued as GNMA securities through 1990, when the coinsurance program was terminated. After coinsurance, issuance shifted back to favor FHA projects, which dominated new originations from 1990 through early 1993. In March of 1993, GNMA lowered its guarantee fee, which reduced the cost of issuing GNMA project securities, and from that time to the present, most new projects have been issued as GNMAs.

PREPAYMENTS

Most project pools consist of one large mortgage loan, unlike single-family pools which are backed by numerous smaller mortgages. Consequently, projects do not trade to estimates of prepayment speeds like single-family mortgage-backed securities. Rather, prepayments on projects are driven by the definite incentives most mortgagors have to prepay their mortgages. The likelihood that a project will prepay is based largely on the economics of the underlying building and the characteristics of the mortgagor, as well as on the specific prepayment restrictions and penalties of each project. A key determinant of prepayment likelihood in projects is whether the borrower is a profit motivated private enterprise or a not-for-profit group. As a general rule, profit motivated developers prepay project mortgages as early as is economically feasible, while non-profit developers are less likely to prepay.

Prepayments on Projects Owned by Non-Profit Groups

Most non-profit groups that operate projects are either state or local housing authorities, church groups or community organizations. As non-profit entities, these groups are not concerned with prepaying a mortgage to access built-up equity nor with refinancing to generate increased tax benefits. Also, non-profit organizations are not likely to convert a rental property to a cooperative or sell out to another developer for a profit, and non-profits often receive government and/or private subsidies that effectively limit default risk. As a result, prepayments on not-for-profit projects are rare. These projects provide reliable call protection, and since their cash flows are consistent, most non-profit projects trade to their final maturity rather than to any assumed prepayment date.

Prepayments on Projects with Section 8

One feature of projects that provides call protection to investors exists when a project has a Section 8 rental subsidy contract between the project owner and the FHA (called a Project-Based Section 8 contract). Under these Section 8 Housing Assistance Payment (HAP) contracts, FHA agrees to pay the difference between what a tenant can afford to pay for rent (based on tenant income) and the prevailing market rate for a similar apartment in the same area. Typically, tenants pay 30% of their monthly income for rent, and Section 8 subsidies cover the balance. To be eligible for Section 8 payments, tenants must be low income families whose incomes do not exceed 50% of the median income for the area; close to four million families are currently served by some form of Section 8 subsidy.

Project-based Section 8 payments are made directly to the owner of the project, which assures a reliable cash flow from the project and makes prepayments from default less likely. Section 8 subsidy payments also provide additional call protection since the project owner may not prepay the mortgage while the HAP contract is in force (most project-based HAP contracts are for 20 years and are renewable). Section 8 contracts cannot be transferred or terminated, and remain with the project under a change of ownership. Section 8 HAP contracts may cover fewer than 100% of the rental apartments in a given project; obviously, projects with higher percentages of Section 8 provide greater call protection.

The Section 8 program has been modified several times in the past decade, as HUD worked to preserve and expand the number of affordable multifamily apartments, and these program changes do effect the prepayment characteristics of bonds backed by Section 8 projects. In the early 1990s, the Low-Income Project Preservation Act (LIPPRA) and successor laws were established to preserve low-income apartments. Section 8 projects covered by LIPPRA are expressly prohibited from prepaying. If the developers of such projects wish to refinance for any reason, they must take a HUD-insured Section 241 second mortgage (see below) rather than prepay the first Section 8 mortgage. Bonds backed by the initial Section 8 project mortgage covered by LIPPRA provide significant call protection.

By 1994, HUD realized that the agency had significant problems brewing, since a substantial majority of their original project-based, 20-year Section 8 HAP contracts were up for renewal between 1999-2003. While the social policy goals of HUD suggested that the agency renew these Section 8 contracts, the subsidized rents at many of these properties exceeded market rents. As a result, concern grew at HUD that the fiscal realities of renewing Section 8 HAP payments could be at odds with the government's goal for a balanced federal budget. Another issue complicated HUD's ability to insure Section 8 housing, since in many cities across the nation, select urban neighborhoods have improved in recent years. Borrowers at Section 8 properties located in these so-called gentrified neighborhoods often did not want to renew their Section 8 contracts, since by refinancing and exiting the Section 8 program, they might generate higher, non-regulated rents from their properties. Political issues and staff reductions slowed HUD's response to these problems, and throughout the late 1990's HUD instituted several different, short-lived programs to address fiscal problems caused by the large number of expiring Section 8 contracts.

As a result of these regular changes in the Section 8 program, estimating the prepayment likelihood of project bonds with Section 8 became difficult. After various studies and pilot programs over several years, the FHA has finally decided to renew some expiring Project-Based Section 8 HAP contracts, while providing Section 8 rental vouchers directly to tenants at other projects. Under HUD's voucher program, low-income tenants are scheduled to receive direct credits which can be used to subsidize their rent at any apartment of their choosing. While Section 8 payments will remain linked to specific properties under the project-based HAP contracts the FHA renews, the new voucher-based Section 8 subsidies are portable. Although this new Section 8 voucher program is untested as of this writing, low income tenants will likely have more choice in selecting where they'll live under Section 8 vouchers than they have under the more established project-based subsidies. This suggest that to the degree the FHA expands voucher-based Section 8 subsidies, investors may anticipate some increase in prepayments on bonds backed by these properties. In the future, the prepayment likelihood of Section 8 projects will depend as much on the location and underlying economics of the property as on the specific type of Section 8 subsidy program at that project.

Prepayments on For-Profit Projects

Private sector, profit-motivated borrowers may refinance projects if interest rates decline, but they also have incentives to refinance loans at current or even somewhat higher rates. While higher interest rates increase the expenses for project owners, the higher debt service costs can often be offset or exceeded by increasing rents. For existing properties that have increased in value, selling the property or refinancing at a higher loan-to-value ratio enables developers to access equity that has built up in a project. The economics of a profit-motivated developer's business often dictate that private sector project borrowers refinance to capitalize available equity. Refinancing a for-profit project may also be driven by a need for the mortgagor to raise money to refurbish or rehabilitate a property without putting up scarce equity. This is very common since most developers maximize profits by gradually increasing rents over time as leases expire and tenants move. The ability to increase rents is obviously dependent on the physical condition of the property. As projects age, developers frequently refinance the mortgage to generate money for refurbishing the building, which in turn protects their long-term investment and encourages higher rents.

As for-profit projects age and the mortgage is paid down, the probabilities increase that private developers will prepay the mortgage to rehabilitate the project or to take out equity. The likelihood and timing of prepayments on profit-motivated projects depends on several factors, including the loan-to-value ratio of the project, the type and location of the project, the physical condition of the property, and the type of borrower. Borrowers are more likely to prepay projects with lower loan-to-value ratios, since this permits them to access a substantial amount of equity quickly. Also, projects built for upper-and middle-income rather than low-income tenants are generally more likely to refinance, since they typically have more amenities (pools, dishwashers, microwave ovens, etc.) that need to be refurbished as they age. For-profit projects are generally in better neighborhoods, and so are more likely to increase in value or be converted to condominiums. Under FHA regulations, if a project does not continue to serve the same use its mortgage must be prepaid; thus, before an owner of a rental project can convert the property to a cooperative or condominium, the HUD mortgage must be prepaid. Moderate and higher income projects also tend to prepay faster since, as the building ages and amenities deteriorate, developers often need to refinance to access equity to refurbish and maintain the project to protect their investment. Also, projects in high growth areas and other favorable locations more frequently increase in value and so tend to prepay faster. Exhibit 2 illustrates that even assuming a conservative 1% annual increase in property values, equity in a project increases by as much as one third after 10-12 years.

Tax considerations also provide motivation for many private investors and limited partnerships to refinance projects. The Tax Reform Act of 1986 curtailed accelerated depreciation, which had provided significant incentives to refinance older projects. Projects originated after 1986 must be depreciated over 27½ years, using a straight line method. However, tax factors remain a consideration in refinancing decisions. The tax shelter provided by deducting mortgage interest payments, coupled with the tax advantages that remain under the current depreciation rules, begin to abate in years 10-12 as the project mortgage amortizes. Exhibit 3 shows that typically, passive tax losses in a project partnership dissipate and begin to generate taxable income by years 10-12. This makes it advantageous for partnerships and individual owners to refinance project mortgages to reset the passive tax losses that are vital to many real estate owners.

Taken together, Exhibits 2 and 3 illustrate how profit-motivated projects often refinance in 10-12 years for two complementary reasons: (1) owners access equity in order to: refurbish their property and maintain competitive rents in their local apartment market, to consolidate ownership by paying off limited partners, and to purchase other projects; and (2) refinancing or sale of the property is a common exit strategy for owners focused on the tax-shelter advantages of projects.

Exhibit 2: Project Equity Accrues over Time

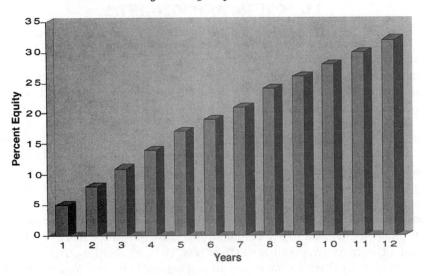

Exhibit 3: Tax Advantages Erode over Time

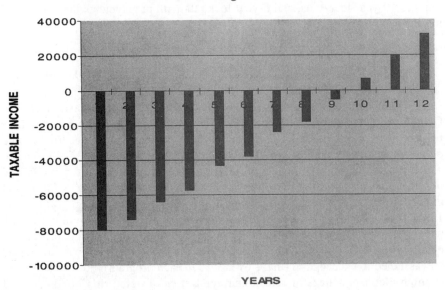

PREPAYMENTS, CALL PROTECTION, LOCKOUTS, AND PENALTIES

FHA/HUD does not prohibit profit-motivated developers from prepaying or refinancing project mortgages, although prepayments on non-profit projects are generally restricted by the agency. Non-profit projects built under several FHA programs may not be prepaid, while under other programs prepayments on non-profit projects are permitted only if the mortgagor is able to secure HUD's approval. In addition, prepayments on projects with Section 8 are restricted, some by formal HUD regulations and others by economic forces (see above).

Most project pass throughs are whole pools backed by one building, and so a full prepayment effectively generates a call at par on the security. As a result, prepayment restrictions and penalties are written into the documentation that governs project trades. HUD has approved three basic types of prepayment restrictions and penalties (see HUD mortgagee letter 87-9): (1) prepayment lock-out restrictions that extend to a maximum of 10 years plus the stated construction period, (2) prepayment penalties of 1% or less, 10 years after the stated construction period, and (3) some combination of prepayment lock-out and penalties with a lockout less than 10 years and a premium no more than 1% 10 years after the stated construction period. At present, the two most common forms of call protection are 10-year lock-outs, and 5-year lockouts with prepayments then permitted in year 6 at a 105% of par, declining to 101% in year 10.

PREPAYMENTS AND DEFAULT: BACKGROUND

Default generates an unanticipated prepayment, received in cash at par for GNMA projects and at 99% in cash or debentures (depending on program) for FHA projects. Defaults on HUD-insured projects have primarily occurred in two older programs: (1) the 221(d)3 Below Market Interest Rate or BMIR program, which insured urban low-income projects in an effort to ameliorate poverty and provide inner-city housing (however, construction design, planning, location and underwriting later proved to be flawed); and (2) the coinsured program of the 1980s. The structural failures of HUD's GNMA coinsurance program are now widely acknowledged (see coinsurance, below). Accurate numbers are difficult to obtain from HUD, but default rates on BMIRs and coinsurance projects are generally assumed to exceed 35% (that's over 35% in each program). For investors, the economic consequences or return characteristics of defaulting bonds depend purely on interest rates. Many investors have reaped windfalls when discount BMIRs defaulted, although other investors have suffered when premium coinsured GNMAs defaulted.

When a project goes into default, the servicer assigns it to the FHA, and over the years the agency has accumulated a significant inventory of defaulted projects. Cumbersome regulations have prevented HUD from foreclosing on many troubled properties, and budget constraints have left HUD ill equipped to manage problem properties. As a result, HUD has begun to sell the projects that have been assigned to the agency. While some of the properties in HUD's inventory are seriously troubled, others are performing, while still other loans have been helped by recovering real estate values and lower interest rates. As HUD continues to liquidate this portfolio, investors can expect to see HUD-insured mortgage pools, senior/subordinate pools, and structured securities transactions backed by these loans.

COINSURANCE

For most of its existence, HUD has been a thinly staffed and lightly funded federal agency. Also, as the nation's largest insurer/provider of multifamily rental housing, HUD has frequently been subject to political pressures at the city, state, and particularly the national levels. Significant political pressures were brought to bear on HUD with the advent of the Reagan administration in the early 1980s, when the department suffered substantial reductions in staffing. FHA loan underwriters and auditors bore the brunt of these cutbacks, and this vitiated HUD's ability to implement strict underwriting standards. In response, in 1983 HUD introduced the coinsurance program.

Under this coinsurance program, private GNMA mortgage bankers took on the role of HUD staffers and were responsible not just for originating loans, but also for all due diligence and underwriting for project loans. In an attempt to preserve credit standards, HUD required mortgage originators to reimburse the agency for 20% of any insurance claims the agency paid out on any projects that defaulted. This 20% liability was intended to keep mortgage bankers in the coinsurance program honest. At that time, the feeling was that the government could minimize risk to the FHA insurance fund by enabling private-sector lenders to risk their own capital on a project in return for greater origination fees. Predictably, the program ran into problems. By the late 1980s, it became clear that underwriting standards had generally received a lower priority than the mortgage bankers' desire for the lucrative fees generated by new loan originations. HUD also lacked the systems needed to monitor the thinly capitalized coinsured mortgage bankers. In addition, cases of outright fraud in loan originations were well publicized, and senior management at HUD became embroiled in several well-publicized scandals. HUD eventually cancelled the coinsurance program in 1990.

A significant number of coinsured GNMA project securities remain in circulation and trade regularly in the secondary market. Since these outstanding projects are in GNMA from, investors are shielded from credit risk by the U.S. government guarantee of Ginnie Mae. However, since most coinsured GNMAs were originated with high coupons, they generally trade at significant price premiums. Investors should exercise caution in evaluating premium projects underwritten with coinsurance; to the degree that questionable underwriting increases the likelihood of default (i.e., par call), the return characteristics of premium coinsured GNMAs can shift dramatically.

CLC/PLC

Under HUD's multifamily insurance programs, the government insures the construction financing of projects as well as the permanent mortgage on the completed structures, unlike single-family mortgage passthroughs in which the government only insures mortgages on completed homes. Investors purchase Construction Projects by investing in bonds that fund construction costs on a monthly basis until the project is built. When construction is completed, the investor's cumulative monthly construction securities are rolled into a permanent mortgage security on the building.

The construction financing portion of a project trades in the secondary market as insured *Construction Loan Certificates* (*CLCs*), in either FHA-insured or GNMA form. CLCs operate as follows: each month during a predetermined construction period (typically 14-18 months), the contractor completes a specified portion of the construction and then submits a bill for the work to the local FHA office. The FHA then sends an inspector to the job site, and after the work meets specifications GNMA issues an insured CLC for that month's work. (FHA issues the insured CLC if the security is in non-GNMA form.) The investor funds the work by fulfilling a commitment to purchase each monthly CLC. When the project is completed, the bond servicer exchanges all the monthly CLCs for an insured *Permanent Loan Certificate (PLC)*.

The PLC is an insured GNMA (or FHA) passthrough security backed by the final mortgage on the completed property. There are vastly more PLCs than CLCs in the market, owing to the long economic lives of project structures, and while CLCs are generally held by one investor over a relatively short construction period, PLCs trade frequently in the secondary market.

Determining the relative value of insured Construction/Permanent securities is a function of the coupon, seasoning, and call protection of the CLC/PLC, as well as the length of the construction period. During construction, each month the investor funds another insured CLC, which represents the construction work completed in the prior month, and bond interest is paid monthly on all the CLCs already funded. The present value of CLC interest payments is primarily a function of the opportunity cost of earning coupon payments as the investment is phased in gradually over the construction time. As a result, CLCs trade at a discount to fully funded Project Securities, and CLCs with shorter construction periods offer more value than do CLCs with lengthy construction periods.

STRUCTURED PROJECT SECURITIES

In 1996, projects began to be used as collateral for structured securitizations, and as of September 2000, $5.8 billion of project loans have been used as collateral for 22 separate structured transactions. A large majority of these securitizations (close to $5 billion) have structured GNMA projects into sequential-pay securities, and have been completed under Fannie Mae's shelf. Structuring projects directs the cash flows and prepayment protection of project collateral to minimize extension risk, target appropriate prepayment scenarios, and so produce more efficiency from the underlying project bond collateral. Also, just as structured financings have increased the market value of many other asset classes, structuring projects has also augmented the secondary trading value of project securities.

SPECIFIC PROJECT PROGRAMS

Since its creation under the National Housing Act of 1934, the FHA has established numerous multifamily insurance programs. Each program serves a specific purpose, and is referred to by the section of the housing act under which it was created. Specific characteristics vary from program to program, since the types of projects, their purposes, allowable mortgage limits, prepayment features and other criteria often differ. As discussed above, regardless of which program a project is insured under, securities backed by insured mortgages may exist in either GNMA form or as FHA passthroughs. A brief discussion of several of the most common multifamily insurance programs is provided in the remainder of this chapter. Exhibit 4 provides a quick reference table on these programs. Exhibit 5 shows a the relative size of each program within the project market.

Multifamily Housing

Section 221(d)4: Rental Housing for
Low- to Moderate-Income Families
The 221(d)4 program is the largest Project program, with $35.1 billion in cumulative insurance issued on 9,960 projects and $28.9 billion insurance remaining in force since the program began in 1959.[1] This program insures mortgages made by private lenders to finance construction or substantial rehabilitation of multifamily rental or cooperative housing for low- to moderate-income or displaced families. Projects insured under Section 221(d)4 must have 5 or more units, and may consist of detached, semi-detached, row, walk-up or elevator structures.

---

[1] All data reported in this chapter are from the U.S. Department of Housing and Urban Development, as of October 31, 1999.

Exhibit 4: Project Quick Reference Chart

SECTION 202

Type of Program:	Direct loans for housing the Elderly or Handicapped
Type of Borrower:	Private, non-profit sponsors (including non-profit cooperatives)
Maximum Loan Amount:	The lesser of: 95% of anticipated net project income or 100% of the project's development costs
Maximum Term:	50 years by Statute, but HUD has limited loans to 40 years
Date Program Enacted:	1959 (amended 1974)
Additional Features:	Older loans fixed rate; newer loans adjust annually at a HUD-determined margin over Treasuries. All projects under Section 202 have 100% Section 8 HAP contracts (see Section 8)
Program Status:	Active
Insurance in Force:	$7.7 billion

SECTION 207

Type of Program:	Construction or rehabilitation of rental housing
Type of Borrower:	Primarily profit-motivated sponsors
Date Program Enacted:	1934
Prepayment Restrictions:	Negotiable
Program Status:	Authorized but not used; multifamily rental projects now issued under Sections 221(d)3 and (4)
Insurance in Force:	$2.9 billion

SECTION 213

Type of Program:	New construction, rehabilitation, acquisition, conversion or repair of Cooperative housing projects
Type of Borrower:	Profit-motivated Co-op sponsors as well as non-profit corporations or trusts
Date Program Enacted:	1950
Prepayment Restrictions:	Negotiable
Program Status:	Authorized but not used; Cooperative projects now issued under Sections 221(d)4, 221(d) 3 and 223(f)
Insurance in Force:	$678 million

SECTION 220

Type of Program:	New construction or rehabilitation of projects in designated Urban Renewal Areas
Type of Borrower:	Profit-motivated and non-profit sponsors
Date Program Enacted:	1949 (expanded 1980)
Prepayment Restrictions:	Negotiable
Program Status:	Active but infrequently used; Urban Renewal projects are being eliminated
Insurance in Force:	$1.1 billion

Exhibit 4 *(Continued)*

SECTIONS 221(D)3 and 221(d)4	
Type of Programs:	Construction or rehabilitation of multifamily rental or cooperative housing
Type of Borrower:	For-profit corporations or partnerships (developers, builders, investors); also nonprofit public or community groups
Maximum Loan Amount:	221(d)4: 90% of FHA-estimated replacement cost (maximum can be higher only with explicit FHA approval) 221(d)3: 100% of FHA-estimated replacement cost
Maximum Term:	40 years from origination
Date Programs Enacted:	221(d)3: 1954; 221(d)4: 1959
Additional Features:	FHA passthroughs auctioned before 1/1/84 have an option that permits investor to put the mortgage to HUD in its 20th year
Prepayment Restrictions:	Negotiable between mortgagor and mortgagee unless project \ has a low income use restriction within a Section 8 HAP contract
Program Status:	Active
Insurance in Force:	221(d)4: $28.9 billion; 221(d)3 Market Rate Only: $2.2 billion
SECTION 223(f)	
Type of Program:	Purchase or refinancing of existing multifamily projects
Type of Borrower:	Primarily profit-motivated sponsors
Maximum Loan Amount:	85% of HUD estimated value (may be raised to 90% with HUD approval)
Maximum Term:	35 years from origination
Date Program Enacted:	1974
Prepayment Restrictions:	Negotiable
Program Status:	Active
Insurance in Force:	$16.4 billion
SECTION 231	
Type of Program:	Rental housing for the elderly or handicapped
Type of Borrower:	Profit-motivated and non-profit sponsors
Maximum Loan Amount:	90% (for-profit project) 100% (non-profit project) of the FHA-estimated replacement cost
Maximum Term:	40 years, or 75% of the project's estimated economic life
Date Program Enacted:	1959
Prepayment Restrictions:	Negotiable
Program Status:	Active
Insurance in Force:	$640 million

Exhibit 4 *(Continued)*

SECTION 232

Type of Program:	Construction or rehabilitation of Nursing Homes, Intermediate Care Facilities, and Board and Care Homes
Type of Borrower:	Profit-motivated and non-profit sponsors
Maximum Loan Amount:	90% of FHA-estimated value of property (includes the value of equipment used to operate the facility)
Maximum Term:	40 years from origination
Date Program Enacted:	1959
Prepayment Restrictions:	Negotiable
Program Status:	Active
Insurance in Force:	$7.4 billion

SECTION 236

Type of Program:	Interest-rate subsidies for low- to moderate-income families and elderly individuals
Type of Borrower:	Profit-motivated and non-profit sponsors
Maximum Loan Amount:	90% of FHA-estimated replacement cost (100% or higher permissible for non-profit sponsors)
Date Program Enacted:	1968
Prepayment Restrictions:	Negotiable
Program Status:	Inactive
Insurance in Force:	$4.9 billion

SECTION 241

Type of Program:	Insured second mortgage for preservation-designated Section 8 projects
Type of Borrower:	Profit-motivated and non-profit sponsors
Maximum Loan Amount:	90% of FHA-estimated replacement cost of first and 241 second mortgage combined
Date Program Reactivated:	1993
Prepayment Restrictions:	Negotiable
Program Status:	Active
Insurance in Force:	$1.5 billion

SECTION 242

Type of Program:	Construction or rehabilitation of public or private Hospitals (includes major movable equipment)
Type of Borrower:	Profit-motivated or non-profit sponsors\
Maximum Loan Amount:	90% of FHA-estimated replacement cost
Maximum Term:	25 years from origination
Date Program Enacted:	1968
Prepayment Restrictions:	Negotiable; non-profit sponsors may only make prepayments with HUD's written consent
Program Status:	Active
Insurance in Force:	$5.4 billion

Exhibit 5: Relative Size of the Various Programs that Constitute the $74 Billion Project Securities Outstanding as of 10/31/99 (HUD Data)

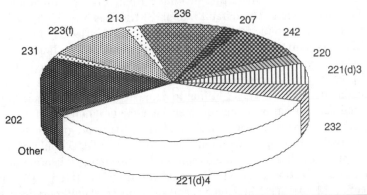

Section 221(d)4 projects may be owned by either non-profit or profit moti-vated developers, and these projects may be insured for up to 90% of their FHA-determined replacement cost. While 100% of the funds invested in project securities is insured, the mortgagor only borrows 90% or less of replacement cost; the balance represents owner equity. The majority of loans insured under Section 221(d)4, and most new loan originations, are unsubsidized, market rate projects. That is, project developers set the rental rates at whatever levels their local real estate market can command (subject to HUD approval), and there are no income restrictions on ten-ants. Since the early 1990's, a significant majority of 221(d)4 issuance has been on these market rate projects. Developers have selected HUD financing as the most cost-efficient way to finance new apartment construction, and most projects insured under Section 221(d)4 are suburban garden apartments and other higher-end apart-ment complexes. Non-market rate projects may also be insured under Section 221(d)4, and most Section 8 subsidized projects have been financed through the 221(d)4 program. Unlike market rent projects, Section 8 projects have restrictions on monthly rents and tenant income (see Section 8, above).

The maximum term of mortgages insured under Section 221(d)4 is either 40-years or 75% of the FHA-estimated remaining economic life of the project, whichever is less. The majority of these projects carry 40-year terms. FHA/HUD does not restrict prepayments on Section 221(d)4 mortgages, although prepayment lockouts and penalties are usually negotiated between the mortgagee and mortgagor (see prepayment section, above). HUD may allow mortgagors to prepay up to 15% of a mortgage per year, unless documents which record the transaction specify in the lockout that the bonds are non-callable in whole or in part for a specified period of time. However, even if documents do not prohibit prepayments, the 15% prepay-ment option is not exercised often, since U.S. government backing makes project financing much less expensive for developers than private financing alternatives.

Section 221(d)3: Rental and Cooperative Housing for Low- to Moderate-Income Families

The 221(d)3 program has two components. The first was an older, below market interest rate program (BMIR) that provided financing to sponsors of lower-income housing projects. The default rate on BMIRs has been high, over 35% as discussed above, and so the BMIR program was closed in 1972 (of the $2.87 billion BMIRs originally insured, only $1.2 billion remain outstanding).

The second component of Section 221(d)3, the market rate program, has been eclipsed by the 221(d)4 program (see above). The market rate 221(d)3 program remains in force, with $3.2 billion in cumulative insurance issued on 2,058 projects and $2.2 billion insurance in force since the program began in 1954. The primary difference between the 221(d)3 and the 221(d)4 program is that Section 221(d)3 provided developers with more leverage, since HUD could insure up to 100% of a project's FHA-determined replacement cost under this program, versus only 90% under Section 221(d)4. The majority of market rate projects insured under Section 221(d)3 have Section 8 rental subsidies, and unlike projects insured under Section 221(d)4, 221(d)3 projects can include cooperatives. Finally, during the first 20 years of a mortgage insured under Section 221(d)3, borrowers must obtain HUD's permission before making any prepayments on the mortgage. Aside from these differences, the 221(d)3 market rate program closely resembles the 221(d)4 program. The program may be used for new construction or substantial rehabilitation of various types of buildings.

7.43 Putable Projects: Older FHA Projects Insured under Sections 221(d)3 and 221(d)4

FHA projects insured under Section 221(d)3 and 221(d)4 prior to 1984 included a 20-year put feature. This put option gives the FHA passthrough holder the right to assign, or put, the mortgage to HUD for a one-year period 20 years after the original mortgage was endorsed by HUD/FHA. When investors put the securities, under the FHA's initial program they received FHA series MM debentures, which are bonds with a 10-year maturity, callable after 6 months. These MM debentures are obligations of the FHA, and as such are unconditionally guaranteed by the U.S government as to payment of interest and principal. The debentures' face value equals the unpaid principal balance of the mortgage that is put to HUD, plus accrued interest.

Prior to December 1983, many FHA projects were auctioned by GNMA. The majority of these projects were purchased by servicers as 7.50% loans, and issued as FHA pass through securities with 7.43 coupons. They are commonly referred to as "7.43's" since the issuers often retained 7 basis points of servicing. The vast majority of 7.43's were auctioned between 1979 and 1983; consequently, most 7.43's are putable between 1999 and 2003, and trade at a spread over comparable treasury bonds. Most of the projects underlying 7.43's carry Section 8 contracts (see above), which provide the investor with a defined cash flow and also limit prepayments. This cash flow certainty coupled with their put feature make putable 7.43's very convex securities.

The exact value of the FHA debentures definitely affects the value of the put option. To compensate for the additional market risk and record keeping associated with debentures, investors have typically valued FHA debentures at 96-to-98 cents on the dollar. However, the FHA changed the put process on 7.43's in 1992. For several years thereafter, investors in 7.43 putable bonds received cash, or par, in lieu of debentures when the bonds were put. As a result, the put option became worth more than the 96% to 98% most investors assumed upon purchase. HUD funded the cash put by auctioning the bonds that were put to the FHA; several successful auctions were held in the mid-1990s, but the auctions stopped by 1996. Since interest rates trended lower during that time, few bonds were put to HUD and the Agency had an insufficient number of bonds to hold further auctions. Consequently, by 1999, the FHA again began paying puts with FHA debentures, and as of this writing, 7.43's are being paid in Series MM debentures, although the cash put auctions are still authorized by HUD.

An accurate valuation of 7.43 puts is linked to the assumed strike price of the put which, in turn, depends primarily on whether HUD funds the put in cash or in debentures. The shift from paying puts in Series MM debentures to paying puts with the cash generated by auctions creates budgetary savings for HUD, and so shaves the Federal budget deficit. As a result, many observers think it likely that HUD will resume their put auctions and reinstitute the change from debenture pay to cash pay. Investors should realize that an overwhelming majority of all 7.43's (just over 7 billion) are eligible to be put in between 2000-2003, while only 2 billion were eligible to be put in the entire period from 1992-1999. Should HUD elect to continue using Series MM debentures to fund the 7.43 puts, the increased supply of debentures could weaken their secondary market value and further erode the value of the put option. Until HUD clarifies the cash versus debenture funding mechanism, the value of 7.43 putable bonds will remain in question.

Finally, investors should note that not all 7.43's are putable; 7.43's issued under some project programs are not putable. Most of these non-putable 7.43's also carry Section 8 contracts, and so provide defined cash flows. Non-putable 7.43's trade in the secondary market at a spread over the U.S. Treasury curve.

Section 223(f): Purchase or Refinancing of Existing Multifamily Projects

The 223(f) program was created to insure the purchase or refinancing of existing rental apartment projects, to refinance existing cooperatives, or to purchase and convert existing rental projects to cooperative housing. Section 223(f) was added to the National Housing Act by the Housing and Community Development Act in 1974, in response to private-sector demands for an FHA-insured refinancing vehicle and to help preserve an adequate supply of affordable housing. Conventionally financed apartment projects, as well as FHA insured housing projects issued under any section of the National Housing Act, can be refinanced by using Section 223(f). Since 1974, 3,823 projects have been originated under Section 223(f), representing $19.4 billion of insurance written with $16.4 billion remaining in force.

Section 223(f) is a market-rate, unsubsidized program created primarily to improve the financing flexibility for profit motivated project developers by making it easier for owners to refinance, convert a project to a co-op, and buy or sell an existing building. To qualify for insurance under Section 223(f), a project must be at least three years old, must contain five or more units, and must have sufficient occupancy to pay operating expenses, annual debt service, and maintain a reserve fund for replacement requirements. A mortgage insured under Section 223(f) cannot exceed 85% of the HUD/FHA estimated value of the project, although this requirement can be raised to 90% for cooperatives and those projects located in Target Preservation Areas as designated by HUD.

The maximum term for mortgages insured under Section 223(f) is either 35 years or 75% of the FHA-estimated remaining economic life of the project, whichever is less. Most 223(f) projects carry 35-year terms. As with other programs, HUD/FHA permits prepayments on mortgages insured under Section 223(f), although prepayment lockouts and penalties are usually negotiated between the mortgagee and mortgagor.

Section 207

Section 207 was enacted in 1934 as the first program used by the FHA to finance construction or rehabilitation of multifamily housing projects. Section 207 projects are primarily moderate income projects sponsored by for-profit developers. The 207 program is rarely used today, as multifamily projects are now originated under Sections 221(d)3 and 221(d)4. However, seasoned Section 207 projects continue to trade in the secondary market. Total cumulative insurance issued under Section 207 was $4.2 billion, with $2.9 billion insurance remaining in force.

Section 213

The Section 213 program was enacted in 1950 to provide mortgage insurance on cooperative projects. Section 213 insurance was used for new construction, rehabilitation, acquisition, conversion or repair of existing housing in several types of cooperative projects that consist of five or more units. The program was available for both non-profit cooperative corporations as well as for profit motivated developers who build or rehabilitate a project and sell it to a cooperative corporation. The 213 program is no longer used, as cooperative apartments are now insured under Sections 221(d)4 and 223(f). Total cumulative insurance written under Section 213 is $1.6 billion on 2,043 projects, with $640 million insurance remaining in force.

Section 220

The Section 220 program was created to insure mortgages and home improvement loans on multifamily projects in urban renewal areas. Before 1980, Section 220 insurance was available in urban renewal areas in which federally assisted slum clearance and urban redevelopment projects were being undertaken. In 1980, the Housing and Community Development Act expanded the scope of the

Section 220 program to include those areas in which housing, development and public service activities will be carried out by local neighborhood improvement, conservation or preservation groups. The main focus of Section 220 is to insure mortgages on new or rehabilitated multifamily structures located within designated urban renewal areas. Over 540 projects have been insured under Section 220, which represents $3.1 billion in total cumulative insurance with $1.1 billion remaining in force.

Section 236: Interest-Rate Subsidies for Low-to Moderate-Income Families and Elderly Individuals

Section 236 was added to the National Housing Act in 1968, but was suspended during the subsidized housing moratorium of 1973 and has never been revived. The 236 program combined governmental mortgage insurance on projects with subsidized payments to reduce the project owners' monthly debt service payments. These reduced interest payments, in turn, are passed on to tenants of the project in the form of lower rents. To qualify for rental assistance under Section 236, tenants' annual income must be less than 80 percent of the median income of the area. The program served both elderly individuals and low-income families.

The maximum mortgage amount for limited-dividend sponsors is 90 percent of replacement cost; for nonprofit sponsors, the maximum mortgage amount can be 100 percent. In certain defined high cost areas, maximums may be increased up to an additional 75 percent. The maximum term under this program is 40 years, and prepayments are prohibited for at least 20 years without prior approval from HUD. Total cumulative insurance issued under Section 236 was $7.5 billion on over 4,000 projects; $4.9 billion insurance remains in force.

Section 241(f): Section 8 Refinancings

Section 241(f) was reactivated early in 1993 to address the refinancing of low-income housing that receives Section 8 rent subsidies (see above). Section 8 projects that fall under the Low Income Housing Preservation Acts of 1987 (Title I) and 1990 (Title II) are designated preservation projects and can not be refinanced. However, owners whose preservation properties have increased in value can access that equity with a second mortgage loan insured under this Section 241, without refinancing the project's underlying Section 8 first mortgage. Under Section 241, HUD reunderwrites the entire project to a maximum 90% loan-to-value, subtracts the remaining balance on the first mortgage, and then insures a 241 loan for the balance. The 241 loan is fully insured by HUD; there is no credit difference between the original HUD mortgage and the new 241 loan. Obviously, given the use of the 241 program, securities backed by first mortgages with Section 8 subsidies provide significant call protection to investors. In addition, the 241 loans are usually originated with 10-years of call protection. Total cumulative insurance written under Section 241(f) is $1.6 billion, with $1.5 billion insurance remaining in force.

Healthcare and Housing for the Elderly

Section 231: Rental Housing for the Elderly or Handicapped

In 1959, Congress enacted Section 231 of the National Housing Act to provide insurance for the construction or rehabilitation of rental housing for the elderly. Section 231 was expanded to include housing for the handicapped in 1964. Residents of projects for the elderly must be at least 62 years old, while residents in projects for the handicapped must be people with a long-term physical impairment that substantially impedes an independent living arrangement, but who could live independently in suitable housing.

Projects must have eight or more units to qualify for insurance under Section 231, and the maximum term for mortgages insured under Section 231 is 40 years or 75% of the project's estimated economic life. In addition, HUD may insure up to 100 percent of the estimated replacement cost for projects originated by nonprofit and public borrowers, but only up to 90 percent of replacement cost for profit-motivated mortgagors. Section 231 is no longer used for new loans; elderly housing is now financed under the 221(d)4 and the 232 programs. Total cumulative insurance issued under Section 231 was $1.1 billion, with $640 million insurance remaining in force.

Section 232: Nursing Homes, Intermediate Care Facilities, and Board and Care Homes

Under Section 232, HUD insures mortgages to finance new construction or rehabilitation of Nursing Homes for patients who require skilled nursing care and related medical services, as well as Intermediate Care Facilities and Board and Care Homes, for patients who need minimum but continuous care provided by licensed or trained people. Section 232 insures mortgages on any of these facilities; also, nursing homes, intermediate care and board and care homes may be combined within the same facility and insured under Section 232. Board and care homes must have a minimum of five one-bedroom or efficiency units, while nursing homes and intermediate care facilities must have twenty or more patients who are unable to live independently but are not in need of acute care. Mortgage insurance under Section 232 may also cover the purchase of major equipment needed to operate the facility. Also, Section 232 may be used to purchase, rehabilitate, and/or refinance existing health care projects already insured by HUD.

Legislation establishing Section 232 was enacted in 1959. Borrowers may include private non-profit associations or corporations as well as for-profit investors or developers. To qualify for insurance under Section 232, sponsors must first qualify for licensing in the State of the facility, and must comply with all relevant State regulations. Total cumulative insurance issued under Section 232 is $8.6 billion on 3,320 projects; total insurance remaining in force is $7.4 billion.

Section 242: Mortgage Insurance for Hospitals

In 1968, Congress enacted Section 242 of the National Housing Act to provide insurance for the construction or rehabilitation of Hospitals. Major equipment used in the hospital may also be included in an insured mortgage under Section 242. Hospitals built or rehabilitated under Section 242 must have appropriate licenses and meet the regulatory requirements of the State in which they are located, and must be approved by the U.S. Department of Health and Human Services. A Section 242 mortgage may not exceed 90% of the FHA-estimated replacement cost, and the maximum term for these mortgages is 25 years.

Borrowers under Section 242 may be either profit-motivated or not-for-profit hospitals. HUD permits full or partial prepayments on profit-motivated Section 242 projects, subject to prepayment restrictions and penalties negotiated between the mortgagor and mortgagee, but prepayments by non-profit mortgagors are permitted only with the written consent of HUD. Total cumulative insurance issued under Section 242 is $7.7 billion on 305 projects, with $5.4 billion insurance remaining in force.

Chapter 5

Lehman Brothers' CMBS Index

Steven Berkley
Managing Director
Lehman Brothers Inc.

Alex Golbin
Senior Vice President
Lehman Brothers Inc.

T he commercial mortgage-backed securities (CMBS) market continues to grow at a very rapid pace with 1998 issuance more than 75% greater than the record $44 billion (105 transactions) set in 1997, and with 1999 issuance just slightly lower ($66.2 billion) than that of 1998. With this high growth, CMBS issuance represented approximately 10% of total mortgage backed securities (MBS) issuance in both 1998 and 1999. Issuance for the record 1998 was $71.6 billion (94 transactions), with average transaction size of $833 million compared to $419 million in 1997 (see Exhibits 1 and 2).

As the investor base for CMBS continued to broaden, Lehman Brothers recognized the need for a formal CMBS Index for use as a performance benchmark. In keeping with our tradition of offering rigorous indices, Lehman Brothers has designed a new index to capture the essential characteristics of the CMBS market. Similar to other members of the Lehman Brothers Global Family of Indices, our CMBS Index was constructed using a rules-based approach. Each security in our CMBS Index must meet all published eligibility criteria (The eligibility criteria are discussed in later in this chapter.) A well-defined set of rules was developed to minimize arbitrary exclusion of securities, assure that included issues have liquidity, and allow for the maintenance of complete market data.

Exhibit 1: Taxable Fixed Income Spread Product Issuance

($ billions)

Sector	1997 Issuance	% of 1997 Issuance	1998 Issuance	% of 1998 Issuance	1999 Issuance	% of 1999 Issuance
US Treasuries	$1,563.4	57.8%	$1,159.1	41.2%	$1,236.0	41.45%
Residential MBS	$368.2	13.6%	$639.8	22.7%	$655.5	21.99%
US Agency	$273.2	10.1%	$386.7	13.7%	$420.2	14.09%
Asset Backed Securities	$176.1	6.5%	$159.0	5.7%	$189.4	6.35%
Corporate Bonds-Inv. Grade	$149.7	5.5%	$269.9	9.6%	$313.5	10.51%
Corporate Bonds-High Yield	$132.1	4.9%	$127.6	4.5%	$100.9	3.38%
CMBS	$44.0	1.6%	$71.6	2.5%	$66.2	2.23%
Total	$2,706.7				$2,981.8	

* As of December, 31, 1999

Exhibit 2: Composition of Outstanding Fixed Income Spread Product Market*

Sector	Total Outstanding	% of Total Outstanding
US Treasuries	$1,544	25.67%
Residential MBS	$2,004	33.32%
Corporate Bonds Inv. Grade	$1,366	22.71%
US Agency	$571	9.49%
Corporate Bonds High Yield	$338	5.62%
Asset Backed Securities	$91	1.51%
CMBS Investment Grade	$101	1.68%
Total	$6,015	

As of 07/31/2000

This approach ensures that the CMBS Index is consistent, objective, reliable, representative of the marketplace, and replicable. As with all our other indices, this index is not influenced by our current inventory positions or by past and future underwriting roles for any issuer. This approach contrasts with sample "basket" or portfolio-based indices where the performance benchmark is an arbitrarily selected set of securities.

INDEX RETURNS AND STATISTICS UNIVERSE

Each Lehman Brothers index consists of two universes of securities—returns and statistics. The "returns universe" is the static set of bonds used to measure the weekly and monthly returns of the index. It is fixed at the start of each month and remains constant throughout that month. The returns universe is not adjusted for securities that become ineligible for inclusion in the index during the month (due to redemption, downgrades, or maturity) or for newly eligible issues (due to upgrades and new issuance). It is adjusted only at the end of the month. Since the returns universe is held constant throughout a month, a fund manager avoids the need to match benchmark moves on a daily basis and is able to rebalance at or near the end of the month.

The "statistics universe" is a dynamic set of bonds that changes daily to reflect the latest composition of the index and becomes the returns universe on the first day of the following month. This universe accounts for changes due to new issuance, redemptions, ratings changes, and remaining maturity. Statistics such as market values, sector weightings, and various averages (i.e., coupon, duration, maturity, yield, price) are updated and reported daily. The statistics universe allows a fund manager to monitor changes in the index throughout a month. Active managers can modify their portfolios as the statistics universe changes, while passive managers can be prepared to execute all rebalancing transactions at or near the end of the month to match the upcoming returns universe. Exhibit 3 shows the returns and statistics universe as of August 31, 2000.

Exhibit 3: CMBS Index Return Statistics as of August 31, 2000

	# of Issues	Price Return	Coupon Return	Paydwn Return	Prepay PenRet	Total Return	Last 3 mo.	Last 6 mo.	Year to Date	Last 12 mo.	Since Inception
CMBS Investment Grade	765	1.25	0.59	0.00	0.00	1.85	5.50	6.39	6.54	8.84	26.91
ERISA-eligible	268	1.19	0.58	0.00	0.00	1.77	5.33	6.32	6.23	8.50	26.74
Not ERISA-eligible	497	1.52	0.63	0.00	0.00	2.16	6.19	6.65	7.76	10.14	27.17
1-3.5 yr	35	0.46	0.57	0.00	0.01	1.03	3.32	4.46	5.08	7.44	25.95
3.5-6 yr	124	0.85	0.57	0.00	0.00	1.42	4.34	5.26	5.36	7.59	25.23
6-8.5 yr	311	1.35	0.59	0.00	0.00	1.94	5.80	6.84	6.67	9.02	27.29
8.5yr+	295	1.55	0.64	0.00	0.00	2.19	6.31	6.83	7.38	9.69	27.85
AAA	274	1.19	0.58	0.00	0.00	1.77	5.33	6.32	6.23	8.51	26.78
1-3.5 yr	35	0.46	0.57	0.00	0.01	1.03	3.32	4.46	5.08	7.44	25.95
3.5-6 yr	113	0.86	0.57	0.00	0.00	1.43	4.33	5.26	5.36	7.57	25.21
6-8.5 yr	95	1.38	0.58	0.00	0.00	1.96	5.81	6.92	6.62	8.96	27.32
8.5yr+	31	1.33	0.62	0.00	0.00	1.95	6.02	6.74	6.67	8.89	27.25
AA	120	1.15	0.61	0.00	0.00	1.76	5.72	6.51	6.69	9.03	27.13
1-3.5 yr	0	0.00	0.00	0.00	0.00	0.00	0.00	0.00	0.00	0.00	0.00
3.5-6 yr	4	0.48	0.65	0.00	0.00	1.13	4.67	5.58	5.38	7.77	5.82
6-8.5 yr	67	1.02	0.60	0.00	0.00	1.61	5.51	6.33	6.32	8.63	26.80
8.5yr+	49	1.41	0.63	0.00	0.00	2.04	6.13	6.83	7.17	9.50	27.43
A	153	1.26	0.63	0.00	0.00	1.89	5.78	6.52	6.93	9.71	26.34
1-3.5 yr	0	0.00	0.00	0.00	0.00	0.00	0.00	0.00	0.00	0.00	0.00
3.5-6 yr	4	0.52	0.66	0.00	0.00	1.19	4.70	5.62	5.49	5.78	5.78
6-8.5 yr	69	1.04	0.61	0.00	0.00	1.65	5.45	6.32	6.46	9.21	23.13
8.5yr+	80	1.59	0.65	0.00	0.00	2.23	6.23	6.84	7.41	10.21	26.71
BBB	218	2.05	0.66	0.00	0.00	2.72	6.95	6.88	9.47	11.63	27.97
1-3.5 yr	0	0.00	0.00	0.00	0.00	0.00	0.00	0.00	0.00	0.00	0.00
3.5-6 yr	3	0.94	0.68	0.00	0.00	1.62	5.25	5.45	6.51	7.45	7.45
6-8.5 yr	80	1.71	0.65	0.00	0.00	2.36	6.39	6.50	8.35	10.53	22.86
8.5yr+	135	2.35	0.68	0.00	0.00	3.03	7.42	7.25	10.07	12.24	28.66
CMBS High Yield	672	3.20	0.96	0.00	0.00	4.16	8.24	9.91	13.12	15.74	37.40
1-3.5 yr	0	0.00	0.00	0.00	0.00	0.00	0.00	0.00	0.00	0.00	0.00
3.5-6 yr	1	2.33	0.75	0.00	0.00	3.08	3.08	3.08	3.08	3.08	3.08
6-8.5 yr	62	2.82	0.80	0.00	0.00	3.62	7.56	9.51	11.69	14.71	7.36
8.5yr+	609	3.27	0.99	0.00	0.00	4.26	8.36	10.00	13.31	15.90	37.64
BB	275	3.97	0.80	0.00	0.00	4.77	8.66	11.26	14.21	16.05	30.76
1-3.5 yr	0	0.00	0.00	0.00	0.00	0.00	0.00	0.00	0.00	0.00	0.00
3.5-6 yr	1	2.33	0.75	0.00	0.00	3.08	3.08	3.08	3.08	3.08	3.08
6-8.5 yr	39	3.13	0.76	0.00	0.00	3.88	7.72	10.09	12.10	14.65	8.66
8.5yr+	235	4.16	0.81	0.00	0.00	4.97	8.87	11.49	14.57	16.33	30.93
B	253	1.94	1.07	0.00	0.00	3.01	7.19	7.73	11.02	14.22	38.49
1-3.5 yr	0	0.00	0.00	0.00	0.00	0.00	0.00	0.00	0.00	0.00	0.00
3.5-6 yr	0	0.00	0.00	0.00	0.00	0.00	0.00	0.00	0.00	0.00	0.00
6-8.5 yr	17	1.66	0.86	0.00	0.00	2.52	6.60	7.84	10.24	14.23	−7.10
8.5yr+	236	1.97	1.09	0.00	0.00	3.06	7.25	7.75	11.09	14.24	38.80
OTHER	144	1.09	1.90	0.00	0.00	2.99	8.32	6.57	11.34	18.14	85.26
1-3.5 yr	0	0.00	0.00	0.00	0.00	0.00	0.00	0.00	0.00	0.00	0.00
3.5-6 yr	0	0.00	0.00	0.00	0.00	0.00	0.00	0.00	0.00	0.00	0.00
6-8.5 yr	6	1.72	1.36	0.00	0.00	3.08	8.79	6.35	10.13	16.56	58.11
8.5yr+	138	1.05	1.93	0.00	0.00	2.98	8.29	6.58	11.40	18.24	85.46
CMBS Interest Only	148	−0.03	1.91	0.00	0.05	1.94	5.19	7.92	13.48	19.02	59.36
Inv Grade Pvt/144A	71	1.03	0.61	0.00	0.00	1.64	5.08	6.06	6.38	8.73	27.19
Commercial Whole Loan	1668	1.30	0.68	0.00	0.00	1.99	5.64	6.67	7.28	9.76	29.33

Exhibit 3 (Continued)

	# of	Mod.Adj.		Avg.		Nominal		Market	% of	% of
	Issues	Durat.	Coupon	Life	Price	Spread	Yield	Value	Index	Main
CMBS Investment Grade	777	5.32	6.83	7.13	96.97	157	7.45	108914	100.00	100.00
ERISA-eligible	271	5.11	6.74	6.73	97.38	143	7.33	86684	79.59	79.59
Not ERISA-eligible	506	6.15	7.15	8.71	95.40	213	7.94	22230	20.41	20.41
1-3.5 yr	37	2.33	6.70	2.67	98.65	113	7.26	5150	4.73	4.73
3.5-6 yr	125	3.74	6.68	4.62	98.13	126	7.25	22735	20.87	20.87
6-8.5 yr	323	5.70	6.65	7.54	95.69	160	7.46	57071	52.40	52.40
8.5yr+	292	6.56	7.43	9.50	98.65	190	7.67	23958	22.00	22.00
AAA	277	5.11	6.74	6.74	97.39	143	7.33	87428	100.00	80.27
1-3.5 yr	37	2.33	6.70	2.67	98.65	113	7.26	5150	5.89	4.73
3.5-6 yr	114	3.73	6.66	4.60	98.12	124	7.24	22310	25.52	20.48
6-8.5 yr	95	5.70	6.58	7.50	95.96	149	7.35	45600	52.16	41.87
8.5yr+	31	6.40	7.44	9.09	100.56	164	7.42	14368	16.43	13.19
AA	122	6.02	6.97	8.29	96.35	181	7.63	6488	100.00	5.96
1-3.5 yr	0	0.00	0.00	0.00	0.00	0	0.00	0	0.00	0.00
3.5-6 yr	4	4.19	7.66	5.26	99.30	183	7.79	154	2.37	0.14
6-8.5 yr	72	5.72	6.73	7.60	95.13	178	7.62	4023	62.00	3.69
8.5yr+	46	6.67	7.35	9.69	98.34	187	7.64	2312	35.63	2.12
A	157	6.14	7.13	8.61	96.23	199	7.80	6983	100.00	6.41
1-3.5 yr	0	0.00	0.00	0.00	0.00	0	0.00	0	0.00	0.00
3.5-6 yr	4	4.35	7.84	5.55	99.56	201	7.95	155	2.22	0.14
6-8.5 yr	71	5.73	6.86	7.68	94.98	193	7.78	3849	55.12	3.53
8.5yr+	82	6.76	7.46	9.98	97.71	206	7.82	2979	42.66	2.73
BBB	221	6.32	7.31	9.20	93.64	257	8.36	8015	100.00	7.36
1-3.5 yr	0	0.00	0.00	0.00	0.00	0	0.00	0	0.00	0.00
3.5-6 yr	3	4.32	7.84	5.53	97.33	251	8.46	117	1.46	0.11
6-8.5 yr	85	5.72	7.15	7.82	93.69	247	8.31	3599	44.90	3.30
8.5yr+	133	6.87	7.43	10.46	93.51	266	8.41	4299	53.64	3.95
CMBS High Yield	687	6.31	6.57	11.83	58.27	792	13.67	7996	100.00	100.00
1-3.5 yr	0	0.00	0.00	0.00	0.00	0	0.00	0	0.00	0.00
3.5-6 yr	1	4.43	7.42	5.85	84.84	513	11.06	41	0.52	0.52
6-8.5 yr	68	5.35	6.51	7.68	69.91	680	12.64	1178	14.73	14.73
8.5yr+	618	6.49	6.57	12.59	56.53	814	13.87	6777	84.75	84.75
BB	280	6.60	6.68	10.80	72.30	557	11.33	5258	100.00	65.75
1-3.5 yr	0	0.00	0.00	0.00	0.00	0	0.00	0	0.00	0.00
3.5-6 yr	1	4.43	7.42	5.85	84.84	513	11.06	41	0.78	0.52
6-8.5 yr	43	5.44	6.76	7.69	77.30	548	11.33	939	17.86	11.75
8.5yr+	236	6.88	6.66	11.53	71.19	559	11.33	4277	81.35	53.49
B	259	6.28	6.47	13.04	51.52	977	15.51	2099	100.00	26.25
1-3.5 yr	0	0.00	0.00	0.00	0.00	0	0.00	0	0.00	0.00
3.5-6 yr	0	0.00	0.00	0.00	0.00	0	0.00	0	0.00	0.00
6-8.5 yr	17	5.19	5.95	7.65	58.40	971	15.56	191	9.10	2.39
8.5yr+	242	6.39	6.51	13.58	50.92	978	15.50	1908	90.90	23.86
OTHER	148	3.99	6.40	16.35	26.91	2122	26.94	640	100.00	8.00
1-3.5 yr	0	0.00	0.00	0.00	0.00	0	0.00	0	0.00	0.00
3.5-6 yr	0	0.00	0.00	0.00	0.00	0	0.00	0	0.00	0.00
6-8.5 yr	8	4.29	5.74	7.71	33.44	2100	26.84	48	7.50	0.60
8.5yr+	140	3.97	6.44	17.05	26.49	2124	26.95	592	92.50	7.40
CMBS Interest Only	150	3.44	1.04	7.66	4.62	471	10.51	6157	100.00	100.00
Inv Grade Pvt/144A	72	4.59	7.11	6.03	97.81	168	7.61	4105	100.00	100.00
Commercial Whole Loan	1700	5.26	6.56	7.41	90.56	213	8.00	127303	100.00	100.00

TOTAL RETURN

Lehman Brothers index results are generally reported on daily, monthly, annual, and since-inception bases. Returns are cumulative for the entire period. Intra-month cash flows (coupons, partial calls, redemptions, prepayment premiums, and final maturities) contribute to monthly returns, but they are not reinvested during the month and thus do not earn a reinvestment return. Intra-month cash flows are reinvested at the beginning of the following month. Thus, index results over two or more months reflect compounding from cash flow reinvestment. Daily, month-to-date, and monthly total returns are calculated based on the sum of price changes, coupons received or accrued, gain or loss on repayment of principal, and where applicable, prepayment premiums, all expressed as a percentage of beginning market value.

If a security is no longer outstanding, the ending price is the level at which the security exited the market. The total return for an index is the weighted average of the total returns of the securities that make up the index; the weighting factor is the full market value (inclusive of accrued interest) at the beginning of the period. Cumulative total returns over periods longer than one month are calculated by compounding monthly returns.

Returns and most summary statistics published for all Lehman Brothers indices are full market value weighted. Returns data are weighted by full market value at the beginning of the period. Some statistics, such as average duration and maturity, are market value weighted based on the end-of-period value. Other statistics, such as average price and average coupon, are weighted by outstanding end-of-period principal amounts.

For index purposes, securities are assumed to settle on the next calendar day. On the last business day of the month, however, the settlement date is always assumed to be the first calendar day of the following month. This procedure allows for calculation of one full month of accrued interest.

CMBS INDEX CRITERIA

As the CMBS market has evolved, newly originated, fixed rate transactions have become the most liquid and most frequently issued type of transaction. Newly originated loans are loans originated and underwritten for securitization. They usually contain structural features that are beneficial in a transaction, such as call protection and reporting requirements. For these reasons, as well as for their homogeneity, these new origination transactions form the base universe of our CMBS Index.

The CMBS Index has four subsectors:

1. CMBS Investment Grade Index — measures return for investment grade classes.

Exhibit 4: Criteria Specific to Each Index

Index	Criteria
CMBS Investment Grade Index	All bonds are rated investment grade by Moody's and are offered publicly.
CMBS High Yield Index	All bonds are not rated investment grade by Moody's and can be offered privately and publicly.
CMBS IO Index	Includes all interest only securities.
Commercial Whole Loan Index	Aggregate of all classes that meet the general CMBS Index criteria.

2. CMBS High Yield Index — measures return for non-investment grade and nonrated classes.

3. CMBS Interest Only Index — measures return for interest-only classes.

4. Commercial Conduit Whole Loan Index — measures return for all bond classes and interest-only classes.

Securities that are assigned split ratings will be categorized according to their Moody's Investors Service, Inc. (Moody's) rating. This is consistent with all the other Lehman Brothers Indices. If securities do not have a Moody's rating, then the Standard & Poor's (S&P) rating will be used. If the securities have neither an S&P nor a Moody's rating, then FitchIBCA will be used, and otherwise Duff & Phelps Credit Rating Co.

A number of specific criteria apply to all the Lehman Brothers CMBS Indices:

1. All transactions must be private label. No agency transactions will be included.

2. The collateral for each transaction must be new origination, that is, originated specifically for securitization.

3. Each original aggregate transaction size must be at least $500 million to be included in the CMBS Index. Aggregate outstanding transaction sizes must be at least $300 million to remain in the CMBS Index.

4. All certificates must be either fixed rate, weighted average coupon (WAC), or capped WAC securities. No floating rate certificates will be included.

5. All certificates must have an expected maturity of at least one year.

Exhibit 4 shows the criteria that are specific to each index.

The CMBS Investment Grade Index is further subdivided into two components:

1. The ERISA-eligible component measures return for all investment grade bonds that are ERISA eligible under the underwriter's exemption.

2. The non-ERISA-eligible component measures return for all investment grade bonds that are not ERISA eligible under the underwriter's exemp-

tion. However, many of these bonds may be ERISA eligible under account-specific exemptions.

CMBS INDEX RETURN COMPONENTS

CMBS Index returns are made up of four elements:

1. *Price return* is the return derived by price changes caused by interest rate movements and spread changes.
2. *Coupon return* is the return associated with the coupon payment on a certificate.
3. *Paydown return* is the return related to expected or unexpected payments of principal. In the case of commercial mortgage loans, prepayments are often accompanied by prepayment premiums. Paydown return may be associated with the related prepayment premium return component (see below).
4. *Prepayment premium return* is the return due to additional premiums paid in connection with certain prepayments. Prepayment premiums are generally distributed to investors as excess interest.

THE CMBS INDEX STATISTICS

As of August 31 2000, there were 123 transactions totaling $130.334 billion market value included in the CMBS Index. These transactions have a total of 1700 certificates outstanding that are categorized into eight rating/type groups. Exhibit 5 shows the composition of the CMBS Index.

Exhibit 5: Composition of the CMBS Index

	Amount Outstanding ($millions)	Number of Deals	Number of Certificates
Deal Sizes ≥ $500,000,000	$130,337	123	1700

Rating/Type	$Market Value ($millions)	Number of Certificates	Percent of Total
AAA	$87,428	277	68.75%
AA	$6,488	122	5.10%
A	$6,983	157	5.49%
BBB	$8,015	221	6.30%
BB	$5,258	280	4.13%
B	$2,099	259	1.65%
NR	$640	148	0.51%
Other (IO/PVT)	$10,262	222	8.07%
TOTAL	$127,173	1,686	100.00%

PRICING AND DATA QUALITY

The Lehman Brothers CMBS trading desk will be the primary source of pricing for the CMBS Index. A database is maintained and updated by Lehman Brothers that tracks deal information including but not limited to class sizes, new issues, and rating changes. Indicative bond data, including updates to certificate sizes and coupons as well as collateral data, will be received each month from Intex. The Lehman Brothers proprietary trading system will provide the cash flows for the transactions. The Lehman Brothers system will also calculate the prices, average lives, durations, and principal windows under the specific pricing assumptions set by the Lehman Brothers traders.

Spreads are updated every Friday and at month-end (when the month-end does not fall on a Friday). Pricing is on the bid side representing 3 p.m. levels. The only exception to this procedure is that new issues are quoted at the offer price during their first month to avoid penalizing a fund manager who recently acquired the certificates.

CMBS RETURN HISTORY

The CMBS Indices have history to December 1996. Historical indicative spreads on the outstanding new origination transactions have been used to create the historical index returns.

Chapter 6

The Efficient Frontier for CMBS and Commercial Mortgages Using a Risk-Return Framework

David P. Jacob
Managing Director
Nomura Securities International, Inc.

Jignesh Patel*
Director
Beyondbond, Inc.

D espite increased investor awareness of the potential risk associated with CMBS, there is still no systematic quantitative approach that enables the investor to fairly compare, on a risk-adjusted basis, the relative value between the various classes in a deal. Investors have no consistent method of answering the following questions. Is a spread of +145 bp on a AAA class better or inferior value to +500 bp on an IO class after adjusting for the risk? Can one combine a position in IO classes and AAA bonds in such a way so that the resulting position has superior risk-return characteristics than a single A security? What is the relative risk between an IO class and BBB rated class? (Which is more risky?) Investors are presented with a stated or nominal spread and a rating. But how can they use this information? Regardless, of the absolute level of spreads, investors always expect to be promised a higher "stated" spread the lower the rating assigned to the class. It is obvious why this is the case. Investors understand that the lower rating means greater risk and therefore, they somehow need to be compensated for assuming that higher risk.

Typically, the stated yield and the rating assigned by the rating agencies are used as proxies for expected return and risk, respectively. Both measures, however, fall short of investors' needs. The stated or nominal spread is simply the internal rate of return usually assuming no default (and possibly no prepayment). The stated spread is achievable under only one scenario, "the pricing scenario." It is not the expected or average return in any sense. In reality there are numerous possible outcomes. While a lower rating tells the investor that a security is more risky, it is not a quantification of risk. The rating is a crude measure of the risk of loss. It does not properly account for the timing of defaults, which can severely impact the perfor-

---

* Jignesh Patel was a Vice President at Nomura Securities International when this chapter was written.

mance of certain classes. The lower rating indicates a possibility of loss. Thus the expected return must be less than the stated yield based on a no default assumption.

In order to overcome these shortcomings, investors run yield tables based on scenarios (default, loss, and prepay assumptions). This is an improvement over the stated yield, but the choice of scenarios is way too arbitrary. In particular investors often use the same set of scenarios for very different pools of collateral. This tends to penalize the better pools and give too much credit to low quality pools. More sophisticated investors might use an option-adjusted approach. More specifically, the option-adjusted spread (OAS) approach.[1] While the OAS provides a measure of return adjusted for defaults, and adjusts the scenarios for the risk of the collateral, it does not directly offer a risk measure. More importantly it can be cumbersome to run the analysis and is not available to most practitioners. In addition, the difficulty in choosing the parameters makes it less useful for some investors.

In this chapter we explore the relationship between risk and return for CMBS. Investors usually arrange their investment opportunities by estimating an expected return and risk for each security, and then create portfolios with the highest expected returns for their target risk levels. In most analyses, risk is computed as the standard deviation of return.[2] In this chapter we outline a framework which allows us to compute the expected returns and standard deviations for CMBS and the underlying loans. The choice of scenarios is directly linked to the quality of the loan pool. Using the results of the simulation, we are able to demonstrate the efficient frontier of investment possibilities.

The efficient frontier represents the set of investments with the highest expected returns for each level of risk. We are able to show where all the CMBS classes including the IO class are situated in a risk-return framework, and thus, equip investors with a tool to evaluate their choice of CMBS and commercial mortgages. We first outline the framework, and then apply it to the summer of 1998 (the period before the market disruption), and to December 1998 (when the market began to return to a more normal period).

ASSUMPTION

In our analysis we used a standard loan pool and CMBS structure as shown in Exhibit 1. The loan pool has a weighted-average coupon of 7.36%, a WAL of 13.26 years, and consists of 15-year balloon mortgages with a weighted average of 341 month amortization schedules. The subordination levels are assumed to be assigned by the rating agencies to reflect the risk of the loan pool.

---

[1] For a full description of this approach see David P. Jacob, Ted C.H. Hong, and Laurence H. Lee, "An Options Approach to Commercial Mortgages and CMBS Valuation and Risk Analysis," Chapter 18 in Frank J. Fabozzi and David P. Jacob (eds.) *The Handbook of Commercial Mortgage-Backed Securities Second Edition* (New Hope, PA: Frank J. Fabozzi Associates, 1999).

[2] While we adopt the use of standard deviation here, other measures of risk such as downside risk might be more appropriate given the asymmetric nature of the return distributions.

Exhibit 1: Deal Structure

Class	Amt. $millions	Cpn (%)	Price (%)	WAL (years)	% of deal	% sub.
Loan Pool	1,000	7.36	100.00	13.26	N/A	N/A
AAA	700	6.62	101.5	12.51	70	30
AA	70	6.90	101.5	15	7	23
A	50	7.13	101.5	15	5	18
BBB	50	7.36	98.67	15	5	13
BB	60	6.00	78.19	15	6	7
B	40	6.00	66.93	15	4	3
UR	30	6.00	31.62	15	3	0
IO	1,000	0.735	5.92	7.15 (cf)	N/A	N/A

METHODOLOGY

Our approach is to simulate the returns of the loan pool and the CMBS classes. The choice of scenarios and their corresponding probabilities will obviously affect the results. A choice of very benign scenarios will cause the lower rated bonds to look better than they should, whereas a too severe set of assumptions will overly bias the results in favor of the senior classes. Our approach to choosing default scenarios is to infer the distribution from the subordination levels assigned by the rating agencies, and the probability of default for each rating category. The idea is that the rating agencies, when they evaluate the collateral and require particular subordination levels, are implicitly using a default and loss distribution. In order for a class to receive its rating, it needs to be able to survive an appropriate portion of the distribution. So we create a set of scenarios to reflect a distribution of outcomes that is consistent with the subordination levels and the assigned ratings.

One of the challenges in this approach, and which is a problem for the industry in general, is the very scant data and history on defaults and default probabilities in the commercial mortgage and CMBS markets. The rating agencies do not publish their default probabilities for CMBS. Instead they look back in history and reference particular periods as reflecting AAA or BBB stress scenarios. On the other hand, the rating agencies have very complete sets of data for corporate bonds going back many years. They also maintain that their rating methodology is consistent across markets so that a AAA in CMBS should have the same risk as a AAA in corporate bonds. Therefore, we decided it would be reasonable to use some of the default experience from the corporate bond market.

Each January, Moody's Investors Service publishes an extensive history of corporate bonds by rating category. In Exhibit 2 we show the 15-year cumulative defaults by rating category as computed by Moody's. The numbers represent the average percent of bonds that defaulted by rating category after 15 years during the period from 1970-1996. Thus, for example, on average after 15 years 50.19% of single B rated bonds defaulted, whereas only 1.55% of Aaa bonds defaulted over 15 years.

Exhibit 2: Moody's 15-Year Cumulative Defaults

Rating	% default
Aaa	1.55
Aa	1.90
A	3.22
Baa	8.18
Ba	30.34
B	50.19

Source: "Historical Default Rates of Corporate Bond Issuers, 1920-1996," Moody's Investors Service, Exhibit 18, p. 17.

Exhibit 3: Loss Distribution

% Loss Breakpoints	Probability
Less than 3%	0.4981
Greater than 3%	0.5019
Greater than 7%	0.3034
Greater than 13%	0.0818
Greater than 18%	0.0322
Greater than 23%	0.0190

In the context of CMBS we will define a default for a class to be the point at which a class begins to experience a loss. For a loss to occur in CMBS, defaults on the underlying loans have to occur, and the losses have to be sufficient to eat through the subordination. Thus, in our context, the default rate of a bond class is a function of the default rate and loss rate on the underlying loans.

Based on this, we created the loss distribution for our collateral shown in Exhibit 3. The numbers in the first column (% loss breakpoints) are taken from the subordination levels of our pool from Exhibit 1. The numbers in the second column correspond to the default probabilities in Exhibit 2.

The next step is to create a set of default and loss scenarios which given the subordination of our pool causes the CMBS classes to default after 15 years at the rate corresponding to their assigned rating. Given the 3% subordination required for the single B CMBS, we need to create a scenario that will lead to 3% losses on the pool causing this bond to default. Once we create this scenario, we will assign a 50.19% probability that there will be at least 3% cumulative losses, since anything greater than 3% losses will cause the single B rated bond to default. This implies that the probability that the losses will be less than 3% is 49.81%. Similarly, given the 23% subordination level of the Aa rated bond, we create a scenario which generates 23% losses, and assign a probability of 1.90% that the cumulative losses will be at least 23%. Then, we create ranges in our probability distribution, which together, cover the whole spectrum of possible losses. For example, the probability that losses will be between 3% and 7% = (0.5019 − 0.3034) = 0.1985. From these ranges of losses, we select discrete loss points and assign a probability to each such point based on the probability of the range.

Exhibit 4: Implied Probability Distribution of Cumulative Defaults

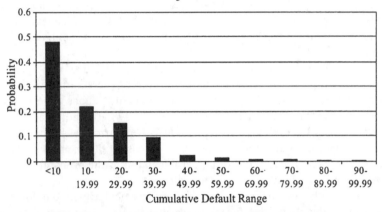

Thus far, we have used the subordination levels to tell us what cumulative loss scenarios we need, and used the ratings to tell us the probabilities of those scenarios. Exhibit 4 graphically shows the implied probability distribution of cumulative defaults for the collateral pool. The exhibit shows there is a 48% probability that between 0% and 10% of the pool will have defaulted over 15 years, whereas there is a less than 10% chance that between 30% and 40% of the pool will have defaulted after 15 years. The average 15-year default rate for this distribution was 14.41%. This is an extremely reasonable number and is not inconsistent with a pool of loans that is between BBB and BB quality. It is also consistent with the numbers obtained using the OAS approach assuming an NOI volatility of between 12% and 16%.[3]

As we vary the assumed recovery rate, the default rate has to be adjusted so that the targeted cumulative loss distribution is created. In our analysis, we assumed three possible recovery rates with the following probabilities:

Recovery Rate	Probability
70%	0.3
60%	0.4
50%	0.3

For each of these recovery rates we created 15 default scenarios, plus one scenario with no default (for a total of 46 scenarios). We then probability-weighted these scenarios so that the losses occurred with the targeted probabilities. In order to create the month-by-month default rates we used the SDA (standard default assumption) promulgated by the PSA (now known as the Bond Market Association). This was used in order to create a pattern of defaults that is

---

[3] See Jacob, Hong, and Lee, "An Options Approach to Commercial Mortgages and CMBS Valuation and Risk Analysis."

consistent with the notion that default rates are not level during the life of a pool, but rather they rise and then peak and plateau several years out, then begin to decline. The assumption of an SDA-type curve is not necessary to the analysis, it just adds to the realism. The practitioner can adjust this to suit the situation. For example, one might adjust the scenarios for the impact of an imminent recession, or downturn in the real estate cycle.

Based on these scenarios we analyzed the deal that was specified in Exhibit 1 at two points in time — the beginning of the summer of 1998, and December 1998. We used spreads that corresponded to those time periods. In Exhibit 5, we show the results for the summer of 1998. The nominal spread and yield are the spread and yields that typical deals were priced at in the summer of 1998. The expected yield is the average yield across all the scenarios taking into account their probabilities, and the standard deviation is the probability weighted standard of deviating from the expected yield.

The results in Exhibit 5 are striking, particularly in the lower rated classes. The exhibit shows that for the scenario distribution we used, the expected or average yield for the Ba and B rated securities was 3.35% and −7.61%, respectively. Obviously long-term investors buying these securities had a very different view on the distribution of future default scenarios. The numbers in the standard deviation column are consistent with the notion that lower rated securities have greater risk. It is interesting to note that the 0.97 standard deviation of the pool is between the standard deviation of the Aaa bond and the Aa bond even though it has an overall quality of between Baa and Ba. It is even more interesting to note the relatively low standard deviation of the IO class. Based on this analysis, the risk of an IO class falls somewhere between the Aa class and the A class.

Even without graphing the results on a risk-return graph, one can see that at this time, only the collateral and the Aaa bond were on the efficient frontier. What this means is that at this time, using this distribution all the other bonds, on a risk-adjusted return basis, were inferior to the collateral and the Aaa bond. These results, if one accepts the scenario distribution, shows how rich the spreads were, particularly on the lower rated bonds in the early part of the summer of 1998.

Exhibit 5: Expected Yields versus Standard Deviations: Summer of 1998

Class	Nominal Spread (bp)	Nominal Yield (%)	Expected Yield (%)	Standard Deviation
Collateral	183	7.47	6.83	0.97
Aaa	90	6.53	6.51	0.04
Aa	117	6.84	6.70	1.27
A	140	7.07	6.20	6.24
Baa	196	7.63	5.87	9.23
Ba	308	8.75	3.35	15.35
B	491	10.58	-7.61	27.83
IO	240	7.88	5.36	3.51

Exhibit 6: Expected Yields versus Standard Deviation: December 1998

Class	Nominal Spread (bp)	Nominal Yield (%)	Expected Yield (%)	Standard Deviation
Collateral	284	7.47	6.83	0.97
Aaa	162	6.24	6.23	0.04
Aa	211	6.78	6.64	1.27
A	236	7.03	6.16	6.25
Baa	319	7.86	6.11	9.17
Ba	650	11.17	6.06	14.48
B	975	14.42	-2.11	25.51
IO	500	9.45	7.10	3.44

Exhibit 6 shows the results for December 1998, when spreads while tighter than during the crisis of October and November, were still wider than the summer, especially in the lower rated bonds and the IO class. The expected spreads are much better than in the summer of 1998, but most still fall somewhat short of the efficient frontier, due to their standard deviations. The major improvement showed up in the IO class, which has an expected yield of 7.10%.

Obviously, the results are dependent on the scenarios. We chose scenarios to correspond to the subordination levels and the ratings. Investors often have different views from the rating agencies, and therefore should use a distribution that reflects their view of the collateral. In order to test the sensitivity of the model, we modified the distribution to make it reflect a less risky portfolio according to the following table:

% default	Probability
Less than 3%	0.75
Greater than 3%	0.25
Greater than 7%	0.15
Greater than 13%	0.04
Greater than 18%	0.02
Greater than 23%	0.01

Under this distribution it is 50% more likely that the default rate will be less than 3%. Using this relatively benign scenario we obtained the following risk-return results shown in Exhibit 7. As expected, the results are much better. However, the only additional bond to make it onto the efficient frontier was the Ba bond. Investors who purchased some of the other classes, ought to try and find out what scenario distribution they had in mind in making their investment decisions. It is interesting to note how robust the standard deviations were. The risk ordering remained the same.

Exhibit 7: Expected Yields versus Standard Deviations: Default Rate Cut in Half

Class	Nominal Spread (bp)	Nominal yield (%)	Expected Yield (%)	Standard Deviation
Collateral	284	7.47	7.08	0.74
Aaa	162	6.24	6.23	0.03
Aa	211	6.78	6.71	0.90
A	236	7.03	6.59	4.44
Baa	319	7.86	6.99	6.54
Ba	650	11.17	8.61	10.55
B	975	14.42	6.14	19.84
IO	500	9.45	8.01	2.62

CONCLUSION

Investors typically make their investment decisions based on their view of the relative risk and expected returns. For structured credit products in general, and CMBS in particular, there are no standard tools or approaches that are used. As a proxy for credit risk, investors use a security's credit rating assigned by the rating agencies, and use the spread or yield as a measure of potential return. As we have discussed in this chapter, neither measure enables an investor to adequately compare the risk-return trade off between two securities. In this chapter we described a systematic approach which enables investors to compute expected returns and standard deviations of those returns using scenarios appropriate to the specific underlying collateral. The results revealed how expensive some of the subordinated classes were in the summer of 1998. In addition, we were able to show that the IO class based on reasonable assumptions has credit risk somewhere between the A and Aa class assuming that there is no risk of voluntary prepayments.

Chapter 7

Structure, Valuation, and Performance of CMBS

Rich Gordon
Director
First Union Securities, Inc.

Lang Gibson
Vice President
First Union Securities, Inc.

In this chapter we discuss the structural features, relative value, risk/return characteristics, hedging strategies, and regulatory environment for CMBS.

RISK, RETURN, AND PRICING IN THE CMBS MARKET

Because of their contractual and structural prepayment protection and sensitivity to credit risk, CMBS spreads are more correlated with corporate bond and swap spreads than residential mortgage securities. From October 1997 to August 1998, the spread between AAA CMBS and AAA corporates held constant at 40 bps. During the bond market discord from August to November 1998, spreads widened to as high as 140 bps in October and have moved in a range of 40 bps–80 bps since November 1998.

The wider spreads found in CMBS versus same-rated corporates can be explained by the following factors:

- *Analytical challenge of studying multiple loans versus corporate cash flow (dependence on ratings).* CMBS require more analysis, so they have wider spreads to compensate investors for analytical complexity. However, the advantage to the investor is that the large number of loans provides ample time to react to credit degradation, whereas corporates have significant event risk.
- *Liquidity premium.* Although liquidity risk took its toll on all spread markets in October 1998, the problem was exacerbated for CMBS, which were hit by a combination of factors: greater financing costs, higher hedge costs as swap spreads widened, dealers aggregating collateral for much larger deals over a longer period than with current smaller joint-issuer deals, and a higher composition of leveraged investors in the CMBS market than is the case now.

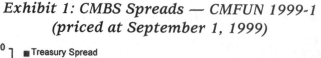

Exhibit 1: CMBS Spreads — CMFUN 1999-1 (priced at September 1, 1999)

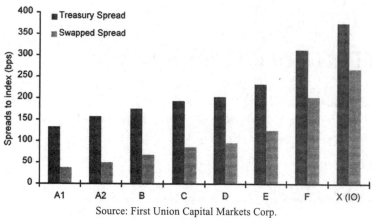

Source: First Union Capital Markets Corp.

- *The unwillingness of natural mortgage security buyers to learn a new collateral class.* Although the rating agencies are conservative in their criteria, many traditional residential mortgage-backed securities (RMBS) buyers have not yet become active in the market. CMBS still tend to trade wider than corporates due in part to a narrower market sponsorship. Therefore, there is an opportunity for those investors willing to learn the characteristics of this younger market.
- *Extension risk.* Most commercial mortgages are underwritten with a stated final maturity of 15–30 years and a balloon payment due after 10 years. The lockout protection in the underlying commercial real estate loans provides excellent protection from prepayment risk, whereas extension will only occur to the extent that borrowers cannot make their balloon payment and make arrangements with the servicer to extend their repayment schedules.
- *Price compression due to prepayments from credit losses.* Although CMBS structures have multiple layers of prepayment protection, unscheduled prepayments can occur. Because of the possibility of unscheduled prepayments, CMBS price appreciation slightly lags that of its bulleted counterparts. Unlike RMBS, this price compression as the bond rises above par is meager. For instance, the AAA tranches might widen about 2 bps per point rise above a price of $103.

As of September 1, 1999, spreads on rated CMBS tranches varied between 125 bps and 375 bps. For example, in the CMFUN 1999-1 deal (Exhibit 1), the 10-year AAA tranche has a 133 bps spread to Treasurys (38 bps swapped back to LIBOR), whereas the BBB- tranche has a 313 bps spread to Treasurys (203 bps swapped back to LIBOR).

Institutional investors that would normally purchase mortgage securities or corporate bonds should consider CMBS as a yield-enhancing investment. Compared with RMBS, CMBS provide significantly higher risk-adjusted returns due to the substantially greater prepayment/extension protection and average life stability. Compared with noncallable corporate bonds, CMBS provide more than adequate spreads to compensate for marginally lower average life stability. Furthermore, with the entry of the Lehman CMBS index into its aggregate fixed-income index, more investors will have to buy CMBS to track and meet their benchmarks.

VALUATION METHODOLOGY

In this section, we outline an analytic framework for the evaluation of CMBS. We believe this methodology provides a sound and consistent framework for the analysis of these structured products. Using FUCMC's proprietary *Bond Analyzer*, we will show how the various risk/return attributes of CMBS tranches can be evaluated.

The process essentially breaks down into three major steps:

- Understand the deal's general structure and the major characteristics of the underlying collateral
- Assess the structural prepayment protection of the deal and tranche being evaluated
- Run loss scenarios to determine the level of credit risk in the tranche

We look at each of these points in detail, using two deals as examples, FULB 1997-C1 and CMFUN 1999-1.

Understanding a Deal's General Structure and the Major Characteristics of the Underlying Collateral

Assess Structural Elements and Levels of Subordination in the Deal
CMBS deal structures are far simpler than most RMBS collateralized mortgage obligation (CMO) structures. The major structural component of a CMBS deal is credit tranching. To have AAA rated tranches, there must be enough credit support from tranches that absorb any losses on the underlying collateral first. In the top right corner of Exhibit 2, we break down FULB 1997-C1 into three major components of credit tranching. Tranches A1, A2, and A3 and the interest-only (IO) tranche are all labeled "Senior." Each of these tranches is Aaa rated, and any permitted discretionary prepayments are applied sequentially, first to the A1 tranche, then the A2 and so on. The tranches rated "Mezzanine Fixed Sequential" are rated anywhere from Aa to Baa3. The tranches with less underlying credit support have lower credit ratings, and the investor is rewarded with commensurately higher yields. The tranches labeled "Junior Fixed Sequentials" are all below investment grade and are the first tranches to absorb losses to principal from credit defaults.

Exhibit 2: Bond Analyzer Commercial Mortgage Collateral Summary

Bond Analyzer Commercial Mortgage Collateral Summary

FIRST UNION-LEHMAN BROTHERS COMMERCIAL MORTGAGE TRUST, SERIES 1997-C1

Report Date 9/29/99

As Of Date Aug-99

FIRST UNION

Quantitative Research Group
First Union Capital Markets

Coll Wac	8.71%
Coll Rem Wam	103
Coll Amort Term	202
Coll Age	30
Coll Factor	0.9740
Coll CurrBal	1,269,393,316
Coll OrigDate	2/1/97
Servicer	FIRST UNION NATIONAL BANK
Trustee	STATE STREET BANK AND TRUST

Mortgage Properties Characteristics

W.A. DSCR	1.37
W.A. CLTV	68.39%
W.A. Year Built/Renewed	

Delinquency, Loss & Pfid Off Statistics

30 & 60 Days	90+	FC & REO	Bankrupt	Paid Off	Assum Loss	Matured
0.00%	1.80%	0.00%		Discharged 0.42%	0.00%	

Top 5 Property Types

Property Type	No. of Loans	Curr. Balance	% of Curr. Balance
Multifamily	120	512,235,994	41.39%
Retail	93	490,973,615	38.68%
Hotel	28	125,145,944	9.86%
Office	14	68,218,910	5.37%
Industrial	11	30,091,282	2.37%
	266	1,227,165,744	96.67%

Top 5 Property States

State	No. of Loans	Curr. Balance	% of Curr. Balance
TX	52	176,865,158	13.93%
FL	30	144,921,988	11.42%
CA	14	100,565,380	7.95%
PA	9	87,844,730	6.92%
MD	10	82,493,933	6.50%
	115	593,109,189	46.72%

Tranche Detail

Tranche	Coupon	Cusip	Orig. Bal	Curr. Bal	Type	Orig Supp	Curr Supp	Maturity
A1	7.13	337J6LAA3	200,000,000	163,944,927	SEN_FIX_SEQ	30.00%	30.80%	Feb-04
A2	7.30	337J6LAB1	318,000,000	318,000,000	SEN_FIX_SEQ	30.00%	30.80%	Dec-06
A3	7.30	337J6LAC9	395,813,000	395,813,000	SEN_FIX_SEQ	30.00%	30.80%	Apr-07
B	7.43	337J6LAE5	78,327,000	78,327,000	MEZ_FIX_SEQ	24.00%	24.60%	Apr-07
C	7.44	337J6LAF2	71,890,000	71,890,000	MEZ_FIX_SEQ	18.50%	19.00%	Apr-07
D	7.50	337J6LAG0	71,890,000	71,890,000	MEZ_FIX_SEQ	13.00%	13.30%	Oct-08
E	7.75	337J6LAH8	19,582,000	19,582,000	MEZ_FIX_SEQ	11.50%	11.80%	Aug-09
F	7.00	337J6LAJ4	71,890,000	71,890,000	JUN_FIX_SBK	6.00%	6.17%	Dec-14
H	7.00	337J6LAK1	13,054,813	13,054,813	JUN_FIX_SBK	5.00%	5.14%	Dec-16
J	7.00	337J6LAL9	26,108,964	26,108,964	JUN_FIX_SBK	3.00%	3.09%	May-17
K	7.00	337J6LAM7	13,054,483	13,054,483	JUN_FIX_SBK	2.00%	2.06%	Mar-20
L	7.00	337J6LAN5	26,108,964	26,108,964	JUN_FIX_SBK	0.00%	0.00%	Apr-27
IO	1.30	337J6LAD7	1,385,448,224	1,269,393,151	SEN_WAC_IC	30.00%	30.80%	Apr-27

CMBS Prepay Restriction Schedule

Due
Open
Point Penalty
Yield
Locked

Top 5 Mortgage Leases

Property Name	Original Balance	Current Balance	% Current Balance	State	Property Type
Pelvere Center	33,409,000	32,895,306	2.6%	CA	Retail
Elmwood Village	30,000,000	29,436,574	2.3%	NJ	Multifamily
Riverview Commons Shopping Center	28,800,000	28,164,354	2.2%	MD	Retail
Riverview Plaza Shopping Center	24,000,000	23,522,174	1.9%	PA	Retail
Mohawk Hills	22,250,000	21,511,568	1.7%	IN	Multifamily
	135,825,977	135,825,977	10.7%		

	Original LTV	Current LTV	Appraised Values	DSCR	NOI	Year Built/Renewed	Rem Maturity
	0.73	0.72		1.13			212
	0.75	0.74		1.23			333
	0.72	0.70		1.33			89
	0.73	0.71		1.28			92
	0.78	0.77		1.24			93

Top 5 Mortgage Leases in Delinquency

Property Name	Original Balance	Current Balance	% Current Balance	State	Property Type
Park Place Apartments	7,924,000	7,766,112	0.6%	FL	Multifamily
SMC-Metrie-408	6,560,000	5,975,121	0.5%	LA	Retail
SMC-Houston-410	4,400,000	3,906,115	0.3%	TX	Retail
SMC-Duluth-249	3,712,500	3,352,047	0.3%	GA	Retail
Snowden Square S.C.-349	2,885,000	2,599,376	0.2%	MD	Retail
	23,678,771		1.9%		

	Original LTV	Current LTV	Appraised Values	DSCR	NOI	Delinquency Status	Rem Maturity
	0.76	0.74		1.42		30	89
	0.55	0.50		3.66		90+	150
	0.58	0.53		2.51		90+	149
	0.66	0.61		6.96		90+	148
	0.54	0.49		3.45		90+	147
		0.60		3.18			

This report has been prepared from original sources and data we believe to be reliable but we make no representations as to its accuracy or completeness. This report is published solely for information purposes and is not to be construed as an offer to sell or as the solicitation of an offer to buy securities in any state where such sale, offer or solicitation would be illegal. First Union Capital Markets Corp., its affiliates and subsidiaries and/or their officers and employees may from time to time acquire, hold or sell a position in the securities mentioned herein. Upon request, we will be pleased to furnish specific information in this regard. If First Union Capital Markets Corp. is used in connection with the purchase or sale of any security discussed in this report, First Union Capital Markets Corp. may act as principal for its own account or as agent for both the buyer and the seller.

When delinquencies and defaults occur, cash flows otherwise due to the sub-ordinated class are diverted to the senior classes to the extent required to meet scheduled principal and interest payments. Thus, subordination allows issuers to create highly rated securities from collateral of various levels of quality. Exhibit 3 highlights the amount of subordination for each of the tranches in the FULB 1997-C1 deal.

General Collateral Specifications

The collateral-remaining weighted average maturity (WAM) is the weighted average time remaining to the balloon date (see the top left corner of Exhibit 2). This section of Exhibit 2 also provides the gross weighted average coupon (WAC) of the underlying collateral and the weighted average final maturity. The number of loans in the underlying pool shows diversification risk. Conduit deals usually have a larger number of smaller deals, whereas fusion deals have a few large loans. The deal we are analyzing has 279 loans, for an average loan size of approximately $4.5 million. Deals with fewer loans are usually considered less liquid and trade at wider spreads. However, buyers who look at the more credit-sensitive tranches sometimes prefer fusion deals because it is easier to analyze the fewer underlying loan credits.

Collateral Concentration by Property Type

The "Top 5 Property Types" (Exhibit 2) shows the respective concentrations of each type of commercial credit exposure to the overall pool of collateral. Heavier concentrations in multifamily loans are usually considered desirable because the loans are relatively short term and the landlord can raise rents to keep up with rising costs. Although multifamily properties are usually more leveraged than other types, historical losses have been lower. The credit strength of retail properties is determined by looking at the strength of retail tenants. Retail properties pose turnover risk. Turnover on retail properties occurs less often than on multifamily properties, but the costs to re-lease are higher. Hotels are analyzed on a going-concern basis because the value of the property lies in the cash flow stability and occupancy rates on the underlying rooms. Office and industrial properties enjoy cash flow stability from long-term leases but carry the highest risk and greatest cost of re-leasing to a different tenant after the lease expires. Indeed, the property is typically adapted to the requirements of a particular lessee, and refitting and re-leasing to a different concern can be costly. It is important for the CMBS investor to be comfortable with the underlying collateral mix as a large concentration to risky sectors is undesirable.

Delinquency and Loss Status of the Collateral

Delinquency rates and default assumptions are key components in assessing the credit risk in the underlying collateral pool. Delinquency rates can be analyzed empirically to determine how future real estate cycles might affect CMBS valuations. Exhibit 4 demonstrates how commercial loan delinquencies have fallen steadily since 1992 to 0.30% as of June 1999.

Exhibit 3: FULB 1997-C1 Subordination Levels

Tranche	S&P Rating	Original Balance	Original Support
A1	Aaa	200,000	30.0%
A2	Aaa	318,000	30.0%
A3	Aaa	395,812	30.0%
B	Aa2	78,327	24.0%
C	A2	71,800	18.5%
D	Baa2	71,800	13.0%
E	Baa3	19,582	11.5%
F	BB	71,800	6.0%
G	BB–	13,055	5.0%
H	B	26,109	3.0%
J	B–	13,054	2.0%
K	144A	26,109	0.0%
IO	Aaa	1,305,448	30.0%

Source: First Union Capital Markets Corp.

Exhibit 4: Commercial Mortgage Loan Delinquency Rates for the 100 Largest Insurance Companies

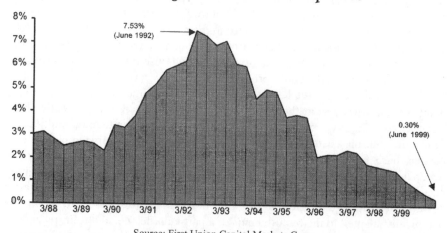

Source: First Union Capital Markets Corp.

In the FULB 1997-C1 deal, only 0.6% of the underlying collateral is 30–60 days past due, 0.42% has been discharged, and no losses have been taken to date.

Geographic Concentration of the Underlying Collateral

It is preferable that the collateral location be reasonably diversified. Collateral concentrations in states or regions where land prices hyperappreciated prior to the origination of the commercial loans may expose the security holder to greater credit and prepayment risks. In the case of FULB 1997-C1, no more than 14% of the collateral is concentrated in one state, and the top five property states represent four distinct geographic regions.

Look at the Major Credit Characteristics of the Collateral Pool and of the Largest Loans in the Pool

Two primary ratios are used to assess the credit of commercial loans: the *debt service coverage ratio* (DSCR) and the *loan-to-value ratio* (LTV). The DSCR reflects the free cash flow generated by the commercial property divided by the debt service requirement. Because of the going-concern nature of commercial properties, this cash flow coverage ratio is really the key to the mortgagee getting paid on the loan. In the pool of collateral in FULB 1997-C1, the weighted average DSCR is 1.37. Obviously, DSCRs of less than 1.0 are cause for concern; it means the property is not providing enough cash flow to cover the debt service payments. Look at the DSCR on the top five mortgage loans in the pool (Exhibit 2). If the largest loans in the pool show signs of credit weakness, such that individual defaults could have a deleterious effect on performance, investors need to factor potential distress on those loans into their analysis and pricing.

LTV is another indicator of risk. When property is liquidated after default, higher LTVs usually result in greater losses on a percentage basis. Again, we look at the characteristics of the largest loans in the pool for signs of potential problems in the future.

The rating agencies set minimum DSCRs and maximum LTVs for different rating classifications based on their analysis of historical loan performance data, qualitative and quantitative reviews of the collateral, and consideration of the security structure. Investors should consider not only the weighted average DSCR and LTV for a deal but also the dispersion.

In the credit tranching process, the goal is to minimize the total cost of funds for the issuer. Consequently, the issuer tries to maximize the size of the higher-rated tranches, which carry lower yields, and minimize the size of the lower-rated tranches, which carry higher yields. However, the size of each tranche is dictated by the leverage ratios required for a targeted rating.

Assessing Structural Prepayment Protection

One of the greatest attractions of CMBS product is the high degree of prepayment protection inherent in the underlying loans. These protections make CMBS a more positively convex product than the majority of RMBS cash flows and structures.

Basic Forms of Call Protection

The basic forms of call protection in a commercial loan are as follows:

Lockouts Most loans prohibit discretionary prepayments for 2–5 years.

Defeasance After the lockout period ends, many loans currently being originated require that, if the loan is prepaid, the cash flows to the mortgagee (and ultimately the security holder) must be maintained. To do this, the mortgagor buys Treasury strips that exactly replicate the cash flows of principal and interest from the prepaid loan. This defeasance serves not only to maintain the cash flow stream but also to improve the underlying credit quality because risk-free government debt is substituted for the credit risk of the underlying borrower. The period that defeasance covers can vary but typically lasts 2–5 years after the lockout period ends. Defeasance improves the "swapability" of the bond to floating rate because the cash flow stream is maintained, and investors have come to prefer defeasance to yield maintenance.

Yield Maintenance Yield maintenance compensates the mortgagee by forcing the mortgagor that is prepaying the loan to "make whole" the mortgagee on an economic basis for the loss of income from the prepayment. The prepayment penalty under a yield maintenance clause can be calculated in several stipulated methods. The most common is for the prepaying mortgagor to pay the mortgagee a penalty equal to the net present value of the future cash flows from the mortgage loan discounted at a rate equal to the yield of the Treasury bond with the same average life as the loan. The lower the yield, the greater the prepayment penalty. This means that as the market rallies and rates fall, the prepayment penalties under most yield maintenance provisions become progressively more onerous. The downside to yield maintenance is that the mortgagee "loses the asset" when it gets prepaid.

Points Prepayment penalties in the form of points are sometimes included in CMBS structures. Point prepayment penalties are typically in place for several years after yield maintenance or defeasance expires. Point penalties usually decline over time.

Factors that Could Trigger an Unscheduled Prepayment
Unlike RMBS, CMBS prepayments are quite insensitive to the level of interest rates. For CMBS, the majority of prepayments are related to credit losses. Other than these credit-induced prepayments, discretionary prepayments are interest-rate-sensitive only to the extent that rates have dropped enough to make the prepayment, with its associated penalties, economically viable. For the most part, such interest-rate-driven prepayments will occur only in booming real estate markets and/or after prepayment penalties have wound down. The following factors could trigger an unscheduled prepayment:

Credit Losses When a default occurs in a pool of CMBS collateral, any loss is absorbed first by the most junior subordinated tranche in the deal. Although the junior tranche absorbs any principal shortfall from the loss, two other tranches also see an impact to cash flow. The credit loss essentially becomes an unscheduled prepayment, and this prepayment is applied as a par redemption to the first sequential tranche in the deal. The other tranche that is directly affected is the WAC IO because the coupon on the IO is reduced as the defaulted loan leaves the pool, diminishing the value of the IO strip.

Real Estate Market Induced Prepayment Prepayments may arise if the economy boosts real estate values and the borrower has an opportunity to refinance the loan with penalties and then leverage the investment economically. The major factors driving such a prepayment include the following:

1. Higher real estate values, which provide a gain to pay for any penalties
2. Lower interest rates, which have an effect similar to that of RMBS
3. Higher marginal tax bracket, which increases the value of a tax deduction for paying prepayment penalties

Exhibit 5 shows the rationale for making an unscheduled prepayment. Lower interest rates five years out provide further incentive to refinance for the same reason a residential mortgage borrower would refinance.

Prepayment Protection Features Winding Down Commercial real estate loans have a wide variety of prepayment penalty structures. In most instances, CMBS are locked out for the first 2–5 years. After the lockout, the yield maintenance period kicks in until several months before maturity, which is usually the 10-year balloon payment. In place of or in addition to yield maintenance, there may be defeasance and prepayment penalties after the lockout. In either case, as these penalties become less onerous, falling rates may induce the borrower to prepay the loan to the extent the interest savings outweigh the after-tax penalty expense.

Exhibit 5: Unscheduled Prepayment Scenario

Property Book Value	$10 million
Borrowed Amount	$7 million (70% LTV ratio)
Marginal Tax Rate	40%
Five Years Later	
Property Market Value	$15 million
Prepayment Penalty	$1 million
Refinance Amount	$10.5 million (70% LTV)
Rationale for Prepayment Quantified	
Gain after Penalty	$4 million (133% ROE)
Tax Deduction	$400,000
Total Gain (with tax benefit)	$4.4 million (147% ROE)

LTV: Loan-to-value; ROE: Return on equity.
Source: First Union Capital Markets Corp.

Exhibit 6: Weighted Average Life Drift — FULB 1997-C1 A2

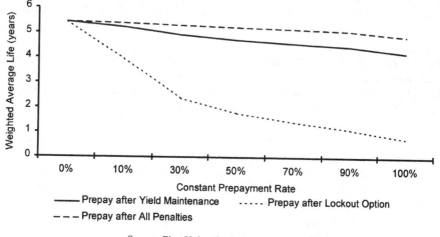

Source: First Union Capital Markets Corp.

To show the structural prepayment protection in CMBS, we looked at the cash flows of the A2 tranche from FULB 1997-C1. When the deal was issued in 1997, the A2 was a 7.75-year bond. The prepayment protection remaining on the whole deal is shown in the CMBS Prepay Restriction Schedule of Exhibit 2. The schedule shows when hard lockout, yield maintenance, and point penalties provide protection from discretionary prepayments.

Next, we ran the A2 tranche on the *Bond Analyzer* under three different prepayment methodologies (Exhibit 6). First, we looked at a scenario where prepayments occur only after all of the forms of prepayment protection expire. Then, we looked at the prepayments and average life variability of the tranche if prepayments occurred after the yield maintenance protection expired. Finally, we looked at the worst case, which assumes prepayments occur after the expiry of the hard lockout period.

We can see in Exhibit 6 the value of yield maintenance. The average life of the cash flows drifts little when the yield maintenance is applied. Sometimes discretionary prepayments are made during the yield maintenance period. However, the structural protection and onerous prepayment penalties imposed in CMBS transactions give comfort to investors that the actual cash flow variability risk is much closer to the first and second potential outcomes.

Stressing the Credit Protection of Individual Tranches

Exhibit 7 depicts how various tranches in the CMFUN 1999-1 deal absorb losses under onerous credit loss scenarios. We used the *Bond Analyzer* to shock tranches under scenarios of rising *constant default rates* (CDRs). Similar to constant prepayment rates (CPRs) in RMBS, the CDR is an annual measure of loss. For instance, a 4% CDR implies that the collateral suffers 4% in defaults annually, an average level not seen since the early 1990s. We also assume a *loss severity rate* (LSR) of 45%, which is higher than indicated in the empirical analysis provided by one rating agency, Fitch IBCA. An LSR of 45% implies that if a $1 million loan defaults, $450,000 is lost.

Using the *Bond Analyzer*, it was found that due to the 26.5% AAA credit support structured into the deal, the AAA 10-year tranche has a constant 7.54% yield over all default scenarios. The A tranche's yield only deteriorates slightly at a 5% CDR assumption, whereas the BBB tranche is hit after 3% CDR and the BBB- tranche starts suffering at 2% CDR. Exhibit 8 enumerates the yields, spreads, and principal outstanding under the different CDR scenarios.

HEDGING CMBS WITH INTEREST RATE SWAPS

Interest rate swaps have become the preferred risk management tool in the marketplace. This is due in part to the relative delinking of Treasury-based products and spread products in the market since the beginning of 1997. Most risk managers use interest rate swaps to hedge part of the interest rate risk in bulleted credit structures. CMBS have structural protections that make the product's cash flow structure similar to that of corporate bonds. In this section, we examine the effectiveness of hedging CMBS positions with interest rate swaps.

Exhibit 7: CMBS Yield Compression under Stressed CDR Scenarios — CMFUN 1999-1 (as of Sept. 1, 1999)

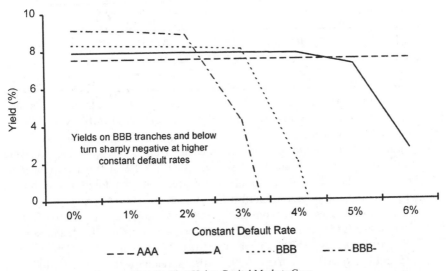

Source: First Union Capital Markets Corp.

Exhibit 8: Impact of Stressed CDR Scenarios—CMFU9901

	Yield (%)				Spreads (bps)				Principal Outstanding (%)			
Tranche:	A2	C	E	F	A2	C	E	F	A2	C	E	F
Rating:	AAA	A	BBB	BBB–	AAA	A	BBB	BBB–	AAA	A	BBB	BBB–
0% CDR	7.54	7.91	8.31	9.12	157	193	233	313	100%	100%	100%	100%
1% CDR	7.54	7.91	8.26	9.04	157	193	227	305	100%	100%	100%	100%
2% CDR	7.54	7.90	8.21	8.85	157	192	221	285	100%	100%	100%	100%
3% CDR	7.54	7.88	8.09	4.27	158	190	207	–174	100%	100%	100%	27%
4% CDR	7.54	7.85	2.03	–8.77	158	186	–396	–1,471	100%	100%	21%	0%
5% CDR	7.54	7.25	–9.70	–15.82	158	124	–1,564	–2,172	100%	87%	0%	0%
6% CDR	7.54	2.71	–15.50	–22.72	159	–329	–2,141	–2,860	100%	31%	0%	0%

CDR: Constant default rate.

Source: First Union Capital Markets Corp.

Exhibit 9: 10-Year AAA CMBS versus Swap Spreads (January 1999-August 1999)

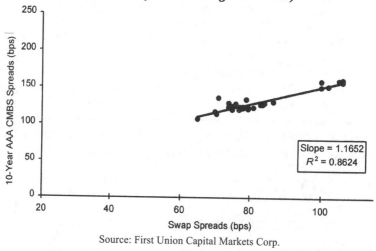

Source: First Union Capital Markets Corp.

Our methodology is to regress CMBS spreads versus swap spreads over three separate time horizons. We looked at the relationship between CMBS spreads and swap spreads over the short term (7 months), the intermediate term (13 months), and the long term (3 years). In each case, 10-year swap spreads were used as the independent variable and 10-year AAA CMBS spreads were used as the dependent variable. The results of each regression are shown in Exhibits 9, 10, and 11 in graph form and in Exhibit 12.

The results show a tight correlation between swap spreads and CMBS spreads in the short term and long term but not in the intermediate term. From August to November 1998, CMBS spreads widened sharply over LIBOR during the period of market contagion (Exhibit 13). After January 1999, CMBS spreads resumed their usual tight relationship to swap spreads and have remained in a relatively tight range since then.

Exhibit 10: 10-Year AAA CMBS versus Swap Spreads (August 1998-August 1999)

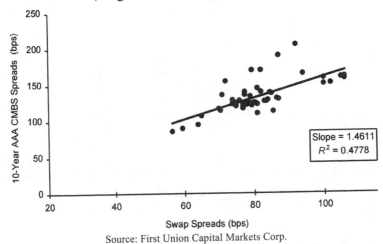

Source: First Union Capital Markets Corp.

Exhibit 11: 10-Year AAA CMBS versus Swap Spreads (September 1996-August 1999)

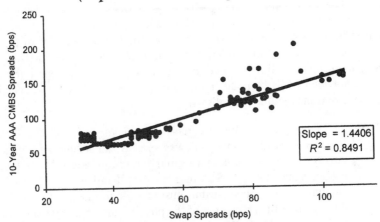

Source: First Union Capital Markets Corp.

Exhibit 12: Summary of Relationship between 10-Year CMBS Spreads and 10-Year Swap Spreads

Period length	R-Squared
Short Term (7 months)	86%
Intermediate Term (13 months)	48%
Long Term (3 Years)	85%

Source: First Union Capital Markets Corp.

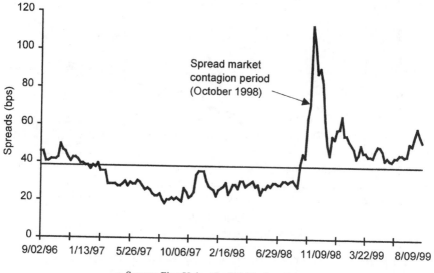

Exhibit 13: 10-Year AAA CMBS Spreads over Swaps (September 1996-August 1999)

Source: First Union Capital Markets Corp.

Liquidity and credit concerns wreaked havoc on the fixed-income spread sector markets from August to November 1998, and CMBS was one of the hardest-hit sectors. However, fundamental structural changes in the CMBS market and the general market climate since then lead us to conclude a similarly sharp disconnect between CMBS spreads and swap spreads is unlikely to occur in the future. These reasons include the following:

Stable financing costs. Higher perceived levels of general credit risk manifest themselves in both wider swap spreads and greater percentage haircuts on financing rates, particularly on more analytically complex products such as CMBS. A haircut of 15% rather than 5% triples the amount of equity the investor must provide for the position and means the effective financing cost of the position increases by approximately 65 bps (Exhibit 14). This happens because the leveraged investor foregoes the earning power of the money invested as equity. The economic opportunity cost of the equity money is approximately LIBOR, which is assumed to be the level of foregone return on the money.

Changes in the haircut increase the cost of financing, similar to the effect of wider swap spreads increasing the hedge cost on the asset side of the transaction. Both erode the income that the position generates. Taken together, the combination can create negative carry, which was the case in 1998. Mark-to-market losses and margin calls in 1998 were the final dagger, and many leveraged investors were forced to sell at distressed levels into an already illiquid market. This fire-sale environment caused CMBS to underperform both Treasurys and LIBOR more than most other spread sectors did in 1998. The CMBS market is generally less leveraged than it was last year, which should curtail any downside spread volatility.

Reduced aggregation risk. Another factor that increased CMBS spread volatility in 1998 was aggregation risk. In 1998, dealers were aggregating collateral for $3–$4 billion deals. In 1999, most deals were smaller, and dealers were partnering up, thereby reducing their downside risk and decreasing the potential spread volatility.

Improved credit climate. Most important, the credit climate is fundamentally different now than it was in 1998 when Russia's default, the Asian flu, and the collapse of Long Term Capital Management sent shock waves through the credit markets, highlighting a high level of inherent credit and liquidity risk. No such credit distress exists now, and this is reflected by the fact that haircuts on CMBS have not been changed.

We conclude CMBS have shown the type of relationship to swap spreads that renders hedging with swaps an extremely useful method of reducing potential spread volatility. Going forward, we do not expect CMBS spreads can or will dislocate from the swaps market to nearly the degree that occurred in 1998.

REGULATORY ISSUES

The more senior tranches of CMBS deals receive favorable regulatory treatment. The Employee Retirement Income Security Act of 1974 (ERISA) sets forth six general conditions that must be satisfied by employee benefit or retirement plans and insurance company separate accounts. In general, the senior tranches rated AAA are ERISA-eligible; however, investors should verify exemption with their legal advisers. In the example CMBS deal (Exhibit 15), the A1, A2, and all of the IO tranche, which represent 73% of the deal, are ERISA-eligible.

Exhibit 14: Adjusted Carry on CMBS Position with Different Haircuts*

Percentage of Haircut	Effective Financing Cost	Asset Yield after Swap	Financing Adjusted Carry
5%	5.25/0.95 = L + 27 bps	L + 42 bps	+15 bps
10%	5.25/0.90 = L + 58 bps	L + 42 bps	−16 bps
15%	5.25/0.85 = L + 92	L + 42 bps	−50 bps

*Assuming 5.25% LIBOR and 10-year AAA CMBS swaps out at LIBOR + 42 bps.
Source: First Union Capital Markets Corp.

Exhibit 15: CMFUN 1999-1

Tranche	Rating	Size	Avg. Life	ERISA	SMMEA
A1	AAA	210,400	5.4	Yes	Yes
A2	AAA	816,866	9.5	Yes	Yes
B	AA	76,870	9.7	No	Yes
C	A	62,894	9.7	No	No
D	A−	20,965	9.8	No	No
E	Baa3	48,917	10.1	No	No
F	BBB−	17,471	10.9	No	No
G	144A	59,400	11.8	No	No
H	144A	10,482	13.6	No	No
I	144A	10,482	13.8	No	No
J	144A	20,965	14.7	No	No
K	144A	6,988	16.3	No	No
L	144A	8,735	16.8	No	No
M	144A	26,206	19.7	No	No
X (IO)	AAA	1,398,640	9.4	Yes	Yes

ERISA: Employment Retirement Income Security Act; SMMEA: Secondary Mortgage Market Enhancement Act.

Source: First Union Capital Markets Corp.

The Secondary Mortgage Market Enhancement Act (SMMEA) was amended in December 1996 to add qualifying CMBS paper. To qualify, the paper must be rated in the top two classes by at least one rating agency and meet certain criteria. In the CMFUN 1999-1 deal, the A1, A2, B, and all of the IO tranche are SMMEA-eligible. Again, investors should verify the interpretation of SMMEA eligibility with the appropriate governing authority or regulatory body.

Chapter 8

Value and Sensitivity Analysis of CMBS IOs

Philip O. Obazee
Vice President
Quantitative Research
First Union Securities, Inc.

ommercial mortgage-backed securities (CMBS) interest-only (IOs) are coupons stripped from an underlying pool of commercial mortgages. Stripping the coupon allows issuers to sell a bond with premium collateral at a price close to par. For example, a 9% coupon commercial mortgage collateral could be stripped to create a 2% IO, so that the bond created out of the collateral would be priced at par with a 7% coupon. In Exhibit 1 we show an example of a weighted average coupon (WAC) IO created from AAA and AA bonds, with 7% and 7.5% coupons, respectively. The collateral-weighted WAC is 9.5%, so 2.5% and 2% coupons are stripped from the AAA and AA bonds, respectively.

To understand the value drivers for an IO, we need to break down CMBS. An investor who purchases CMBS holds a long position in a noncallable bond, a short call option, and default put option. When selling the options, the investor is compensated in the form of enhanced coupon payments. Part of this enhanced coupon is stripped off to create the IO, hence the basic value drivers for IOs come largely from prepayments and default put options. Unlike residential mortgage-backed securities (RMBS) for which the prepayment option predominates, the default option has greater impact in a CMBS transaction. The option embedded in a CMBS transaction derives its value from the following:

Exhibit 1: A Typical WAC IO Structure

Bond Class	Principal Balance	Investment Class Coupon	Pool WAC	Class WAC IO
AAA	375	7.00%		2.500%
AA	125	7.50%		2.000%
WAC IO	0		9.50%	
Total	500	7.125%		2.375%

WAC IO: Weighted average coupon interest-only.
Source: First Union Securities, Inc.

- time to maturity of the underlying collateral
- collateral coupon and scheduled and unscheduled principal payments
- interest rate
- volatility of the interest rate
- prepayment restriction (e.g., lockout)
- net operating income (NOI) from the collateral and the volatility of the NOI
- correlation between the interest rate and the NOI
- collateral default clause

Although this option-theoretic approach is useful in identifying the factors that determine the value of CMBS, the analytical complexity it presents makes investors more likely to value IOs by looking at the contribution to return from prepayment and default as well as the sensitivity of their IO position to changing prepayment and default assumptions.

In this chapter, we examine the various types of IOs and show how the value of an IO is affected by a number of scenarios related to the magnitude and timing of prepayments, defaults, and interest rates.

TYPES OF CMBS IOS

There are four types of CMBS IOs: fixed-rate IOs, WAC IOs, notional IOs, and component IOs. Each type of IO is discussed below.

Fixed-Strip IOs

The holder of a *fixed-strip IO* receives a fixed-stripped coupon off a collateral WAC. For example, a 1% IO stripped off a 9% collateral WAC will pay an 8% coupon to the bond classes. Any change in the collateral WAC is absorbed by the bond classes. Thus, if the collateral WAC changes to 8.5%, the IO will remain at 1% with the WAC bond changing to 7.5%.

WAC IOs

With *WAC IOs*, bondholders receive a fixed coupon and the change in the WAC is passed on to the IO holders. For example, if a 1% IO is stripped off a 9% collateral WAC, the coupon to the bond classes is 8%, and the change in the collateral WAC to, say, 8.5% will result in a new IO coupon of 0.5%. As the loan with the high coupon prepays, the WAC IO coupon is lower and, conversely, as the loan with the low coupon prepays the coupon on the WAC IO is higher.

Notional IOs

The holder of a *notional IO* receives varying strips of coupons from different tranches. For example, the notional IO structure could consist of 1.5% stripped from the A1 tranche and 1% from the A2 tranche. Both bonds are off collateral WAC, so that as the collateral WAC changes the coupon on the bond changes and the IO remains the same. Moreover, the cash flow of a notional IO is affected by the pay-down in the bond class; the cash flow decreases the most as the bond with the higher stripped coupon pays down.

Component IOs

A *component IO* is a combination of a WAC and notional IOs. The WAC IO is stripped from the collateral and the notional IO is stripped from the bond classes. Changes in the collateral WAC are passed on to the WAC IO, and the notional IO remains unchanged.

IMPACT OF PREPAYMENT ON CMBS IOS

A CMBS IO has low convexity cost because, unlike residential mortgages that can prepay in response to refinancing incentives, commercial mortgages usually have prepayment restrictions. The restrictions in CMBS structures are lockouts, defeasance, point penalties, and yield maintenance.

Lockouts

The lockout period, generally 2–5 years, prohibits a borrower from prepaying a loan prior to the scheduled maturity.

Defeasance

From an investor's perspective, a loan that is defeased is locked out from prepayment. In a defeased structure, prepayments from borrowers do not change the cash flows to investors. The borrower replaces a mortgage with a series of U.S Treasury strips that match the payment stream of the mortgage loan. The defeasance option improves the credit quality of the collateral with a corresponding decline in yield. For example, NASC 98-D6 is backed by collateral with defeasance.

Penalty Period

The penalty period, which follows a lockout period, allows a borrower to repay a loan by compensating the lender for the right to terminate early. There are two types of penalties: yield maintenance and fixed percentage penalty points.

Yield Maintenance

Yield maintenance is designed to compensate the lender for interest lost as a result of prepayments by making borrowers indifferent to prepayments. If the prevailing market rate is higher at the time of prepayment than at origination, the borrower would not be required to make a penalty payment. The key variable determining yield maintenance is the reference rate, which is the comparable maturity Treasury rate or the comparable maturity Treasury plus spread. Investors prefer Treasury flat because it results in higher present value in terms of prepayment penalty. As the term to maturity of the mortgage shortens, the yield maintenance as a percentage of the remaining balance decreases and the remaining loan payment represents a lower percentage of total investor return.

Fixed Percentage Penalty Points

Fixed percentage points assess a percentage penalty on the remaining loan balance, and this percentage declines over the life of the loan. Typically, the points penalty is distributed as follows:

Lockout: 5 Years

Year	Penalty (%)
6	5
7	4
8	3
9	2
10	1

Significant movement in interest rates and increases in property values would affect these fixed economic disincentives to prepay a penalty loan because the penalties do not change with interest rates.

ALLOCATION OF PREPAYMENT PENALTIES

The allocation of prepayment penalties differs by deal. In general, for a deal issued prior to and including 1996 the prepayment penalties were 75% to 100% allocated to IOs and the penalties paid to the coupon bondholders were capped between 0% and 25%. Recent deals allocate the prepayment penalties such that the currently paying bonds are "whole" and the remaining penalties distributed to the IOs. In this newer allocation method, the investor holding the currently paying bond receives compensation for the early return of principal in a lower-rate environment. The IO holder generally receives 65% to 75% of the penalty, and the current principal paying bond receives the remainder — making it "whole" to the bond's coupon and not flat to Treasurys. The penalty point allocated to a bond is computed as the product of the prepayment distribution and yield maintenance.

PREPAYMENT RESTRICTIONS AND RELATIVE VALUE ISSUES

The cash flow variability in lockout and defeased bonds comes from credit events. Movements in interest rates, spread levels, and the credit performance of the underlying loan determine total return. Lockout and defeased structures are not exposed to prepayment risk. Exhibit 2 shows the yield to maturity of NASC 98-D6 PS1 under different prepayment restrictions. The yield is not affected by prepayment protection because of it defeasance feature. NASC 98-D6 PS1 exhibits greater average life stability than FULBA 98-C2 (Exhibit 3). As a rule of thumb, a change in average life of less than half a year as prepayment speed increases from 0 conditional prepayment rate (CPR) to 100% CPR is a good indicator of how well a structure is call protected. For example, NASC 98-D6 PS1 has approximately two months weighted average life (WAL) drift for an increase in prepayment speed from 0 CPR to 100% CPR.

Although yield maintenance leaves investors indifferent to prepayments, the variety of securities within a deal and differences across deals cause diverse bond performance depending on the prepayment and rate scenarios. The credit performance of the loan, interest rates, prepayment speed, and the allocation of penalties will determine the yield of a bond with a yield maintenance provision. Market convention is to assume the loans do not prepay during the yield maintenance period and to assume a pricing speed of 100% CPR for an IO. If the actual prepayment is less than 100% CPR, the investor benefits. For example, Exhibit 4 shows a yield pickup of 77 bps if the realized prepayment for FULB 98-C2 is 20% CPR. Exhibit 5 shows the yield to maturity of FULBA 98-C2 with prepayments that occur under different prepayment scenarios. Exhibit 6 shows the pickup in yield that results in a drop or slope in spread; that is, the exhibit shows the difference between the actual prepayment speed and the pricing speed.

Exhibit 2: Yield to Maturity of NASC 1998-D6 PS1 by Prepayment Restriction

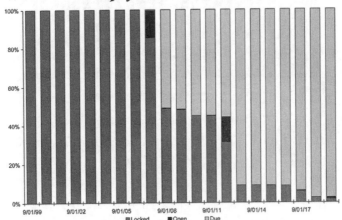

Source: First Union Securities, Inc.

Exhibit 3: Yield to Maturity and WAL of NASC 1998-D6 PS1 by Prepayment Scenario

	Prepay after Lockout Option					Prepay after Yield Maintenance					Prepay after All Penalties				
CPR	0	10	20	50	100	0	10	20	50	100	0	10	20	50	100
Yield	10.70	10.70	10.69	10.67	10.50	10.70	10.70	10.69	10.67	10.50	10.70	10.70	10.69	10.67	10.50
WAL	9.83	9.82	9.82	9.80	9.67	9.83	9.82	9.82	9.80	9.67	9.83	9.82	9.82	9.80	9.67

CPR: Conditional prepayment rate; IO: Interest-only; WAL: Weighted average life; YTM: Yield to maturity.
*Pricing assumption: 470 bps at 100 CPR.

Source: First Union Securities, Inc.

Exhibit 4: Yield to Maturity and WAL of FULBA 1998-C2 IO by Prepayment Scenario

	Prepay after Lockout Option					Prepay after Yield Maintenance					Prepay after All Penalties				
CPR	0	10	20	50	100	0	10	20	50	100	0	10	20	50	100
Yield	10.73	8.81	7.49	5.37	4.03	10.73	10.47	10.30	10.01	9.53	10.73	10.71	10.69	10.63	10.31
WAL	9.37	8.56	8.14	7.61	7.36	9.37	9.12	8.99	8.82	8.61	9.37	9.35	9.34	9.31	9.15

CPR: Conditional prepayment rate; IO: Interest-only; WAL: Weighted average life; YTM: Yield to maturity.
* Pricing assumption: 375 bps at 100 CPR.

Source: First Union Securities, Inc.

Exhibit 5: Yield to Maturity of FULBA 1998-C2 IO by Prepayment Restriction

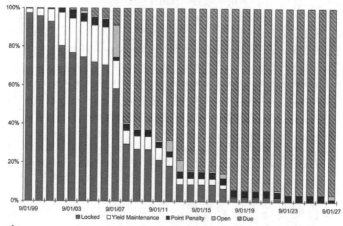

IO: Interest-only.

Source: First Union Securities, Inc.

Exhibit 6: Yield Pick-UP from the Slope in Spread for FULBA 98-C2 IO

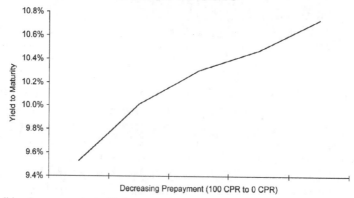

CPR: Conditional prepayment rate; IO: Interest-only

Source: First Union Securities, Inc.

Exhibit 7: Yield to Maturity and WAL of FULBA 1998-C2 IO by Prepayment Scenario – Shock versus No Shock

	Prepay during Yield Maintenance (no shock)					Prepay during Yield Maintenance (shock + 300 bps)				
CPR	0	10	20	50	100	0	10	20	50	100
Yield	10.71	11.26	11.75	12.63	13.56	10.71	9.46	8.59	7.06	6.53
WAL	9.37	8.56	8.14	7.60	7.16	9.37	8.56	8.14	7.60	7.16

CPR: Conditional prepayment rate; IO: Interest-only; WAL: Weighted average life; YTM: Yield to maturity.
Source: First Union Securities, Inc.

Exhibit 8: Yield to Maturity of FULBA 98-C2 IO by Prepayment Scenario during Yield Maintenance

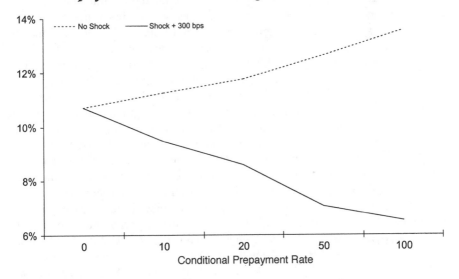

IO: Interest-only.
Source: First Union Securities, Inc.

In general, IOs benefit as prepayment speed increases during the yield maintenance period. The present value of the yield maintenance penalty paid to the IO is usually greater than the present value of the forgone interest that would have been received from the loan that prepaid. If interest rates rise to the level where there is no prepayment penalty, the IO holder does not benefit from faster prepayments and the IO loses the income from the prepaid loan and does not receive a compensating penalty payment.

Unlike a defeased IO, an IO from a deal backed by yield maintenance offers investors the potential for a higher return with faster prepayment under stable interest rate scenarios. Exhibits 7 and 8 show the yield to maturity of FULBA 98-C2 IO for an unchanged rate and a 300 bps rate increase.

IMPACT OF DEFAULT ON CMBS IOS YIELD

The impact of defaults on a CMBS bond depends on various factors. Some of these factors are the bond's position in the distribution priority, loan characteristics in the pool, timing of default, amount of recovery, and servicer advance feature. For an IO, the lower the default rate and the later the default occurs, the better the IO's performance profile. To assess the default probability and the timing of the default, the investor has to understand the characteristics of each of the loans in the pool. In a WAC IO, one approach is to take the difference between each of the loan rates and the current weighted average coupon and determine which loans contribute the most to the IO, and then examine these loans by using the historical default rate for that type of loans.

Investors generally make assumptions about the default rate. A recent study of default rates on commercial mortgages held by insurance companies showed the 10-year cumulative default rate ranged from 9% for 1977 origination to about 28% for 1986.[1] These cumulative default rates translate to about 1% and 4% conditional default rates (CDRs), respectively, for 10-year collateral. Although this study provides useful insights into default rates, there are differences between insurance companies and mortgage conduit originations. Another study that examined default rates on conduit loans originated and securitized between 1995 and 1999 showed the cumulative default rate was 0.78% on a loan basis and 0.48% on a balance basis.[2] We believe this impressive performance is partly explained by the absence of term defaults for these loans (that is, a default that occurs prior to the balloon date), the strong real estate market, and the oversight and discipline provided by the capital markets and the rating agencies.

Although there is no standard CDR to use, there is an emerging consensus favoring a 2% to 3% CDR with 30% to 35% loss severity and 12 months to recover as reasonable numbers to evaluate conduit IOs. In Exhibits 9 and 10, we show the results for FULBA 98-C2 and NASC 98-D6 using various CDRs. At 3% CDR, FULBA 98-C2 suffers a yield loss of 381 bps and NASC 98-D6 incurs a yield loss of 335 bps. We decided to look at the degree of structural leverage in the FULBA 98-C2 and NASC 98-D6 IOs. What we found is that, on average for a 1% change in CDR, there is 10.31% yield compression for FULBA 98-C2 and 10.24% for NASC 98-D6. However, when we examine the volatility of the yield compression, FULBA 98-C2 has a standard deviation of 3% compared with 1.4% for NASC 98-D6. FULBA 98-C2 suffers a 15.7% yield compression for the first 1% of CDR shock compared with 10.5% for NASC 98-D6. Ignoring that series for a moment, the average and standard deviations of the yield compression for FULBA 98-C2 become 8.97% and 0.2%, respectively, compared with 10.17% and

---

[1] Howard Esaki, Steven L'Heureux and Mark P. Snyderman, "Commercial Mortgage Defaults," *Real Estate Finance* (Spring 1999).

[2] Richard Parkus and John F. Tierney, "The Conduit Loan Market: A Statistical Analysis of Default Activity," Deutsche Bank (July 21, 1999).

1.6% for NASC 98-D6. A telling detail is that there is a larger swing in yield for the FULBA 98-C2 IO for the first 1% default rate, but the yield stabilizes as the default rate increases. Exhibits 11 and 12 contain the results for percentage yield compression for the FULBA 98-C2 and NASC 98-D6 IOs.

PUTTING IT ALL TOGETHER:
CMBS IOS SENSITIVITY ANALYSIS

To properly evaluate the prepayment and default risk in CMBS IOs in one shot, we suggest a sensitivity analysis that contains carefully chosen scenarios that we believe will help investors identify relative value in this sector. Typically, investors need to see the effect of a large number of scenarios relating to the magnitude and timing of prepayments, defaults and interest rates. The scenarios we suggest investors use are defined in terms of prepayment and default risk measures and are listed below:

- *Scenario 1*: base scenario at 0 CPR and 0 CDR, no yield shock
- *Scenarios 2-4*: prepay at 10%, 50%, and 100% CPR after all penalties (measures the effect of prepayments at the tail of a deal)
- *Scenarios 5-7*: prepay at 10%, 50%, and 100% CPR after yield maintenance (measures the effect of prepayments during and after fixed-point penalty periods)

Exhibit 9: Yield to Maturity of FULBA 1998-C2 IO by Varying CDR

CPR	0						100					
CDR	1.0%	2.0%	3.0%	4.0%	5.0%	6.0%	1.0%	2.0%	3.0%	4.0%	5.0%	6.0%
Yield	9.33	7.84	6.95	6.11	5.26	4.42	8.14	6.63	5.72	4.93	4.10	3.28
WAL	8.94	8.55	8.19	7.85	7.54	7.24	8.26	7.94	7.64	7.36	7.09	6.83

CDR: Conditional default rate; CPR: Conditional prepayment rate; IO: Interest-only; WAL: Weighted average life; YTM: Yield to maturity.

Source: First Union Securities, Inc.

Exhibit 10: Yield to Maturity of NASC 1998-D6 PS1 by Varying CDR

CPR	0						100					
CDR	1.0%	2.0%	3.0%	4.0%	5.0%	6.0%	1.0%	2.0%	3.0%	4.0%	5.0%	6.0%
Yield	9.63	8.52	7.36	6.10	5.12	4.25	9.42	8.31	7.15	5.88	4.89	4.01
WAL	9.40	9.00	8.62	8.26	7.93	7.61	9.26	8.87	8.50	8.16	7.83	7.53

CDR: Conditional default rate; CPR: Conditional prepayment rate; WAL: Weighted average life; YTM: Yield to maturity.

Source: First Union Securities, Inc.

Exhibit 11: Yield and Percentage Yield Compression for FULBA 98-C2 IO and NASC 1998-D6 by Varying CDR

CDR	FULBA 98-C2 Yield	NASC 98-D6 Yield	FULBA 98-C2 Yield Compression	NASC 98-D6 Yield Compression
0.01	9.33	9.63		
0.02	7.84	8.52	15.7%	10.5%
0.03	6.95	7.36	9.3%	11.0%
0.04	6.11	6.10	8.8%	12.0%
0.05	5.26	5.12	9.0%	9.3%
0.06	4.42	4.25	8.8%	8.3%
		Average	10.3%	10.2%
		Standard Deviation	3.0%	1.4%

CDR: Conditional default rate.

Source: First Union Securities, Inc.

Exhibit 12: Percentage Yield Compression for FULBA 98-C2 IO and NASC 1998-D6

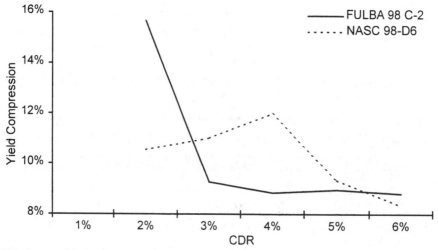

CDR: Constant default rate

Source: First Union Securities, Inc.

- *Scenarios 8-10*: prepay at 10%, 50%, and 100% CPR after lockout periods (measures the effect of prepayments during and after yield maintenance and fixed-point penalty periods)
- *Scenarios 11-13*: prepay at 10%, 50% and 100% CPR after lockout periods with negative 1% yield shock (lower rates mean higher yield maintenance penalties)
- *Scenarios 14-16*: prepay at 10%, 50%, and 100% CPR after lockout periods with plus 1% yield shock (higher rates mean lower yield maintenance penalties)

- *Scenarios 17-19*: prepay at 10%, 50%, and 100% CPR after lockout periods with plus 2% yield shock (higher rates mean lower yield maintenance penalties)
- *Scenarios 20-23*: no prepayment, default at 1%, 2%, 3%, and 4% CDR (measures the effect of defaults in the absence of prepayments)
- *Scenarios 24-27*: prepay at 100% CPR after lockout periods, default at 1%, 2%, 3%, and 4% CDR (measures the effect of defaults in situations with high prepayments and penalties); loss severity of 25% is assumed for Scenarios 20-27 and recovery is assumed to be 12 months

Exhibits 13 and 14 show the sensitivity analysis results for the FULBA 98-C2 and NASC 98-D6 IOs, respectively. The exhibits allow an investor to effectively evaluate the interaction among prepayments, defaults, interest rates, loan penalty terms, and deal structures.

CONCLUSION

Determining value in CMBS IOs may look daunting, but the challenges can be easily overcome if the investor understands the contribution of each value driver—prepayments and defaults. From a prepayment perspective, the market convention of pricing an IO at 100% CPR provides a "drop" advantage that is the difference in spread using 0% and 100% CPRs. Although there is a dearth of historical data on commercial mortgage prepayments, from the little we know about the pools issued by Resolution Trust Corp. the lifetime prepayment speeds for those pools were 20%-30%. More important, these deals did not enjoy the type of prepayment protections found in recent deals. In this respect, we believe the market convention of pricing IOs with a 100% CPR assumption provides the potential for higher yield if the actual prepayment is below the pricing speed.

On the default front, a report by the American Council of Life Insurance (ACLI) shows the delinquency rate on loans held by insurance companies fell to 0.30% in the second quarter of 1999 — the lowest level in the past 34 years. Moreover, an industry study of defaults on commercial mortgages originated in the conduit loan market shows a cumulative default of 0.48% from 1995 to 1999. A spate of negative reports about the viability of some retail-type properties notwithstanding, we believe the short-term fundamentals on the credit front are sound.

Exhibit 13: CMBS Sensitivity Report for FULBA 1998-C2 IO

CMBS Sensitivity Analysis

Issue	fulb98c2
Tranche	IO
Cusip	337367ag1
Price	3 50/64
Settle Date	10/1/99
Price Date	9/28/99

Yield Curve   9/28/99

3MO	6MO	1YR	2YR	5YR	10YR	30YR
4.851	4.988	5.165	5.575	5.700	5.808	5.994

	10% CPR	50% CPR	100% CPR
Yield Change (bp) for Prepayments After LO,YM, and Penalties	-2	-10	-42
Yield Change (bp) for Prepayments During Penalty Period	-26	-72	-120
Yield Change (bp) for Prepayments During YM (Yield Curve Unch)	53	186	170
Yield Change (bp) for Prepayments During YM (Yield Curve -100bp)	57	200	193
Yield Change (bp) for Prepayments During YM (Yield Curve +100bp)	-15	-21	-114
Yield Change (bp) for Prepayments During YM (Yield Curve +200bp)	-120	-349	-499

	1% CDR	2% CDR	3% CDR	4% CDR
Yield Change (bp) for Defaults Assuming No Prepayments	-126	-261	-392	-486
Yield Change (bp) for Defaults Assuming 100 CPR During YM (Yield Curve -100 bp)	-118	-242	-377	-502

Exhibit 13 (Continued)

Scenario #	PrePay Assumptn Unit	Rate	Yield Shock(bps)	Default Assumptn Unit	Rate	Prepay when ...	Yield	Wal	ModDur	Sprd(bp)	TSY Mat	Win Beg	Win End
1	CPR	0.00%	0	CDR	0.00%	After All Penalties	10.732	9.369	3.954	494	9.37	Nov-99	May-28
2	CPR	10.00%	0	CDR	0.00%	After All Penalties	10.708	9.354	3.950	491	9.35	Nov-99	May-28
3	CPR	50.00%	0	CDR	0.00%	After All Penalties	10.628	9.307	3.942	484	9.31	Nov-99	May-28
4	CPR	100.00%	0	CDR	0.00%	After All Penalties	10.314	9.145	3.933	452	9.15	Nov-99	Apr-28
5	CPR	10.00%	0	CDR	0.00%	After Yield Maintenance	10.473	9.123	3.895	468	9.12	Nov-99	May-28
6	CPR	50.00%	0	CDR	0.00%	After Yield Maintenance	10.012	8.821	3.835	423	8.82	Nov-99	Apr-28
7	CPR	100.00%	0	CDR	0.00%	After Yield Maintenance	9.528	8.610	3.816	375	8.61	Nov-99	Apr-28
8	CPR	10.00%	0	CDR	0.00%	After Lock Out Periods	11.267	8.561	3.671	549	8.56	Nov-99	May-28
9	CPR	50.00%	0	CDR	0.00%	After Lock Out Periods	12.596	7.611	3.186	684	7.61	Nov-99	Apr-28
10	CPR	100.00%	0	CDR	0.00%	After Lock Out Periods	12.435	7.358	3.050	668	7.36	Nov-99	Apr-28
11	CPR	10.00%	−100	CDR	0.00%	After Lock Out Periods	11.306	8.561	3.672	553	8.56	Nov-99	May-28
12	CPR	50.00%	−100	CDR	0.00%	After Lock Out Periods	12.731	7.611	3.175	697	7.61	Nov-99	Apr-28
13	CPR	100.00%	−100	CDR	0.00%	After Lock Out Periods	12.664	7.358	3.028	691	7.36	Nov-99	Apr-28
14	CPR	10.00%	100	CDR	0.00%	After Lock Out Periods	10.586	8.561	3.748	481	8.56	Nov-99	May-28
15	CPR	50.00%	100	CDR	0.00%	After Lock Out Periods	10.519	7.611	3.419	476	7.61	Nov-99	Apr-28
16	CPR	100.00%	100	CDR	0.00%	After Lock Out Periods	9.596	7.358	3.400	385	7.36	Nov-99	Apr-28
17	CPR	10.00%	200	CDR	0.00%	After Lock Out Periods	9.534	8.561	3.852	376	8.56	Nov-99	May-28
18	CPR	50.00%	200	CDR	0.00%	After Lock Out Periods	7.238	7.611	3.812	148	7.61	Nov-99	Apr-28
19	CPR	100.00%	200	CDR	0.00%	After Lock Out Periods	5.746	7.358	3.979	−1	7.36	Nov-99	Apr-28
20	CPR	0.00%	0	CDR	1.00%	After All Penalties	9.472	8.948	3.926	369	8.95	Nov-99	May-29
21	CPR	0.00%	0	CDR	2.00%	After All Penalties	8.120	8.557	3.865	234	8.56	Nov-99	May-29
22	CPR	0.00%	0	CDR	3.00%	After All Penalties	6.814	8.193	3.800	104	8.19	Nov-99	May-29
23	CPR	0.00%	0	CDR	4.00%	After All Penalties	5.873	7.855	3.834	11	7.85	Nov-99	May-29
24	CPR	100.00%	−100	CDR	1.00%	After Lock Out Periods	11.486	7.084	3.022	574	7.08	Nov-99	Apr-29
25	CPR	100.00%	−100	CDR	2.00%	After Lock Out Periods	10.240	6.826	3.001	450	6.83	Nov-99	Apr-29
26	CPR	100.00%	−100	CDR	3.00%	After Lock Out Periods	8.894	6.584	2.960	316	6.58	Nov-99	Apr-29
27	CPR	100.00%	−100	CDR	4.00%	After Lock Out Periods	7.647	6.355	2.942	192	6.35	Nov-99	Apr-29

CMBS: Commercial mortgage-backed securities; IO: Interest-only.

Source: First Union Securities, Inc.

Exhibit 14: CMBS Sensitivity Report for NASC 1998-D6 IO

CMBS Sensitivity Analysis

Issue	nas98d06
Tranche	PS1
Cusip	655356J3
Price	8 25/64
Settle Date	10/1/99
Price Date	9/28/99

Yield Curve   9/28/99

3MO	6MO	1YR	2YR	5YR	10YR	30YR
4.851	4.988	5.165	5.575	5.700	5.808	5.994

	10% CPR	50% CPR	100% CPR
Yield Change (bp) for Prepayments After LO,YM, and Penalties	–1	–3	–20
Yield Change (bp) for Prepayments During Penalty Period	–1	–3	–20
Yield Change (bp) for Prepayments During YM (Yield Curve Unch)	–1	–3	–20
Yield Change (bp) for Prepayments During YM (Yield Curve –100bp)	–1	–3	–20
Yield Change (bp) for Prepayments During YM (Yield Curve +100bp)	–1	–3	–20
Yield Change (bp) for Prepayments During YM (Yield Curve +200bp)	–1	–3	–20

	1% CDR	2% CDR	3% CDR	4% CDR
Yield Change (bp) for Defaults Assuming No Prepayments	–103	–207	–314	–423
Yield Change (bp) for Defaults Assuming 100 CPR During YM (Yield Curve –100 bp)	–102	–207	–314	–423

Exhibit 14 (Continued)

Scenario #	PrePay Assumptn Unit	PrePay Assumptn Rate	Yield Shock(bps)	Default Assumptn Unit	Default Assumptn Rate	Prepay when ...	Yield	Wal	ModDur	Sprd(bp)	TSY Mat	Win Beg	Win End
1	CPR	0.00%	0	CDR	0.00%	After All Penalties	10.702	9.828	4.104	490	9.83	Oct-99	Apr-20
2	CPR	10.00%	0	CDR	0.00%	After All Penalties	10.697	9.823	4.103	489	9.82	Oct-99	Apr-20
3	CPR	50.00%	0	CDR	0.00%	After All Penalties	10.669	9.802	4.100	486	9.80	Oct-99	Apr-20
4	CPR	100.00%	0	CDR	0.00%	After All Penalties	10.501	9.671	4.084	470	9.67	Oct-99	Jan-20
5	CPR	10.00%	0	CDR	0.00%	After Yield Maintenance	10.697	9.823	4.103	489	9.82	Oct-99	Apr-20
6	CPR	50.00%	0	CDR	0.00%	After Yield Maintenance	10.669	9.802	4.100	486	9.80	Oct-99	Apr-20
7	CPR	100.00%	0	CDR	0.00%	After Yield Maintenance	10.501	9.671	4.084	470	9.67	Oct-99	Jan-20
8	CPR	10.00%	0	CDR	0.00%	After Lock Out Periods	10.697	9.823	4.103	489	9.82	Oct-99	Apr-20
9	CPR	50.00%	0	CDR	0.00%	After Lock Out Periods	10.669	9.802	4.100	486	9.80	Oct-99	Apr-20
10	CPR	100.00%	0	CDR	0.00%	After Lock Out Periods	10.501	9.671	4.084	470	9.67	Oct-99	Jan-20
11	CPR	10.00%	−100	CDR	0.00%	After Lock Out Periods	10.697	9.823	4.103	489	9.82	Oct-99	Apr-20
12	CPR	50.00%	−100	CDR	0.00%	After Lock Out Periods	10.669	9.802	4.100	486	9.80	Oct-99	Apr-20
13	CPR	100.00%	−100	CDR	0.00%	After Lock Out Periods	10.501	9.671	4.084	470	9.67	Oct-99	Jan-20
14	CPR	10.00%	100	CDR	0.00%	After Lock Out Periods	10.697	9.823	4.103	489	9.82	Oct-99	Apr-20
15	CPR	50.00%	100	CDR	0.00%	After Lock Out Periods	10.669	9.802	4.100	486	9.80	Oct-99	Apr-20
16	CPR	100.00%	100	CDR	0.00%	After Lock Out Periods	10.501	9.671	4.084	470	9.67	Oct-99	Jan-20
17	CPR	10.00%	200	CDR	0.00%	After Lock Out Periods	10.697	9.823	4.103	489	9.82	Oct-99	Apr-20
18	CPR	50.00%	200	CDR	0.00%	After Lock Out Periods	10.669	9.802	4.100	486	9.80	Oct-99	Apr-20
19	CPR	100.00%	200	CDR	0.00%	After Lock Out Periods	10.501	9.671	4.084	470	9.67	Oct-99	Jan-20
20	CPR	0.00%	0	CDR	1.00%	After All Penalties	9.676	9.399	4.089	388	9.40	Oct-99	Apr-20
21	CPR	0.00%	0	CDR	2.00%	After All Penalties	8.629	8.997	4.076	284	9.00	Oct-99	Apr-20
22	CPR	0.00%	0	CDR	3.00%	After All Penalties	7.561	8.618	4.061	178	8.62	Oct-99	Apr-20
23	CPR	0.00%	0	CDR	4.00%	After All Penalties	6.468	8.262	4.043	70	8.26	Oct-99	Apr-20
24	CPR	100.00%	−100	CDR	1.00%	After Lock Out Periods	9.477	9.257	4.070	368	9.26	Oct-99	Apr-20
25	CPR	100.00%	−100	CDR	2.00%	After Lock Out Periods	8.430	8.867	4.057	265	8.87	Oct-99	Apr-20
26	CPR	100.00%	−100	CDR	3.00%	After Lock Out Periods	7.360	8.501	4.041	158	8.50	Oct-99	Apr-20
27	CPR	100.00%	−100	CDR	4.00%	After Lock Out Periods	6.266	8.155	4.022	50	8.15	Oct-99	Apr-20

CMBS: Commercial mortgage-backed securities; IO: Interest-only.

Source: First Union Securities, Inc.

Chapter 9

Valuation and Analysis of Credit-Sensitive CMBS Tranches

Philip O. Obazee
Vice President
Quantitative Research
First Union Securities, Inc.

In this chapter, we have examined both the traditional and modern analytical frameworks for evaluating credit-sensitive commercial mortgage-backed securities (CMBS). We contend the credit rating and credit spread are two market observables that contain the information necessary to price the probability of the default and recovery rate risks. In addition, the rating class reflects the agency's assessment of the frequency and severity of expected future defaults. In assigning a rating, agencies look at

- Loan credit quality
- Origination quality
- Servicer capability and flexibility
- Pool diversification and concentration

Understanding these elements is important, but investors may not have the resources to evaluate and monitor them. Investors who do not have access to analytical tools to do extensive fieldwork on the loans in a CMBS deal look to the credit rating and rating agencies in assessing the probability of default.

Continuous monitoring of a deal is important for investors in the credit-sensitive tranches. Investors should examine remittance and surveillance reports for delinquencies and specially serviced loans. There are five major trustees involved in conduit deals, and remittance reports on these deals are available at their Web sites. For troubled loans, investors should talk with the special servicers and participate in special servicers' conference calls. It is important to know what the special servicers are doing to maximize proceeds from troubled loans.

It is also important for investors to monitor property market fundamentals and real estate market conditions, particularly as they relate to property value. Monitoring the property value over the life of a loan provides indications of the potential proceeds that could be realized if a loan defaults and the property is foreclosed and liquidated. In addition, investors should monitor the current LTV distribution of a deal because a decline in property value increases LTV, which raises the risk of default. For example, if the property value of a loan declines by 20%, for example, and the current LTV on the loan is 75%, that decline in value would push the current LTV to 95%.

A traditional analytical framework does not provide guidance on how to model the recovery rate, and we believe the simple approach we suggest in this chapter should be taken as a first-cut in dealing with this problem. Our approach could be extended to account for multiple factors. The flexibility of this technique is that by making the recovery rate dynamic, a link is established between the credit spread and the recovery rate. This would account for any changes in the credit spread that come from either the change in the probability of default or the change in the recovery rate conditional on default changes. Moreover, credit spreads are correlated with the term structure, which suggests the probability of default and the recovery rate in the event of default may depend on macroeconomic conditions as well as structural changes in the economy and property market trends.

To evaluate the relative attractiveness of credit-sensitive CMBS, we introduce in this chapter two sets of tools: break-even yield analysis and default option-adjusted spread (DOAS). Break-even yield adjusts the yield to maturity of a credit-sensitive CMBS bond by taking into consideration the default and recovery rates. The greater the differences between the bond yield and the break-even yield, the more attractive the bond. The break-even formula can be used to back out the implied default rate the market expects by solving for the default rate that makes the bond yield equal the break-even yield. The spread differential between the bond yield and the break-even yield should be seen as the premium for liquidity risk, prepayment risk and forecast errors about default probabilities and the recovery rate.

Although break-even yield is easy to compute, DOAS is more difficult to implement and it uses an option-based technique. Unlike residential mortgage-backed securities (RMBS) OAS, where the prepayment model is exogenously determined, the recovery rate that drives DOAS is endogenous to the model. The recovery rate is keyed off the credit spread; that way, one of the major inputs into the DOAS model is determined from market variables. We believe DOAS will become a useful tool in identifying relative value in the CMBS sector.

OVERVIEW

The CMBS market achieved a phenomenal growth rate in the last five years of the 1990s. Renewed interest in this sector began with the successful Resolution Trust Corp. program in the early 1990s that provided the framework for modern securitization and secondary market conventions. One hallmark of modern CMBS securitization is the senior/subordinate structure, which provides an efficient way of allocating credit risk and yield across different classes of securities. Subordination levels reflect the amount of additional principal available to each tranche to pay any loss sustained by an underlying pool of commercial mortgages. Subordination levels are expressed either as a percentage of the original deal or the current balance. Tranche paydown increases the credit enhancement level and, conversely, increases in realized losses decrease the credit enhancement level. The mezzanine tranches are subordinated to the senior tranches and superior to the subordinated pieces (Exhibit 1). The first loss piece is unrated, and it absorbs the initial losses from the mortgage pool. In this chapter, credit-sensitive tranches refer to the mezzanine and subordinated tranches.

Typically, 70%-75% of a deal's original balance is assigned a AAA rating, which amounts to 25%-30% credit enhancement. The subordination level is inversely related to the credit quality of the underlying collateral. The better the credit of the underlying collateral, the lower the level of subordination required to achieve a given rating class. Exhibit 2 shows the credit enhancement ranges for various rating classes, and Exhibit 3 shows the credit enhancement levels for FULBA 1998-C2.

Exhibit 1: Senior/Subordinated Structure

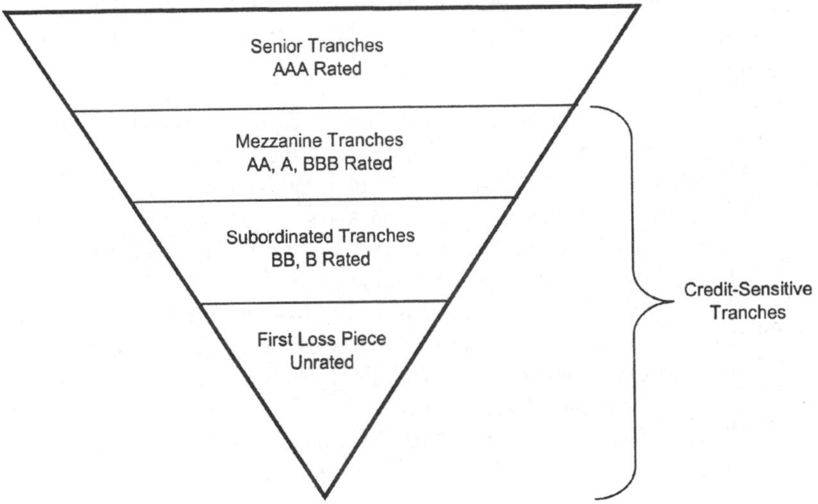

Source: First Union Securities, Inc.

Exhibit 2: Credit Enhancement Ranges by Rating Class

Rating	AAA	AA	A	BBB	BBB-	BB	B	NR
Credit Enhancement Levels	25%–30%	20%–24%	14%–19%	10%–13%	8%–9%	4%–7%	2%–3%	—

NR: Not rated.

Source: First Union Securities, Inc.

Exhibit 3: Credit Enhancement Levels for FULBA 1998-C2

Class	Current Balance ($000)	Coupon	Type	Rating	Original Credit Enhancement	Current Credit Enhancement	Rating Agency
A1	707,814	6.28	Fixed Rate	AAA/Aaa	28.00%	28.44%	S&P/Moody's
A2	1,693,794	6.56	Fixed Rate	AAA/Aaa	28.00%	28.44%	S&P/Moody's
B	170,403	6.64	Fixed Rate	AA/Aa2	23.00%	23.36%	S&P/Moody's
C	170,402	6.73	Fixed Rate	A/A2	18.00%	18.28%	S&P/Moody's
D	204,483	6.78	Fixed Rate	BBB/Baa2	12.00%	12.19%	S&P/Moody's
E	68,161	6.78	Fixed Rate	BBB-/Baa3	10.00%	10.16%	S&P/Moody's
F	51,121	6.78	Fixed Rate	8.50%	8.63%		
G	102,242	7.00	Fixed Rate	5.50%	5.59%		
H	17,040	7.00	Fixed Rate	5.00%	5.08%		
J	34,080	6.15	Fixed Rate	4.00%	4.06%		
K	51,121	6.15	Fixed Rate	2.50%	2.54%		
L	34,080	6.15	Fixed Rate	1.50%	1.52%		
M	17,040	6.15	Fixed Rate	1.00%	1.02%		
N	34,080	6.15	Fixed Rate	0.00%	0.00%		

S&P: Standard & Poor's Corp.

Source: First Union Securities, Inc.

Besides the senior/subordinate structure, another novelty in CMBS is the taxonomy of the deals by pool loan size. The types of deals are conduit, large loan, and fusion.

- *Conduit.* Conduit deals are initiated by financial companies engaged in commercial mortgage origination with the intent of selling the loans through securitization rather than holding the loans in their portfolios. For the purpose of classifying pooled loans, a conduit refers to securitized loans with an average loan balance of less than $5 million, with the largest loan to a property type not exceeding $50 million.
- *Large loan.* A pool of small loans backed by one large property type (e.g., a superregional mall) or a few commercial mortgages is known as a large loan. Insurance companies favor this type of deal because they can readily analyze the number of loans involved.
- *Fusion.* Fusion deals are CMBS transactions of large and conduit-sized loans.

With either senior or subordinated tranches, the investment characteristics of CMBS depend on the underlying collateral, which is commercial mortgages. Some of the salient features of commercial mortgages are as follows:

- *Nonrecourse.* The lender cannot look into the personal assets of the borrower to satisfy a claim in the event of a default.
- *Credit event.* The borrower's ability to generate income from the property and service the debt obligation on the mortgage loan is a basic determinant of a credit event.

- *Prepayment protection.* The types of prepayment protection found in commercial mortgages are lockouts, defeasance, fixed-point penalties, and yield maintenance. Commercial mortgages have prepayment protection provisions that prevent the borrower from prepaying the loan in the first 2-5 years followed by a penalty period (point penalties and yield maintenance).
- *Balloon and extension risk.* Most commercial mortgages are structured to amortize over 20-30 years but mature with a balloon payment in 5-10 years. If the borrower cannot make the payment at maturity, the loan may be extended.

TRADITIONAL VALUATION ANALYSIS

The qualitative and quantitative toolkits used by CMBS professionals vary according to their experience, be it in bonds or real estate. Market participants with a real estate background are mostly found in the B-piece market, where there is the greatest need to examine the underwriting criteria, loan files, property management expertise, and environmental and engineering reports. In general, the traditional set of tools used by professionals' fall into one of the groups below with the depth of analysis increasing as a function of the credit rating of the tranche the investor desires to hold. Although these sets of tools are useful in understanding the nature of a CMBS deal and developing relevant stress-level numbers, we caution that they do not lend themselves directly to determining the market or theoretical value of the bond. Invoking Nobel Laureate Paul Samuelson's famous dictum, "a dollar is dollar" a CMBS is a bond, and we argue a CMBS's value is the expected discounted cash flow adjusted for the risks priced in the market. For CMBS, in addition to interest rates and prepayment risks, the other inherent risks are default and the recovery rate. For these risks, there are two market variables — credit rating and credit spread — that contain the information necessary to price CMBS.

Credit Quality Metric

The debt service coverage ratio (DSCR) and loan-to-value (LTV) are the strongest indicators of the probability of default used by market professionals. The DSCR measures net operating income relative to mortgage payments. The higher the ratio, all else being equal, the lower the default risk. A higher DSCR provides the investor with some comfort as to the ability of the borrower to meet mortgage payments in the event of an economic downturn. For an investor considering a credit-sensitive tranche, the distribution of the DSCR in a deal provides a better indication than the weighted average. Exhibit 4 shows the distribution of the DSCR for FULBA 1998-C2. In general, conduit deals' weighted-average DSCRs fall within the range of 1.30×-1.45×, and the percentage of the deals in which the DSCR is less than 1.25× is considered to be a weaker credit quality.

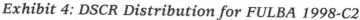

Exhibit 4: DSCR Distribution for FULBA 1998-C2

Weighted Average	1.47
Minimum	0.98
Maximum	3.86

Source: First Union Securities, Inc.

The LTV is used to measure the likelihood of default as well as the potential loss severity after foreclosure and liquidation. The LTV is the ratio between the loan amount and the property value. The property value is estimated as the stabilized net operating income divided by the appropriate capitalization rate, which is the minimum acceptable rate of return for the level of cash flow variability inherent in the property type. Which capitalization rate to use is a thorny question. However, whatever rate is chosen, it must reflect the operating and financial risks of the property type. Operating risk depends to a large extent on the nature of the property type and to a lesser degree on the operating leverage — the mix of fixed and variable costs. In contrast, financial risk depends principally on financial leverage — the mix of debt to equity. By approaching the analysis this way, we see that LTV estimation is built on two fundamental principles: incremental benefits (identification and estimation of the cash flow) and risk-return trade-off (consideration of the risk when determining a required rate of return). We make this point to emphasize the importance of property value and the LTV in assessing credit risk. After all, the default options embedded in CMBS transactions give the borrowers the right to put the property back to the trust. From the borrower's perspective, it is optimal to exercise this right when the LTV is greater than or equal to one. If a borrower exercises this option, the credit-sensitive tranche holders look to how much could be recovered from liquidating the property — the recovery rate risk. Furthermore, the property value estimate could be made separately from the borrower's cash flow projection, which mitigates the moral hazard evident in the principal-agent relationship in the loan contract. Exhibit 5 shows the LTV distribution of FULBA 1998-C2.

Typically, conduit deals' weighted-average LTV falls within the range of 65%-75%, and the percentage of deals with a weighted-average LTV greater than 75% has been used as an indicator of weak credit quality. We feel property value and LTV are good indicators of the likelihood of refinancing a property, thus mitigating balloon date default.

Exhibit 5: Loan-to-Value Distribution for FULBA 1998-C2

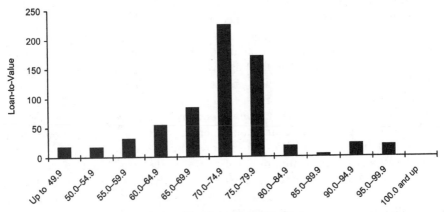

Source: First Union Securities, Inc.

Exhibit 6: Change in Market Value by Property Type

Property Type	Change in Market Value*
Office	−50.2%
Industrial	−33.6%
Retail	−26.4%
Apartment	−16.6%

* From the first quarter of 1986 to the third quarter of 1995.
Source: National Council of Real Estate Investment Fiduciaries and Standard & Poor's Corp.

In Exhibit 6, we show the change in market value for different property types as reported by the National Council of Real Estate Investment Fiduciaries (NCREIF).

The NCREIF data indicate that from the first quarter of 1986 to the third quarter of 1995, the value of office property declined 50.2%. These numbers reflect changes in market value at the national level and could vary in local economies. Moreover, this past performance further reinforces the argument that property value and recovery rate are more important to the credit quality of CMBS bonds, at least for most investors, than temporal phenomena such as frequency of defaults.

Prepayment Protection

Although prepayments have a greater effect on senior rather than lower-rated tranches, the need exists to understand how prepayments affect the mezzanine class as it becomes current principal paying bonds. In particular, prepayment protection has a countervailing effect on CMBS transactions. A loan that prepays effectively does not require any more credit support; however, prepayment restrictions, for example, lockouts, which discourage early prepayment, are not favorable to credit-sensitive tranches. The types of prepayment restrictions found in

CMBS structures are lockouts, defeasance, point penalties, and yield maintenance. Exhibit 7 shows the prepayment protection in FULBA 98-C2, and Exhibit 8 shows the prepayment protection schedule.

Because borrowers are not required to pay a penalty in a higher interest rate environment, but pay the par amount, a fast prepayment during the penalty period would result in a higher yield for investors owning those short average life AAA bonds that share a prepayment penalty and are priced at a discount. Borrowers would prepay during high-rate scenarios because they sold or refinanced the property. If the interest rate is unchanged or a lower-rate environment exists, prepayments during the yield maintenance period would increase the bond yield. However, as the yield increases, the average life of the bond shortens and, for some investors, the shortening mitigates the benefits of the higher yield. Those bonds rated AAA that do not share prepayment penalties would generally not experience an increase in yield as prepayments increase during yield maintenance. However, if interest rates increase sufficiently so the bonds trade at a discount, the yield would increase as prepayment speed rises during yield maintenance.

Exhibit 7: Prepayment Protection in FULBA 98-C2

Prepayment Protection	No. of Loans	Balance ($)	% Balance	WAC	Remaining Term (months)	DSCR	LTV
Lockout	490	2,446,099,898	72.97	7.19	128	1.44	71.3
Lockout then Penalty	161	815,503,079	24.33	7.34	157	1.38	73.6
Points at 1%	1	13,502,536	0.40	7.34	101	1.40	73.1
Yield Maintenance	12	77,111,345	2.30	7.74	109	1.26	77.2

DSCR: Debt service coverage ratio; LTV: Loan-to-value; WAC: Weighted average coupon.
Source: First Union Securities, Inc.

Exhibit 8: Prepayment Restriction Schedule for FULBA 98-C2

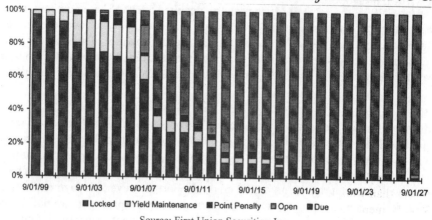

Source: First Union Securities, Inc.

Exhibit 9: Yield to Maturity and WAL of FULBA 1998-C2 Prepayment Scenario after Yield Maintenance

	AA Rated Class					A Rated Class					BBB Rated Class				
CPR	0	10	20	30	50	0	10	20	30	50	0	10	20	30	50
Yield	7.40	7.50	7.64	8.06	9.27	7.61	7.81	7.87	8.30	9.61	8.42	8.90	9.00	9.44	11.63
WAL	10.16	8.31	6.66	4.23	2.07	11.75	8.40	7.77	5.08	2.48	13.23	8.78	8.24	6.46	3.13

CPR: Conditional prepayment rate; WAL: Weighted average life.
Source: First Union Securities, Inc.

Because mezzanine bonds, for example, a AA bond, have higher sensitivity to interest rates as a result of their higher duration, these bonds will likely trade at a discount for smaller increases in interest rates than a short average life AAA bond. In rising rate scenarios, AA bonds that do not share yield maintenance penalties would experience an increase in yield. However, for bonds sharing yield maintenance penalties, the prepayment speed will determine whether the investor receives a higher yield than the base case 0% conditional prepayment rate (CPR). In this case, prepayment must be fast enough to retire the AAA bond during the yield maintenance period for the yield to increase in the AA bond. If the AAA bonds are retired during the yield maintenance period, the AA bond becomes the current principal paying bond and would receive yield maintenance penalties and, if not, it does not receive any prepay penalties. In either case, the weighted average life (WAL) shortens. Exhibit 9 shows the yields and the WAL of FUBLA 1998-C2 for the mezzanine tranches for prepayments after the yield maintenance period.

Diversification and Concentration

The sustainability of property value and expected cash flow depend largely on regional and local economies. To reduce credit risk concentration to one regional or local economy, analysts and rating agencies examine the effective diversity of CMBS transactions.

The Herfindahl Index used by Moody's Investors Service, Inc., is one way to quantify the effective diversity of a deal. This index is the reciprocal of the sum of the squared pool shares of all the loans in a deal, and it equates a portfolio of loans of unequal size into an equivalent number as if they were equal in size. For example, FULBA 1998-C2 has a Herfindahl index score of 117.43, which means the 664 loans in the pool have an effective diversity score of 117 loans. Moody's studies indicate conduit deals originated in 1997 had diversity scores of 80-90; 1998 origination diversity scores were higher, hitting 141 for the third quarter albeit declining in the fourth quarter. With the trend moving away from the larger deal sizes in 1998, the diversity scores have fallen to the 80s and 90s. For example, the diversity score for CMFUN 1999-1 is 70, which is slightly lower than what is considered to be reasonably diverse in the current small deal environment. Moody's considers a Herfindahl index score of 80-90 reasonably diverse. See Exhibit 10 for the quarterly diversity scores for CMBS deals.

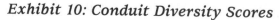

Exhibit 10: Conduit Diversity Scores

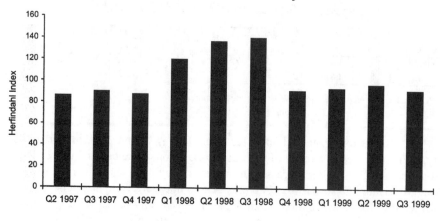

Source: First Union Securities, Inc.

Although the Herfindahl index is a useful measure, we believe using it in conjunction with economic diversity analysis provides the true value of pool diversification. Economic diversity in a deal allows investors to

- Quantify the exposure of a deal to a particular economic sector
- Compare relative exposure to a specific economic sector among the loans in a pool
- Compare one deal to another in terms of economic diversity score, as well as compare any industrial concentration in CMBS deals to the industrial concentration of other asset classes in a portfolio

To measure economic diversity, Moody's, for example, examines the industry mix in the pool relative to the U.S. benchmark, metropolitan statistical area (MSA) level diversity and geographic dispersion. Moody's will add economic diversity scores to all CMBS transaction rated after January 1, 2000.

Diversification is highly valued by rating agencies because it is difficult to predict individual loan defaults. Exhibit 11 shows the state distribution for FULBA 1998-C2; as rule of thumb, in conduit transactions, a concentration of 40% or more in one state is considered an unacceptable threshold.

Loan Underwriting

Unlike residential mortgage deals, which are pools of homogenous loans with clearly stated underwriting standards, commercial mortgage deals are more heterogeneous and the underwriting standards vary widely among lenders. Because of the nature of CMBS, underwriting procedures and policies have a direct effect on the likelihood of losses for a given pool of assets. Some of the issues that investors should look into are as follows:

Exhibit 11: State Distribution of FULBA 1998-C2

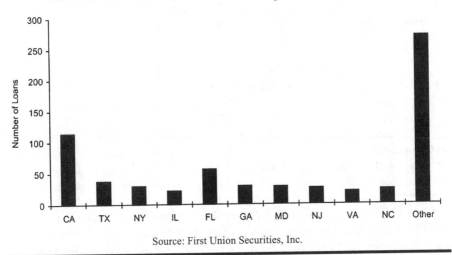

Source: First Union Securities, Inc.

- *Loan sourcing.* How do the originators source their loans? How are the originators compensated? Originators compensated on the basis of the quality and quantity of the loans originated are generally preferable.
- *Underwriting procedure.* What are the policies, procedures and controls for underwriting loans? How detailed and thorough is the scope of the policies? How well does the underwriter conform to written guidelines? How does the originator underwrite the cash flow for each property type? How does the originator account for reserves for real estate taxes, insurance, tenant-initiated improvements, leasing commissions and capital improvements?
- *Loan approval.* How is the loan approved? Is the loan approval process done independently or is it centralized? What are the sources of information used for loan approval? Does the credit search involve credit and legal screening?
- *Loan closing.* What is the procedure to identify documents and monitor changes to the loan document? How is the auditing process handled (internally or externally) with respect to compliance with guidelines?

Industry studies on the underwriting quality of conduit originators in terms of credit performance have been inconclusive. Although one of these studies suggests bank-originated collateral exhibits a better credit performance than nonbank-originated collateral, another study shows that some bank-contributed loans have exhibited higher delinquency rates than some nonbank contributed collateral. Given that conduit origination came of age in 1995, and the real estate market has been strong since then, richer statistical data is too sparse at best to conclusively lend support to the quality of loan underwriting claims. That said, we believe the quality of loan underwriting will continue to improve as surveillance efforts and market discipline increase. Moreover, we believe the market perception that bank-originated collateral will exhibit on average a better credit performance than nonbank-originated loans to be a valid extrapolative assessment based on commercial banks' history in the credit management arena.

Analysis by Property Type

The property types found in CMBS transactions are multifamily, office, retail, industrial and other types of income-producing properties. Exhibit 12 shows the property-type distribution in FULBA 98-C2.

Retail exhibits great uncertainty because of concern about the impact of an economic downturn on supply and demand, the realignment of the retail industry as a result of the Internet revolution, personal income growth and spending. Although we do not suggest a direct correlation between industry categories and property-type performance, it is instructive to note Standard & Poor's Corp. (S&P) reports a default rate of 12.7% for the consumer/service sector from 1981 to 1998. A large percentage of the consumer/service sector is retail property tenants. Moreover, the spate of bankruptcy activities among retailers, for example, Hechingers Co., Caldor Corp., Service Merchandise Inc., Jumbo Sports, Inc., and others, has increased delinquency and default frequencies in CMBS transactions. The market trend in the property market as reported in the Korpacz Real Estate Investor Survey for the third quarter of 1999 is shown in Exhibit 13.

In assessing the ability of a property to sustain long-term projected cash flow and value, analysts must address the following issues:

• Visibility and accessibility (ingress and egress) of the property
• Convenience of the property to major thoroughfares and economic centers (e.g., employment, retail)
• Proximity of the property to educational, cultural and recreational facilities

Exhibit 12: Property Distribution of FULBA 98-C2

Property Type	No. of Loans	Balance ($mm)	% of Total Balance
Multifamily	228	1,067.4	31.8
Retail	167	916.6	27.3
Office	71	667.5	19.9
Other	73	226.8	6.8
Lodging	45	226.8	6.8
Industrial	44	127.3	3.8
Health Care	12	64.0	1.9
Mixed Use	9	25.0	0.7
Self-Storage	10	21.1	0.6
Mobile Home	5	13.3	0.4
Warehouse	0	0.0	0.0
Total	664	3,355.9	100.0

Source: First Union Securities, Inc.

Exhibit 13: Market Trends by Property Type

Property Type	Subcategories	Market Trends
Office	National CBD	CBD reports low single-digit vacancy rate Growth in rental rate declining
	National Suburban	Overbuilding in some markets
	Key Markets	
	Atlanta	Improving market fundamentals and overbuilding threaten some submarkets
	Chicago	Vacancy rate expected to rise with construction in suburbs and downtown
	Dallas	Construction in suburbs negatively affecting vacancy rates
	Los Angeles	High vacancy rate downtown and favorable market conditions in the submarkets
	Manhattan	High investment interest and transaction activity
	San Francisco	Class A office property trading at a high price with moderate projected price increases in the next 12 months
	Washington, DC	Strong preleasing expected to keep vacancy rate low
Multifamily	National	Overbuilding negatively affecting occupancy rates, rental rates and income growth; some markets still tight and price adjustment occurring
Retail	National Regional Mall	Debate over the effects of e-commerce on regional markets and reduced buying pool for top-tier properties
	National Strip Mall	Limited concern about overbuilding and effects of e-commerce
Industrial	National	Construction continues with bulk warehousing the preferred property
Hotel	National Full-Service	Decline in transactions and strong investor interest
	National Economy/ Limited Service	Concern of overbuilding and diminished investment opportunity
	National Luxury	Highest occupancy rate and average daily room rates, and strongest hotel segment
	National Extended Stay	Fastest-growing hotel segment; construction expected to continue in this riskiest of all hotel segments

CBD: Central business district.
Source: First Union Securities, Inc. and Korpacz Real Estate Investor Survey.

- Sustainability (in terms of the locale's ability to support the real estate value) and compatibility of the property to other property nearby
- Regional analysis of competition, supply and demand trends, demographic data, absorption rate and land use
- Management control and building construction quality

We briefly summarize some of the qualitative issues with respect to the multifamily, office, retail and industrial property types.

Multifamily

The market for multifamily properties is competitive, and the supply and demand dynamics are governed to a large extent by demographic trends. Changes in supply and demand are driven by the lease terms. Because of the short-term nature of apartment leases, the turnover rate is high, especially in markets experiencing newer construction with improved amenities. Basic analytical issues are the age and condition of the property, management quality and market conditions (growth rate, expected property turnover rate, rental rates and expense ratios).

Office

Office properties are differentiated by market area. For example, the characteristics of central business district (CBD) office properties are different from suburban properties. The economic viability and sustainability of office properties depend on the market area. The main issues are whether the market area economy can support a stable tenant base, the age of the building (technological functionality and obsolesce), competition, rollover risk, management quality and capitalization.

Retail

Retail properties range from superregional malls to neighborhood shopping centers. Visibility, accessibility, demographics, anchorage and income growth and distribution of the area are primary issues.

Industrial

Warehouses are evaluated on structural characteristics, such as bay depth, clearance, divisibility, ease-of-truck maneuverability and spacing. In particular, access to the labor pool, transportation medium (road and rail) and proximity to suppliers and customers are important factors in assessing the cash flow viability of industrial properties.

MONITORING DEFAULT PROBABILITIES

Additional risks inherent in CMBS transactions are the default probability and the recovery rate. Market participants look to the credit rating in assessing the probability of default. Rating agencies continually monitor a deal to determine if the current rating correctly reflects the credit risk. Evaluations are based on the following sources:

> *Trustee.* The trustee provides transaction-level information including certificate balances, collateral balances, cumulative realized losses, delinquencies and cumulative advances. The trustee depends on the master and primary servicers for this information.

Exhibit 14 lists five major trustees involved in conduit deals, and Exhibit 15 lists all the trustees, master servicers and special servicers on CMBS deals.

> *Master and primary servicers.* By mandate, there is only one master servicer in a deal who is responsible for supervising the primary servicer while the loan is performing. The primary servicer collects loan payments, operating financial statements and other information specified in the pool and servicing agreement.

Exhibit 14: CMBS Conduit Deal Trustee Web Sites

Trustee Bank	URL
Bankers Trust (Deutsche Bank)	http://www-apps.gis.deutsche-bank.com
Chase Manhattan Bank	http://www.chase.com/chase/gx.cgi/FTes?evalpage=Chase/Href&url-name=corpinst/trust/whychase
LaSalle National Bank	http://www.lnbabs.com
Norwest Bank	http://securitieslink.net
State Street Bank and Trust	http://corporateTrust.statestreet.com

Source: First Union Securities, Inc.

Special servicer. Troubled loans and loans 60-90 days delinquent are transferred to a special servicer. The effectiveness of the special servicer is reflected in its ability to maximize the proceeds from troubled loans.

Borrowers and property management companies. On single-transaction deals, borrowers and property management companies are good sources of information.

Rating agencies review information from these sources and other pertinent information to determine whether a rating alert or action is required. A rating action would result in an affirmation, an upgrade or a downgrade (Exhibit 16). Because of the sequential nature of the CMBS transactions, senior tranches are more likely to be upgraded than lower-rated classes. Moreover, a correlation exists between credit quality and default remoteness, that is, the higher the credit rating of a bond, the lower the probability of default. Conversely, the lower the original rating, the shorter the time to default.

Affirmation. Most rating actions affirm the existing rating, which indicates no material change in the rating agency's assessment of the probability of a tranche's default.

Upgrade. The key determinant of an upgrade is the current level of credit enhancement. Rating agencies also consider the diversification and concentration of the remaining loans in a deal. As the loan pays down and realized losses are low or none, the credit enhancement in the senior tranches increases. Upgrades include those transactions without prepayment lockouts, with no or low prepayment penalties and with some seasoned loans. From 1993 to the third quarter of 1999, Fitch IBCA upgraded 363 tranches totaling $9.7 billion.

Downgrade. Unlike upgrades driven by increases in credit enhancement, downgrades are caused by decreases in credit enhancement that result from losses. High delinquency rates that lead to decreases in projected credit enhancement could, in rare cases, result in a deal being downgraded. Fitch IBCA downgraded 47 tranches totaling $1.3 billion from 1993 to the third quarter of 1999. The ratio of downgrades to upgrades is 0.12.

Exhibit 15: CMBS Conduit Deal Trustee, Master Servicer and Special Servicer

Deal Name	Trustee	Master Servicer	Special Servicer
Amresco Commercial Mortgage Funding I Corp., Series 1997-C1	LaSalle National Bank	Amresco Services	Midland Loan Services
Asset Securitization Corp., Series 1995-D1	LaSalle National Bank	Midland Loan Services	Banc One (originally Crimmi Mae)
Asset Securitization Corp., Series 1996-D3	LaSalle National Bank	Amresco Services	Banc One (originally Crimmi Mae)
Asset Securitization Corp., Series 1997-D4	LaSalle National Bank	Amresco Services	Amresco Services
Asset Securitization Corp., Series 1997-D5	LaSalle National Bank	Amresco Services	Amresco Management
Bear Stearns Commercial Mortgage Securities, Series 1998-C1	LaSalle National Bank	Banc One Mortgage Capital Markets	GMAC Commercial Mortgage (originally Amresco Management)
Bear Stearns Commercial Mortgage Securities, Series 1999-C1	LaSalle National Bank	GE Capital Loan Services	GE Capital Realty Group
Capco America Securitization Corp., Series 1998-D7	LaSalle National Bank	Amresco Services (originally Capital Company of America)	Amresco Services
Chase Commercial Mortgage Securities Corp., Series 1996-1	LaSalle National Bank	Chase Manhattan Bank	Lennar Partners
Chase Commercial Mortgage Securities Corp., Series 1996-2	LaSalle National Bank	Chase Manhattan Bank	Lennar Partners
Chase Commercial Mortgage Securities Corp., Series 1997-1	LaSalle National Bank	Chase Manhattan Bank	Midland Loan Services
Chase Commercial Mortgage Securities Corp., Series 1997-2	State Street Bank and Trust	Chase Manhattan Bank	Lennar Partners
Chase Commercial Mortgage Securities Corp., Series 1998-1	State Street Bank and Trust	Chase Manhattan Bank	Crimmi Mae Services
Chase Commercial Mortgage Securities Corp., Series 1998-2	State Street Bank and Trust	GMAC Commercial Mortgage Corp.	GMAC Commercial Mortgage Corp.
Commercial Mortgage Acceptance Corp., Series 1998-C1	LaSalle National Bank	Midland Loan Services	Midland Loan Services
Commercial Mortgage Acceptance Corp., Series 1998-C2	Norwest Bank Minnesota	Midland Loan Services	Midland Loan Services
Commercial Mortgage Acceptance Corp., Series 1999-C1	LaSalle National Bank	Midland Loan Services	Banc One Mortgage Capital Markets
Chase Manhattan Bank-First Union National Bank Commercial Mortgage Trust, Series 1999-1	State Street Bank and Trust	Chase Manhattan Bank	Orix Real Estate Capital Markets
Credit Suisse First Boston Mortgage Securities Corp., Series 1995-WF1	LaSalle National Bank	Wells Fargo Bank	Wells Fargo Bank
Credit Suisse First Boston Mortgage Securities Corp., Series 1997-C1	Chase Manhattan Bank	First Union National	Bank Lennar Partners
Credit Suisse First Boston Mortgage Securities Corp., Series 1997-C2	Norwest Bank Minnesota	First Union National Bank	Lennar Partners
Credit Suisse First Boston Mortgage Securities Corp., Series 1998-C1	State Street Bank and Trust	Banc One Mortgage Capital Markets	Lennar Partners, Inc
Credit Suisse First Boston Mortgage Securities Corp., Series 1998-C2	Chase Manhattan Bank	First Union National Bank	Lennar Partners
DLJ Mortgage Acceptance Corp., Series 1995-CF2	Chase Manhattan Bank	Midland Loan Services (originally Boatmen's National Mortgage)	Lennar Partners
DLJ Mortgage Acceptance Corp., Series 1996-CF1	LaSalle National Bank	GMAC Commercial Mortgage Corp. (originally Mellon)	Banc One (originally Crimmi Mae Services)
DLJ Mortgage Acceptance Corp., Series 1996-CF2	Chase Manhattan Bank	Midland Loan Services (originally Boatmen's National Mortgage)	Banc One (originally Crimmi Mae)
DLJ Mortgage Acceptance Corp., Series 1997-CF1	LaSalle National Bank	GMAC Commercial Mortgage Corp. (originally Mellon)	Lennar Partners

Exhibit 15 (Continued)

Deal Name	Trustee	Master Servicer	Special Servicer
DLJ Mortgage Acceptance Corp., Series 1997-CF2	LaSalle National Bank	Banc One Mortgage Capital Markets (originally Crimmi Mae)	Crimmi Mae
DLJ Commercial Mortgage Corp., Series 1998-CF1	Norwest Bank Minnesota	Banc One Mortgage Capital Markets	Clarion Partners
DLJ Commercial Mortgage Corp., Series 1998-CF2	Norwest Bank Minnesota	Banc One Mortgage Capital Markets	Banc One Mortgage Capital Markets
DLJ Commercial Mortgage Corp., Series 1998-CG1	Norwest Bank Minnesota	GE Capital Loan Services	Midland Loan Services
DLJ Commercial Mortgage Corp., Series 1999-CG1	Norwest Bank Minnesota	GE Capital Loan Services	Banc One Mortgage Capital Markets
DLJ Commercial Mortgage Corp., Series 1999-CG2	Norwest Bank Minnesota	GE Capital Loan Services	Banc One Mortgage Capital Markets
Deutsche Mortgage & Asset Receiving Corp., Series 1998-C1	LaSalle National Bank	Banc One Mortgage Capital Markets	Banc One Mortgage Capital Markets
First Union-Lehman Brothers Commercial Mortgage Trust, Series 1997-C1	State Street Bank and Trust	First Union National	Bank Banc One (originally Crimmi Mae)
First Union-Lehman Brothers Commercial Mortgage Trust, Series 1997-C2	LaSalle National Bank	First Union National Bank	Banc One Mortgage Capital Markets (originally Crimmi Mae)
First Union-Lehman Brothers-Bank of America Commercial Mortgage Trust, Series 1998-C2	Norwest Bank Minnesota	First Union National Bank	Crimmi Mae
First Union Commercial Mortgage Trust, FUNB Series 1999-C1	Norwest Bank Minnesota	First Union National Bank	Lennar Partners, Inc.
First Union-Chase Manhattan Commercial Mortgage Trust, Series 1999-C2	Norwest Bank Minnesota	First Union National Bank	Banc One Mortgage Capital Markets
GMAC Commercial Mortgage Securities Corp., Series 1996-C1	State Street Bank and Trust	GMAC Commercial Mortgage Corp.	GMAC Commercial Mortgage Corp.
GMAC Commercial Mortgage Securities Corp., Series 1997-C1	LaSalle National Bank	GMAC Commercial Mortgage Corp.	
GMAC Commercial Mortgage Securities Corp., Series 1997-C2	State Street Bank and Trust	GMAC Commercial Mortgage Corp.	GMAC Commercial Mortgage Corp.
GMAC Commercial Mortgage Securities Corp., Series 1998-C1	LaSalle National Bank	GMAC Commercial Mortgage Corp.	GMAC Commercial Mortgage Corp.
GMAC Commercial Mortgage Securities Corp., Series 1998-C2	LaSalle National Bank	GMAC Commercial Mortgage Corp.	GMAC Commercial Mortgage Corp.
GMAC Commercial Mortgage Securities Corp., Series 1999-C1	Norwest Bank Minnesota	GMAC Commercial Mortgage Corp.	GMAC Commercial Mortgage Corp.
GMAC Commercial Mortgage Securities Corp., Series 1999-C2	LaSalle National Bank	GMAC Commercial Mortgage Corp.	GMAC Commercial Mortgage Corp.
GS Mortgage Securities Corp. II, Series 1998-C1	LaSalle National Bank	GMAC Commercial Mortgage Corp.	Lennar Partners
GS Mortgage Securities Corp. II, Series 1999-C1	LaSalle National Bank	GMAC Commercial Mortgage Corp.	Amresco Management/ Banc One
JP Morgan Commercial Mortgage Finance Corp., Series 1995-C1	State Street Bank and Trust	Banc One Mortgage Capital Markets	Amresco Management/ Banc One
JP Morgan Commercial Mortgage Finance Corp., Series 1996-C2	State Street Bank and Trust	Banc One Mortgage Capital Markets	Banc One Mortgage Capital Markets
JP Morgan Commercial Mortgage Finance Corp., Series 1996-C3	State Street Bank and Trust	Banc One Mortgage Capital Markets	Banc One Mortgage Capital Markets
JP Morgan Commercial Mortgage Finance Corp., Series 1997-C4	State Street Bank and Trust	Banc One Mortgage Capital Markets	Banc One Mortgage Capital Markets
JP Morgan Commercial Mortgage Finance Corp., Series 1997-C5	LaSalle National Bank	Midland Loan Services	Midland Loan Services
JP Morgan Commercial Mortgage Finance Corp., Series 1998-C6	State Street Bank and Trust	Midland Loan Services (originally Dover House Capital)	Banc One (originally Crimmi Mae)

Exhibit 15 (Continued)

Deal Name	Trustee	Master Servicer	Special Servicer
JP Morgan Commercial Mortgage Finance Corp., Series 1999-C7	State Street Bank and Trust	Midland Loan Services	Midland Loan Services
JP Morgan Commercial Mortgage Finance Corp., Series 1999-C8	State Street Bank and Trust	Midland Loan Services	Midland Loan Services
LB Commercial Conduit Mortgage Trust II, Series 1996-C2	LaSalle National Bank	GMAC Commercial Mortgage Corp.	Banc One (originally Crimmi Mae)
LB Commercial Conduit Mortgage Trust, Series 1995-C2	LaSalle National Bank	GMAC Commercial Mortgage Corp.	Banc One Mortgage Capital Markets (originally Lennar, then Crimmi Mae)
LB Commercial Mortgage Trust, Series 1998-C1	LaSalle National Bank	GMAC Commercial Mortgage Corp.	GMAC Commercial Mortgage Corp.
LB Commercial Mortgage Trust, Series 1998-C4	LaSalle National Bank	First Union National Bank	Lennar Partners
LB Commercial Mortgage Trust, Series 1999-C1	Norwest Bank Minnesota	First Union National Bank	GMAC Commercial Mortgage Corp.
Mortgage Capital Funding, Series 1995-MC1	State Street Bank and Trust	GMAC Commercial Mortgage Corp. (originally Citibank)	Banc One Mortgage Capital Markets (originally Je Roberts, then Crimmi Mae)
Mortgage Capital Funding, Series 1996-MC1	State Street Bank and Trust	GMAC Commercial Mortgage Corp.	Hanford/ Healy Asset Management Co.
Mortgage Capital Funding, Series 1996-MC2	LaSalle National Bank	GMAC Commercial Mortgage Corp.	GMAC Commercial Mortgage Corp.
Mortgage Capital Funding, Series 1997-MC1	LaSalle National Bank	Banc One Mortgage Capital Markets (originally Crimmi Mae)	Banc One Mortgage Capital Markets (originally Crimmi Mae)
Mortgage Capital Funding, Series 1997-MC2	LaSalle National Bank	Midland Loan Services	Banc One Mortgage Capital Markets (originally Crimmi Mae)
Mortgage Capital Funding, Series 1998-MC1	LaSalle National Bank	Amresco Services	Banc One Mortgage Capital Markets (originally Crimmi Mae)
Mortgage Capital Funding, Series 1998-MC2	State Street Bank and Trust	Crimmi Mae Services	Banc One Mortgage Capital Markets (originally Crimmi Mae)
Mortgage Capital Funding, Series 1998-MC3	LaSalle National Bank	Amresco Services	Allied Capital Corp.
Merrill Lynch Mortgage Investors, Series 1995-C1 (originally Bankers Trust, then Mellon)	Bankers Trust	GMAC Commercial Mortgage Corp.	Crimmi Mae Services
Merrill Lynch Mortgage Investors, Series 1995-C3	Bankers Trust	GMAC Commercial Mortgage Corp. (originally Bankers Trust, then Mellon)	Banc One Mortgage Capital Markets (originally GE Capital Realty Group)
Merrill Lynch Mortgage Investors, Series 1996-C1	Bankers Trust	GMAC Commercial Mortgage Corp. (originally GE Capital Asset Management)	Banc One Mortgage Capital Markets (originally GE Capital Realty Group)
Merrill Lynch Mortgage Investors, Series 1996-C2	State Street Bank and Trust	First Union National Bank	Banc One Mortgage Capital Markets (originally Crimmi Mae)
Merrill Lynch Mortgage Investors, Series 1997-C1	LaSalle National Bank	Crimmi Mae Services (originally GE Capital Asset Management)	Banc One Mortgage Capital Markets (originally GE Capital Realty Group)
Merrill Lynch Mortgage Investors, Series 1997-C2	State Street Bank and Trust	GE Capital Loan Services	Banc One Mortgage Capital Markets (originally GE Capital Realty Group)
Merrill Lynch Mortgage Investors, Series 1998-C2	Norwest Bank Minnesota	First Union National Bank	Crimmi Mae Services
Merrill Lynch Mortgage Investors, Series 1998-C3	Chase Manhattan Bank	GE Capital Loan Services	GE Capital Realty Group
Midland Realty Acceptance Corp., Series 1996-C1	LaSalle National Bank	Midland Loan Services	Midland Loan Services

Exhibit 15 (Continued)

Deal Name	Trustee	Master Servicer	Special Servicer
Midland Realty Acceptance Corp., Series 1996-C2	LaSalle National Bank	Midland Loan Services	Midland Loan Services
Morgan Stanley Capital I, Series 1995-HF1	LaSalle National Bank	Heller Financial	Fleet Real Estate Capital
Morgan Stanley Capital I, Series 1996-C1	LaSalle National Bank	GMAC Commercial Mortgage Corp. (originally Fleet, then Mellon)	Lennar Partners
Morgan Stanley Capital I, Series 1996-WF1	LaSalle National Bank	Wells Fargo Bank	Wells Fargo Bank
Morgan Stanley Capital I, Series 1997-C1	LaSalle National Bank	GMAC Commercial Mortgage Corp.	GMAC Commercial Mortgage Corp.
Morgan Stanley Capital I, Series 1997-HF1	LaSalle National Bank	Amresco Services	Amresco Services
Morgan Stanley Capital I, Series 1997-WF1	LaSalle National Bank	Wells Fargo Bank	Banc One (originally Crimmi Mae)
Morgan Stanley Capital I, Series 1998-Cf1	LaSalle National Bank	Amresco Services	Lennar Partners
Morgan Stanley Capital I, Series 1998-HF1	LaSalle National Bank	Amresco Services	Lennar Partners
Morgan Stanley Capital I, Series 1998-HF2	LaSalle National Bank	GMAC Commercial Mortgage Corp.	GMAC Commercial Mortgage Corp.
Morgan Stanley Capital I, Series 1998-WF1	LaSalle National Bank	Wells Fargo Bank	Banc One Mortgage Capital Markets (originally Crimmi Mae)
Morgan Stanley Capital I, Series 1998-WF2	Norwest Bank Minnesota	Wells Fargo Bank	Banc One (originally Crimmi Mae)
Morgan Stanley Capital I, Series 1999-WF1	LaSalle National Bank	Wells Fargo Bank	GMAC Commercial Mortgage Corp.
Nomura Asset Securities Corp., Series 1998-D6	LaSalle National Bank	Amresco Services	Banc One Mortgage Capital Markets (originally Crimmi Mae)
Nationslink Funding Corp., Series 1996-1	Chase Manhattan Bank	Amresco Services	Amresco Services
Nationslink Funding Corp., Series 1998-1	Norwest Bank Minnesota	Midland Loan Services	Lennar Partners
Nationslink Funding Corp., Series 1998-2	Norwest Bank Minnesota	Midland Loan Services	Lennar Partners
Nationslink Funding Corp., Series 1999-LTL-1	LaSalle National Bank	Midland Loan Services	Midland Loan Services
Nationslink Funding Corp., Series 1999-1	Norwest Bank Minnesota	Banc One Mortgage Capital Markets	Banc One Mortgage Capital Markets
Painewebber Mortgage Acceptance Corp. IV, Series 1995-M1	Bankers Trust	GMAC Commercial Mortgage Corp. (originally Bankers Trust, then Mellon)	
Painewebber Mortgage Acceptance Corp. IV, Series 1996-M1	LaSalle National Bank	GMAC Commercial Mortgage Corp. (originally Mellon)	
Prudential Securities Secured Financing Corp., Series 1995-C1	LaSalle National Bank	Midland Loan Services Lennar Partners	
Prudential Securities Secured Financing Corp., Series 1995-MCF2	LaSalle National Bank	Midland Loan Services	Lennar Partners
Prudential Securities Secured Financing Corp., Series 1998-C1	Chase Manhattan Bank	National Realty Funding	National Realty Funding
Prudential Securities Secured Financing Corp., Series 1999-C2	Chase Manhattan Bank	National Realty Funding	National Realty Funding
Salomon Brothers Mortgage Securities VII, Series 1996-C1	LaSalle National Bank	Midland Loan Services	Midland Loan Services
Salomon Brothers Mortgage Securities VII, Series 1999-C1	Chase Manhattan Bank	GMAC Commercial Mortgage Corp.	BNY Asset Solutions
Credit Suisse First Boston Mortgage Securities Corp., Series 1995-M1	LaSalle National Bank	GMAC Commercial Mortgage Corp. (originally GE Capital Asset Management)	GE Capital Realty Group

Source: First Union Securities, Inc.

Exhibit 16: Rating Actions by Fitch IBCA from March 1993 to September 1999

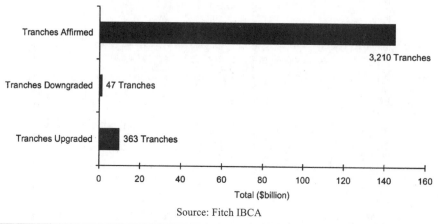

Total ($billion)

Source: Fitch IBCA

COLLATERAL PERFORMANCE AND DETERMINANTS OF DEFAULT

Recently, we have seen several industry reports on commercial mortgage-backed securities (CMBS) default studies and collateral performance analysis. One such report updates a study by Mark Snyderman's default analysis of commercial mortgages originated by insurance companies.[1] This report found that commercial mortgages held by insurance companies showed a 10-year cumulative default rate ranging from 9% for 1997 originations to 28% for 1986. These cumulative default rates translate into 1% and 4% conditional default rates (CDRs), respectively, for 10-year collateral. A recent quarterly report issued by the American Council of Life Insurance shows the delinquency rate on loans held by insurance companies fell to 0.30% in the second quarter of 1999 — the lowest level in 34 years (Exhibit 17).

Other industry reports have focused on deals originated in the conduit loan market. One of these reports, which is based on analysis that tests for the statistical significance of its findings, showed a cumulative default rate of 0.78% on a loan basis and 0.48% on a balance basis for commercial mortgages originated and securitized from 1995 to 1999. Furthermore, this report follows the lead of a 1998 Fitch IBCA study that cited the following factors as statistically significant in explaining defaults:[2]

---

[1] Howard Esaki, Steven L'Heureux, and Mark Snyderman, "Commercial Mortgage Default: An Update," *Real Estate Finance* (Spring 1999).
[2] Rodney Pelletier and Andrew Rudenstein, "Trends in Commercial Mortgage Default Rate and Loss Severity — 1997 Update."

Exhibit 17: Life Insurance Companies' Commercial Mortgage Delinquencies

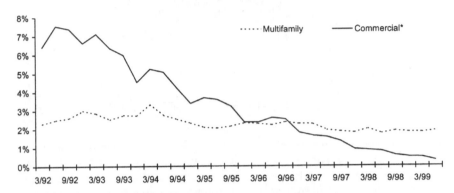

*Apartments, retail, office, industrial, hotel and motel, mixed use and others.
Source: American Council of Life Insurance.

- *Loan to value (LTV) and debt service coverage ratio (DSCR).* The incidence of default rises with the LTV, that is, if all other factors are held constant, the probability of default for a loan increases as the LTV increases, but the increases are not equal. For example, an increase in the original LTV from 60% to 70% resulted in about a 50% rise in the probability of default from 0.54% to 0.80% CDR. An increase in the LTV from 50% to 60% raised the probability of default by 0.18%, whereas increasing the LTV from 80% to 90% boosted the probability of default by 0.58%.

  Unlike the LTV, where the probability of default increases as the LTV rises, the incidence of default is a decreasing function of the DSCR. The relationship between the DSCR and the probability of default is, however, weaker than the relationship between the LTV and default. One explanation is that borrowers have an incentive to negotiate with lenders about payment rescheduling and debt restructuring, but that incentive wanes quickly when the LTV is significantly greater than 1.0.

- *Age.* The incidence of default increases with age. On a loan count basis, the aging curve is steeper in the 12-24-month range with the CDR rising from 0.2% to 1.0% and remaining at 1.0% thereafter.

- *Property type.* A 1999 Fitch IBCA study examined 9,760 commercial mortgage loans in 69 conduit deals issued since 1993 and found loans secured by hotel properties have the highest cumulative default rate, at 1.07%, followed by multifamily loans at 0.81%.[3] Exhibit 18 shows the defaults by property type.

---

[3] Mary Stuart G. Freydberg and Keith Lee, "CMBS Conduit Loan Defaults by Property Type," Fitch IBCA April 6, 1999.

Exhibit 18: Commercial Mortgage Default by Property Type

Property Type	No.of Loans	% of Total Loans	No of Defaults	% of Total Defaults
Multifamily	3,078	33.2	25	50.0
Retail	2,373	25.6	7	14.0
Other/Mixed	1,534	16.6	4	8.0
Office	905	9.8	3	6.0
Hotel	839	9.1	9	18.0
Industrial	535	5.8	2	4.0
Total	9,264	100.1	50	100.0

Source: Fitch IBCA

- *Coupon spread.* The difference between the loan rate and the average interest rate of a loan cohort is a determinant of default. A loan cohort is defined in terms of origination month, property type and loan size. In the home equity loan market, for example, the initial coupon spread is used as an indicator of involuntary prepayment. In theory, borrowers willing to pay a high initial credit spread have weak credit histories, which implies an extended period of credit curing. Therefore, they are assigned a higher probability of default — a higher percentage of the standard default assumption (SDA) curve. In contrast, commercial mortgage loans with a higher-than-average coupon in a cohort reflect the increased likelihood of default.
- *Loan size.* Large loans have lower default probabilities than small loans. For example, an industry study showed the probability of default for a $2 million loan was 2.5 times greater than for a $20 million loan with the same characteristics. One explanation is that the management quality and control for borrowers seeking larger loans are far superior to those for borrowers of small loans.
- *Amortization schedule.* The conventional wisdom that the quicker a loan amortizes the lower the default risk was not supported by the industry study. A loan with a 240-month amortization schedule has about a 35% greater probability of default than a similar loan with a 360-month schedule.
- *Loan underwriting.* Bank-originated collateral exhibited a better credit performance than nonbank-originated collateral. An industry study showed, on average, bank-originated collateral has a 0.27% default rate on a balance basis compared with 0.56% for nonbank conduits. The study claims the difference in performance is attributable to the banks' superior underwriting standards. This finding that bank-originated loans have better collateral performance than nonbank-originated loans has sparked so much debate among the investment banking community that some analysts in Wall Street firms have been mining databases and surveillance reports trying to refute this evidence.

DEFAULT RATE AND LOSS SEVERITY

The price of credit-related transactions generally incorporates the credit rating. The credit rating reflects the rating agency's assessments of the likelihood of default. For each rated class, an applicable credit spread provides information about the following:

- Likelihood of default
- Expected recovery rate in the event of default
- Market credit risk premium

Dividing credit spread into its various components allows us to write the following equation for the price of a credit-sensitive bond:

Price of a zero coupon credit-sensitive bond
= Price of a risk-free bond with the same maturity (or average life)
− Loss severity × Adjusted probability of default
× Price of risk-free bond with the same maturity (or average life)

The loss severity is equal to 1.0 minus the recovery rate. Pricing a security in the absence of an arbitrage opportunity requires that a credit-sensitive bond trade at a value less than its risk-free counterparts. This means that the credit-sensitive bond's yield will be higher than that of a corresponding risk-free yield (e.g., Treasury). The difference in yields is the credit spread. In the equation, the value of the credit-sensitive bond equals the value of a risk-free bond of the same average life minus the adjustment for the default risk. This adjustment is the product of the adjusted probability of default, loss severity and the value of a risk-free bond of the same average life. So, the equation expresses a credit event as the product of the frequency of default and loss severity. Another way of interpreting the equation is that the value of a credit-sensitive bond is the expected value of all its possible cash flows (for both default and no default scenarios) discounted at the risk-free rate.

Under the pricing rule that makes the equation consistent, one cannot value securities using the objective probability but must price them using a normalized probability, that is, the equivalent probability measure. This measure is the product of a risk-adjustment factor for the default risk premium and the objective probability. For a given frequency of default associated with a deal, the market consensus — the risk adjustment factor for the default risk premium — must be taken into consideration. We observed that when valuing a deal, the correct probability measure is the equivalent (risk-neutral) measure, whereas in scenario analysis the objective probability is more appropriate. In short, the frequency of default must be adjusted based on the market's prevailing default premium. For example, in October 1998, when CMBS spreads widened, the frequency of default was not necessarily increasing but the adjustment for the default premium was. The market determines the adjustment factor for the default risk premium.

Could this explain why bank-originated CMBS are fairly priced in the market? The market may be looking at bank-originated deals, recognizing banks' conservative credit culture and their expertise in credit management, then correctly adjusting risk for the default risk premium. On the contrary, some of our colleagues are working on theories using objective default probabilities with no adjustment, then questioning why bank-originated deals are spread tightly and challenging the authenticity of market levels.

The most important points in valuing credit-related instruments such as CMBS are as follows:

- The frequency of default does not directly enter the equation because it must be adjusted as a function of the default risk premium.
- The loss severity, which is 1.0 minus the recovery rate, enters the equation directly.

For CMBS, aside from interest rate and prepayment risks, the other inherent risks are default and recovery rate. For these risks, two market observables — credit rating and credit spread — contain the information necessary to price them. Moreover, the frequency of default enters into the equation indirectly, whereas loss severity enters the equation directly. Thus, we conclude the frequency of default matters, but how much is recovered in the event of default matters more for most investors.

RELATIVE VALUE ISSUES

In Exhibit 19, we show the spread history of the senior tranche rated AAA relative to the mezzanine A and BBB rated tranches. As with the rest of the credit sensitive sector, CMBS languished during the crisis in October 1998, with the spreads of A rated bonds and BBB rated bonds widening 150 bps and 185 bps, respectively, from their 1997 highs. Although spreads have recovered from their wides, they are still wide relative to levels seen prior to October 1998. In particular, spreads in the below-investment-grade sector have tightened modestly from their October 1998 levels. This suggests the valuations in the below-investment-grade CMBS are attractive. Exhibits 20 and 21 show indicated spreads of CMBS subordinates and spread statistics, respectively.

Note the standard deviation of the B rated class and the range of the high and low spreads is tight, which indicate this tranche does not trade actively in the market. Indeed, the B-piece holders are mainly buy-and-hold accounts.

To show the impact of the frequency of default and loss severity on subordinated CMBS, we considered the mezzanine tranche of FULBA 1998-C2, in particular, class C, rated A/A2, and the result of this analysis is as follows:

Case 1: At a loss severity of 0%, the yield to maturity increases as the CDR rises and the WAL decreases (Exhibit 22).

Exhibit 19: AAA, A and BBB Rated CMBS Spreads

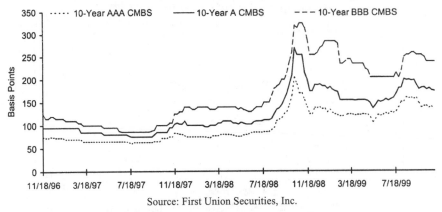

Source: First Union Securities, Inc.

Exhibit 20: Indicative Spreads of CMBS Subordinates

Rating	Spread 11/08/99	Spread 10/26/99	Change (bps)
AA	149	210	−61
A	169	255	−86
BBB	240	325	−85
BBB−	330	425	−95
BB	535	575	−40
B	815	850	−35

Source: First Union Securities, Inc.

Exhibit 21: Descriptive Spread Statistics for CMBS Subordinates *

Rating	Mean (bps)	Median (bps)	Standard Deviation	Maximum (bps)	Minimum (bps)
AA	155	155	21	220	122
A	178	176	29	270	137
BBB	249	245	34	325	205
BBB−	340	330	38	425	290
BB	560	550	23	625	520
B	821	815	10	850	800

*Data for Oct. 12, 1998, to Nov. 8, 1999.

Source: First Union Securities, Inc.

Case 2: Holding the CDR at the same level, for example, at 2%, the yield to maturity decreases as the loss severity increases and the WAL also increases (Exhibit 23). Note the "hockey stick" shapes, a common feature of structures with embedded optionality.

Case 3: Holding loss severity at the same level, for example, 35%, the yield to maturity decreases as the CDR and the WAL increase (Exhibit 24).

Exhibit 22: Change in Yield and WAL for Change in CDR, Assuming Loss Severity of 0%

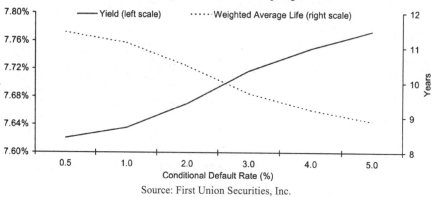

Source: First Union Securities, Inc.

Exhibit 23: Change in Yield and WAL for Change in Loss Severity, Assuming 2% CDR

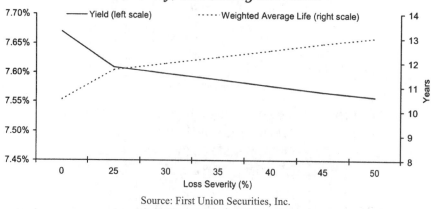

Source: First Union Securities, Inc.

Exhibits 25 and 26 show the sensitivity of yield and WAL to changes in CDR and loss severity. Exhibit 27 shows the yield compression that results from changes in CDR and loss severity.

One quick and simple way to evaluate a credit-sensitive CMBS is to compare the current yield of the bond to its break-even yield. The break-even yield is computed by adjusting the yield to maturity by the frequency of default and loss severity. The formula is

Break-even yield

$$= \frac{\text{Treasury yield} + \left[\text{Default rate} \times (1 - \text{Recovery rate}) + \text{Default rate} \times \left(\frac{\text{CMBS Yield}}{12} \right) \right]}{(1 - \text{Default rate})}$$

Exhibit 24: Change in Yield and WAL for Change in CDR, Assuming 35% Loss Severity

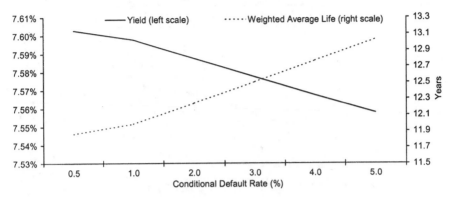

Source: First Union Securities, Inc.

Exhibit 25: Sensitivity of Yield to Change in CDR and Loss Severity

Loss	Conditional Default Rate(%)					
Severity (%)	0.5	1	2	3	4	5
0	7.62	7.64	7.67	7.72	7.75	7.77
25	7.61	7.61	7.61	7.61	7.61	7.61
30	7.61	7.60	7.60	7.59	7.59	7.58
35	7.60	7.60	7.59	7.58	7.57	7.56
40	7.60	7.59	7.58	7.56	7.55	7.54
45	7.60	7.59	7.57	7.55	7.54	7.51
50	7.59	7.58	7.56	7.55	7.52	7.46

Source: First Union Securities, Inc.

Exhibit 26: Sensitivity of Weighted Average Life to Change in CDR and Loss Severity

Loss	Conditional Default Rate(%)					
Severity (%)	0.5	1	2	3	4	5
0	11.5	11.1	10.5	9.7	9.2	8.9
25	11.7	11.7	11.7	11.7	11.7	11.7
30	11.8	11.9	12.0	12.1	12.2	12.4
35	11.9	12.0	12.2	12.5	12.8	13.0
40	11.9	12.1	12.5	12.9	13.2	13.5
45	12.0	12.3	12.8	13.2	13.5	14.7
50	12.1	12.4	13.0	13.3	14.2	16.8

Source: First Union Securities, Inc.

Exhibit 27: Yield Compression Matrix for Change in CDR and Loss Severity

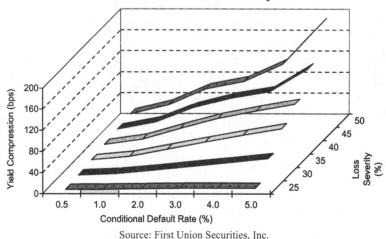

Source: First Union Securities, Inc.

Exhibit 28: 10-Year Treasury, 10-Year BBB CMBS and Break-Even Yields

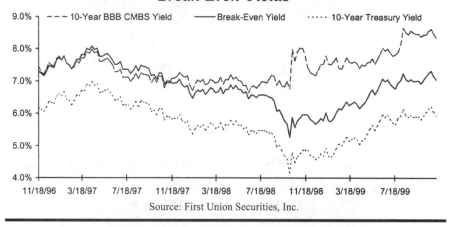

Source: First Union Securities, Inc.

Exhibit 28 shows the 10-year Treasury, the 10-year BBB CMBS and the break-even yield from November 1996 to November 1999. In calculating the break-even yield, we assumed a default rate of 3% and a 65% recovery rate (i.e., a 35% loss severity). By comparing the bond yield to the break-even yield, we can evaluate the relative attractiveness of the bond at any point in time. The greater the difference between the bond yield and the break-even yield, the more attractive the bond. From November 1996 to November 1999, the average spread (the 10-year CMBS yield minus the break-even yield) was 59 bps with a maximum spread of 215 bps during October 1998. Another way of interpreting the difference between

CMBS bond yield and the break-even yield is the premium an investor requires for liquidity risk and forecasts errors from the default and recovery rates (Exhibit 29).

SERVICER FLEXIBILITY AND LOSS SEVERITY

When a loan is defaulted, it can either be restructured or foreclosed. If a loan is foreclosed, the property value and foreclosure and liquidation costs are important determinants of the recovery rate. Whether a loan is restructured or foreclosed, the servicer's effectiveness and flexibility are important in working out successful outcomes for the defaulted loans. Some of the factors that contribute to loss severity are as follows:

- Foreclosure process (state laws and ownership structure)
- Ease of sale (property type, condition of the property and location)
- Foreclosure and liquidation costs (legal fees, carrying costs, improvement costs and commissions)

The amount recovered in the event of default is the cash flow of the property estimated over the foreclosure period minus the foreclosure and liquidation costs. An important role for the servicer is to maximize the cash flow from a defaulted loan. In performing this role, the servicer has the flexibility to decide whether modifying or foreclosing the loan would maximize returns for the stakeholders. The servicer's flexibility in modifying a defaulted loan is crucial to loss mitigation. For example, a 1998 Fitch IBCA study showed a slight trend toward lower losses when servicers had more flexibility.[4] Servicers can modify a defaulted loan in the following ways:

Exhibit 29: 10-Year BBB CMBS Yield Less Break-Even Rate

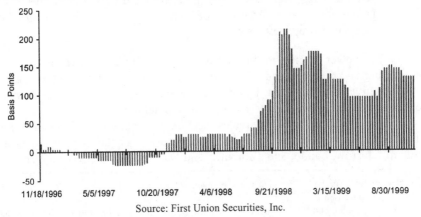

Source: First Union Securities, Inc.

---

[4] Pelletier and Rudenstein, "Trends in Commercial Mortgage Default Rate and Loss Severity — 1997 Update."

• Adjust the interest rate and amortization schedule
• Extend the loan maturity
• Forgive interest or principal
• Change other terms of the loan

NEWER ANALYTICAL FRAMEWORK

Market participants have witnessed the growth of instruments designed to reallocate credit risk between investors and issuers. Three basic types of structures have been used:

• *Event risk covenants.* These are triggering events, such as a rating downgrade, that give the investor the right to put the debt back to the issuers.
• *Credit-sensitive debt.* Issuers can buy the right to put the debt back to the investors, in which case the investor enjoys enhanced coupon payments.
• *Credit risk derivatives.* Credit derivatives are agreements between two parties that transfer specific credit risk from one party to the other. Credit (default) swap, total return swap, the credit option and the downgrade option are examples of credit derivatives. Among these examples, a total return swap is the most prevalent in the CMBS market. A buyer of a CMBS total return swap receives the total return on a basket of CMBS bonds and in exchange pays LIBOR plus a spread. The swap provides a means for market participants, for example, a hedge fund, to buy CMBS without repeatedly looking to the repo market for financing. Originators use total return swaps to protect against spread risk. The majority of the activities in the CMBS total return swap market have been in the 10-year AAA tranches, and activities in the lower-rated tranches have been slow taking off because of the lack of liquidity that makes the pricing of the associated swap inefficient.

The newer pricing model is based on the fundamental relationship of credit rating and credit spread. This relationship is encapsulated in the value of credit sensitive bond equation. Examining the equation, we know that to value a credit-sensitive bond, we need term structure and default models.

The discussion below provides the elements that go into implementing a default option-adjusted model. The development draws on the work of Jarrow and Turnbull,[5] Jarrow, Lando, and Turnbull,[6] and Das and Tufano.[7] The appendix to

---

[5] R. Jarrow and S.M. Turnbull, "Pricing Options on Financial Securities Subject to Credit Risk," *Journal of Finance* (1995), pp. 53-86.

[6] R. Jarrow, D. Lando, and S.M. Turnbull, "A Markov Model for the Term Structure of Credit Risk Spreads," Working paper, Cornell University (1994).

[7] S.R. Das and P. Tufano, "Pricing Credit-Sensitive Debt When Interest Rates, Credit Ratings and Credit Spreads are Stochastic," *Journal of Financial Engineering* (1996), pp. 161-198.

this chapter shows the pricing of credit-sensitive bonds, modeling the recovery rate, and cumulative probability of default, and computing the default risk premium.

Term Structure Models

A term structure model establishes a mathematical relationship that determines the price of a zero-coupon bond for all dates between now and when the bond matures. The term structure shows the relationship between the yield to maturity and the time to maturity of the bond. To compute the value of a security that depends on the term structure, we specify the dynamic of the interest rate process (e.g., a zero coupon bond) and apply the no-arbitrage condition. A term structure model satisfies the arbitrage restriction if there is no opportunity to invest risk-free and be guaranteed a positive return.

Several term structure models have been proposed with subtle differences. However, the basic differences amount to how the dynamic of interest rates is represented, the number of factors that generate the rate process and whether the model is closed by equilibrium or arbitrage arguments. The most popular models are those closed by arbitrage argument and that assume the distribution of rates is either normal or lognormal. We summarize the assumptions and issues concerning these popular models in Exhibit 30. However, term structure models such as Heath, Jarrow and Morton that allow for path dependency and for which the history of interest movement is taken into account when evaluating a bond provide a richer analytical framework for credit-sensitive CMBS.

The Default Model and the Recovery Rate

The default model parameterizes the probability of default and the recovery rate in the event of default. To extract these values from market data, an analyst generally uses the information in the credit rating and the credit spread. For example, because the credit ratings are supposed to reflect the likelihood of default, an analyst generally relies on this information as a way of characterizing the probability of default. As the quality of the bond transits from one rating level to another, information in the credit spread is used to assess the recovery rate in the event of default. Because credit spread is correlated with the interest rate, the recovery rate needs to be correlated with the term structure.

Unlike term structure models where the object of valuation — the zero coupon bonds — has been properly delineated, default models suffer from a lack of intrinsic pricing primitives. Proposed models either

- Assume a generating process for the value of the issuer and then treat a credit-sensitive bond as an option, or
- Assume a generating process for the credit quality of each bond and the recovery rate in the event of a default

Exhibit 30: Assumptions and Issues Concerning Popular Term Structure Models

Hull and White (1990)/Extended Vasicek (1977)

ASSUMPTIONS
- Evolution of interest rates are driven by the short rate (one factor)
- Short rates are normally distributed
- Instantaneous standard deviation of the short rate is constant
- Short rates are mean-reverting with a constant revision rate

ISSUES
- Computational advantages (speed and convergence)
- Analytical solution exists for pricing some European-style derivatives
- Normally distributed interest rates imply a finite probability of rates becoming zero or negative

Ho and Lee (1986)

ASSUMPTIONS
- Evolution of interest rates are driven by the short rate (one factor)
- Short rates are normally distributed
- Instantaneous standard deviation of the short rate is constant
- Short rates are not mean-reverting

ISSUES
- Computational advantages (speed and convergence)
- Closed-form solution exists for pricing European-style derivatives
- Nonexistence of the mean-reverting parameter on the model simplifies the calibration of the model to the market data
- Normally distributed interest rates imply a finite probability of rates becoming zero or negative
- Nonexistence of the mean revision in the model implies all interest rates have the same constant rate, which is different from market observations (the short rate is more volatile than the long rate)

Cox, Ingersoll and Ross (1985)

ASSUMPTIONS
- Evolution of interest rates is driven by the short rate (one factor)
- Short rates are normally distributed
- Instantaneous standard deviation of the short rate is the constant times the square root of the interest rate
- Short rates are mean-reverting with a constant revision rate

ISSUES
- Eliminating the possibility of negative interest rates
- Analytical solution is difficult to implement, if you find one
- Popular among academics because of its general equilibrium overtone

Black, Derman and Toy (1990)

ASSUMPTIONS
- Evolution of interest rates are driven by the short rate (one factor)
- Short rates are lognormally distributed
- Instantaneous standard deviation of logarithmic short rate is constant
- Logarithmic short rates are not mean-reverting

ISSUES
- Eliminating the possibility of negative interest rates
- No closed-form solution

Exhibit 30 (Continued)

Black and Karasinski (1991)

ASSUMPTIONS
• Separated the reversion rate and volatility in Black, Derman and Toy
• Provide a procedure for implementing the model using binomial lattice with time steps of varying length

ISSUES
• Whether mean reversion and volatility parameter should be a function of time. By making it a function of time, it is possible to fit the volatility at time zero correctly. However the volatility structure in the future may be dramatically different from today.

Heath, Jarrow and Morton (1992)

ASSUMPTIONS
• Evolution of interest rates are driven by the forward rates (one factor or multifactor)
• Involves specifying the volatilities of all forward rates at all times
• Non-Markovian, that is, the history of the rate process is taken into account
• Expected drift of forward rate in a risk-neutral world is calculated from the forward rate's volatilities

ISSUES
• Difficult to implement
• Useful in valuing path-dependent securities such as mortgages

---

The basic inputs into a default model are

• Credit spread
• Transition probability of default
• Recovery rate
• Recovery rate volatility
• Correlation between recovery rate and interest rates

Default Process

A typical CMBS has a credit rating range from AAA to NR (the first loss piece). Suppose we index the rating level by $i = 1, 2, ..., K$, where the first loss piece is equal to K. The first loss is absorbed by K, and subsequent losses are passed on to the next rating class. Suppose we assume a transition probability — a suitable analytical candidate is the so-called Markov chains — that governs the movement from one default event to another. This transition probability allows us to calculate the probability of loss to a rating class and can be represented in a matrix, in which the last row is the absorbing state. The transition probability matrix for a given deal can be obtained from historical data on rating changes and defaults. Rating agencies such as S&P publish transition probability matrices for corporate bonds.

Another technique used by investors and rating agencies to model the probability of default is called survival analysis. A survival analysis model relates a credit rating probability of default to factors such as the original credit rating, current rating and the historical volatility of the credit quality based on rating actions (upgrades and down-grades). One of these approaches, developed by Edward Altman and based on actuarial theory,[8] corrects for the potential biases in the traditional default measurement in that it recognizes the likelihood of default changes with the age of the underlying collateral. This approach computes the marginal and cumulative mortality rates as follows:

> Marginal Rate$_t$
> = [Dollar Amount (or issuer number) of Bonds Defaulting in Period t]/
> [Dollar Amount (or issuer number) of Bonds at the Start of Period t]

and

$$\text{Cumulative Rate}_t = [1 - (\Pi SR_t)]$$

where SR_t is the survival rate in period t, which is equal to (1 − Marginal rate at period t), and Π is a product operator that multiplies across the survival rate in each period.

Whether an analyst uses the transition probability matrix or survival models, we reiterate that consistent pricing convention requires securities not be valued off objective probability; instead, such securities should be priced using a normalized probability, that is, the equivalent probability measure. It is equivalent in the sense the objective and normalized probability assign the same measure to impossible events. More important, we need a price for each state in the transition probability matrix so that for each rating class there is a risk adjustment factor associated with the default risk premium. The matrix that results from the scalar transformation is called the equivalent probability measure matrix, which has a multiplicative relationship with the original measure. For example, if we let p_{ij} be the objective transition probability for moving from state i to state j (states are defined here with respect to credit quality), an equivalent probability measure is $q_{ij} = p(i)p_{ij}$ and $p(i)$ is the risk adjustment factor for default risk premium. As noted earlier, when pricing is the concern, the correct probability measure is the equivalent (risk-neutral) measure, whereas in scenario analysis the objective probability is more appropriate.

Recovery Rate

For each of the rated CMBS tranches, there is a maturity-specific spread over the comparable Treasury that the bond will trade. For example, an A rated conduit paper may be quoted as 160 bps over the curve and a BBB conduit paper at 240 bps. From the quoted spread, we can construct a term structure of forward credit spread for each of the tranches. Because the recovery rate determines the credit spread, the forward credit spread is a function of the amount recovered in the

---

[8] Edward Altman, "Measuring Corporate Bond Morality and Performance," *Journal of Finance* (1989), pp. 909-922.

event of default at some forward date. Hence, the recovery rate is dynamic and cases where a constant value is assumed for the loss severity do not tell the whole story. By making the recovery rate dynamic, a link is established between the credit spread and the recovery rate. Any changes in the credit spread that come from either the change in probability of default or the change in recovery rate conditional on the default changes are accounted for. Moreover, credit spreads are correlated with the term structure, which suggests the probability of default and the recovery rate may depend on macroeconomic conditions. For example, the rating agencies use property value and LTV to determine the probability of term or balloon default. In assessing the property value, the rating agency and the real estate analyst look at national, regional and local economic trends.

To specify the dynamic of recovery rate, it simplifies the analysis to assume one of the factors — either probability of default or recovery rate — is correlated with the term structure. For example, if the recovery rate depends on the term structure, the expected cash flow as a function of the recovery rate is then equal to the expected cash flow as a function of the expected recovery rate conditional on the spot rate (the term structure). This verbiage is neatly written as $E_{r\beta}[C(\beta)] = E_r\{C[E(\beta|r)]\}$, where C is the cash flow, β is the recovery rate, r is the spot rate and $E(\bullet)$ is the expectation operator. With this set-up, we can use lattice, for example, the binomial tree, to obtain at each node the expected value of recovery rate $\beta(t)$ given the value of the spot rate $r(t)$ at that node.

TOWARD DEFAULT OPTION-ADJUSTED SPREAD (DOAS)

To tie all this new analytical framework together in a way that is amenable to consistent relative value analysis, we broach the notion of DOAS. An investor who purchases CMBS holds a long position in noncallable bond, short position in call, and default put options. For selling, the options investor is compensated in the form of enhanced coupon payments. Because of the sequential nature of the CMBS structure, where any prepay is passed onto the senior tranches (current paying bond), it is reasonable to argue that the voluntary prepayment impact on the credit-sensitive tranches is negligible. Accepting this contention, we further argue that a large portion of the enhanced coupon received by the investor holding credit-sensitive tranches comes from the default put option. The default put option value consists of intrinsic and time value, and to the extent that the option embedded in CMBS is delayed American-exercise style, the time value component therefore dominates. Hence, in valuing credit-sensitive CMBS, the value of the option that is associated with the probability of default and recovery rate needs to be evaluated.

We believe one way to value the option is to appeal to the option-adjusted technology that is prevalent in RMBS. In RMBS OAS analysis, the prepayment forecast plays a key role, and in CMBS we propose that role for the recovery rate in the event of default. The binomial tree can be used to obtain at each node the expected value of recovery rate given the value of the spot rate at that node (discussed earlier). Because we are concerned about forecasting the recovery rate, a simulation tree would suffice. In a simulation tree, the evolution of the spot and recovery rates are simulated using a random tree. Thorough analysis of how to implement a simulation tree is beyond the scope of this chapter. Exhibit 31 provides a schema for DOAS tree implementation.

DOAS uses an option-based technique to evaluate credit-sensitive CMBS under different recovery rate scenarios. DOAS is the numerical difference between the forward credit spread and the default option cost. Option cost is associated with the variability in cash flow that results from the change in probability of default or the change in recovery rate conditional on default changes. There are two main inputs that determine the DOAS of a credit-sensitive bond:

- Generate cash flows as a function of probability of the default and recovery rates
- Generate interest rate paths under an assumed term structure model

At each cash flow date, there is a spot rate that determines the discount factor for each cash flow conditional on the recovery rate. The present value of the cash flows is equal to the sum of the product of the cash flows and their discount factors. Assume the current market price of a credit-sensitive CMBS is $P_m(\bullet)$, and the DOAS is a constant value (α) added to the spot rate for every rate path such that the market price equals the theoretical value, $P(\bullet)$. DOAS is a relative value tool that helps an investor identify what is cheap or rich in a credit-sensitive market.

Exhibit 31: Schematic of DOAS Tree Implementation

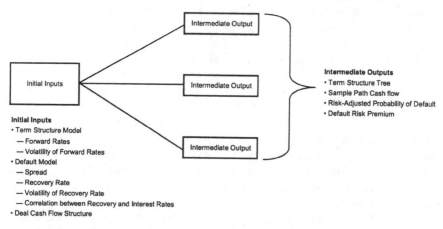

DOAS: Default option-adjusted spread.

Source: First Union Securities, Inc.

TECHNICAL APPENDIX

Pricing Credit-Sensitive Bonds

The price of credit-sensitive bonds,

$$P(r, t,\bullet) = B(r, t) - \delta(\bullet) \times Q(\bullet) \times B(r, t)$$

where r is the risk-free rate of interest, t is the maturity date, $P(\bullet)$ is the price of a zero coupon credit-sensitive bond, $B(\bullet)$ is the price of a risk-free bond with the same maturity (or average life), $Q(\bullet)$ is the probability of default, $\delta(\bullet)$ is equal to $(1 - b(\bullet))$, that is, the loss severity, and $b(\bullet)$ is the recovery rate.

Modeling the Recovery Rate

The purpose of the modeling recovery rate is to price credit-sensitive tranches; this exercise should depend on market observables as much as possible. However, in evaluating scenario analysis, the empirical framework based on historical data about property values and rents is useful. Using a binomial lattice to model the spot rate at each node in the tree, we can compute the expected recovery rate conditional on the spot rate, and it is given by

$$E[\beta(t)|r(t)] = E[\beta(t)] - \rho \frac{\sigma_\beta}{\sigma}\{r(t) - E[r(t)]\}$$

and,

$$E[\beta(t)] = \int_{\infty}^{\infty}\left[1 + \frac{1 - \beta_0}{\beta_0}\exp(\sigma_\beta \varepsilon \sqrt{t})\right]^{-1}\phi(\varepsilon)dt$$

$$\varepsilon \sim N(0, 1)$$

$$\phi(\varepsilon) = 1/\sqrt{2\Pi}\exp\left[-\frac{\varepsilon^2}{2}\right]$$

$$E[r(t)] = f(0, t) + \sum_{j=0}^{\frac{t}{h} - t}(jh, h)h$$

where, $E[\beta(t)|r(t)]$ is the expected recovery rate at time t conditional on the spot rate at time t, $E[\beta(t)]$ is the expected recovery rate at time t, $E[r(t)]$ is the spot rate at time t, ρ is a correlation between the recovery rate and the spot rate, β_0 is the initial recovery rate, σ_β is the volatility of the recovery rate, σ is the volatility of the spot rate, $\phi(\bullet)$ is the cumulative normal distribution function, ε is the random sample from the standard normal distribution, and $f(0, t)$ is the forward interest rate over the period $(0, t)$.

Cumulative Probability of Default

Let t be now and $q_{ik}(mh)$ the cumulative probability of default at time $(t + mh)$. Define $q_{ik}^0(mh)$ as the one period probability of default over the period from $[t + (m - 1)h]$ to $[t + mh]$. The first passage time probability (or the probability of default in the period indexed by m without a default having occurred) is given by

$$\{1 - q_{ik}[(m - 1)h]\}q_{ik}^0(mh)$$

The cumulative probability of default ending in the period indexed by m is given by

$$q_{ik}(mh) = q_{ik}[(m - 1)h] + \{1 - q_{ik}[(m - 1)h]\}q_{ik}(mh)$$

and one period probability of default in the period indexed by m is

$$q_{ik}^0 = \frac{q_{ik}(mh) - q_{ik}[(m - 1)h]}{1 - q_{ik}[(m - 1)h]}$$

Computing the Default Risk Premium

Computing the default risk premium from the binomial lattice is somewhat involved. First, define the state prices derived from term structure model as $w(t, n)$. Second, let $f(t, \cdot)$ be the forward rate and $s_j(\cdot)$ be the credit spread. The one period probability of default can be computed from the tree as follows:

$$q_{ik}^0\left(\frac{T}{h}\right) = \frac{A - B + C}{D}$$

where,

$$A = \sum_{m = \frac{t}{h} + 1}^{\frac{T}{h} - 1} \left[\sum_{n - 1}^{m} w(mh, n)\{1 - q_{ik}[(m - 1)h]\}q_{ik}^0(mh)\beta(mh, n) \right]$$

$$B = \exp\left[-h \sum_{j = \frac{t}{h}}^{\frac{T}{h} - 1} [f(t, jh) + s_i(jh)] \right]$$

$$C = \sum_{n - 1}^{m} w\left(\frac{T}{h}, n\right)\left[1 - q_{ik}\left(\frac{T}{h} - 1\right) \right]$$

$$D = \sum_{h = 1}^{m} w\left(\frac{T}{h}, n\right)\left[1 - q_{ik}\left(\frac{T}{h} - 1\right) \right]\left[1 - \beta\left(\frac{T}{h}, n\right) \right]$$

Chapter 10

An Empirical Framework for Estimating CMBS Defaults

Dale Westhoff
Senior Managing Director
Bear Stearns & Co.

V.S. Srinivasan
Associate Director
Bear Stearns & Co.

Mark Feldman
Managing Director
Bear Stearns & Co.

I deally, an expected default rate for a given set of commercial or residential loans is derived from a complete history of default frequencies on identical collateral through multiple real estate cycles. In reality, historical default information is often very limited in scope and not reflective of current underwriting standards or regional economic trends. This leaves investors with few alternatives beyond static scenario analysis to assess the default risk of a commercial mortgage portfolio.

To address the need for a more rigorous, empirical framework for default analysis, Bear Stearns has developed a powerful new approach based on the rich historical data available on actual commercial real estate values and rents. This data set consists of 13 years of property value and rent data on four different property categories (apartments, industrial/warehouse, office, and retail) in 38 regions. The breadth of this data allows us to dynamically simulate future property values and rents in a manner consistent with that observed historically, accounting for both regional and property type variations in the data. In this framework, we can ascertain financial solvency for individual properties across thousands of randomly generated property value/rent paths to derive an expected periodic default rate. By aggregating these individual results, we can then derive an "expected" default curve for any given set of commercial properties. The key to this approach is that the simulations are calibrated to match the observed volatility and serial correlation in actual real estate values at the regional level. Once this is done, it is a simple matter to track an individual loan's performance along each simulated path given its property type, initial debt service coverage ratio (DSCR), and initial loan-to-value (LTV). Furthermore, this framework allows investors to perform more rigorous and sophisticated scenario analysis that is rooted in actual historical experience. For example:

1. Investors can modify the property value/rent volatility assumption to measure the sensitivity of a security to real estate cycles that are, on average, more severe or less severe than what we have seen historically.
2. Investors can impose a long-term price or rent trend on the simulation process.
3. Investors can define a specific price/rent scenario if they have a strong view on where we are in the current commercial real estate cycle.

The advantage of this statistical framework is that it does not rely on historical default information which is often limited in scope, biased by inconsistent underwriting standards, and linked to specific periods in regional economic cycles. These data problems tend to make traditional default analysis more subjective in nature. Using simulation, we eliminate these problems while still accounting for the intrinsic characteristics of the loans and the regional and property specific influences on commercial default behavior. Furthermore, we believe this approach is particularly well suited to large, diversified commercial loan portfolios where extensive loan-level due diligence may be difficult to perform.

THE PRICE AND RENT DATA

Our historical price and rent data come from the National Real Estate Index which is owned and operated by CB Commercial. This organization publishes property value and rent indices on four different property types (apartments, offices, warehouse/industrial, and retail) in 38 regions. The indices span 13 years including the severe commercial real estate recession from the late 1980s through the early 1990s. The property value index is derived from actual sales prices on 50,000 properties reported by brokers, title companies, REITs, and appraisers. The rent price indices are derived from quarterly surveys of asking rents for the same properties.

THE SIMULATION PROCESS

Just as we sample alternative interest rate paths in an option-adjusted spread framework, we can simulate real estate price and rent paths in the commercial market to determine the probability of default in any given period. However, in this case we sample from actual historical price and rent data using a statistical method known as "bootstrapping."

In this procedure, for a given property type and region, we repeatedly sample its historical price and rent data series to construct a simulation that is consistent with actual price and rent volatility and serial correlation[1] observed at the regional real estate market level. By simply repeating this procedure, we can generate thousands of random paths over which we can evaluate individual loan performance. For example, once price and rent simulations are constructed we can track DSCRs and LTVs along every path to determine if default conditions are met. The probability of default for an individual loan in any given period is simply the ratio of the predicted default occurrences across all paths divided by the number of paths. The "expected" default rate for a collection of commercial loans is calculated as the weighted average of the individual probabilities. This analysis can be further stratified by region, property type, or loan attribute to define areas of concentrated default risk.

Conditions that Trigger a Default

We assume a mortgage will default when the following two conditions are met:

1. the net operating income (NOI) is less than the scheduled mortgage payment (i.e., the DSCR is less than one), and
2. the market value of the property is less than the outstanding value of the debt (i.e., the LTV ratio is greater than 1).

Both conditions must be met before a default occurs. For example, if the DSCR is less than 1 but the LTV is also less than 1, we assume the owner would attempt to sell before defaulting. Conversely, if the LTV is greater than 1 but the DSCR is also greater than 1, the owner is unlikely to default unless forced to sell.

Simulating the Debt Service Coverage Ratio

DSCR is defined as (Revenue − Operating Expenses)/Debt Service and is a critical measure of a borrower's ability to meet debt obligations. The probability of a default is inversely correlated to DSCR and values below 1.0 indicate insufficient income to meet debt payments. We simulate DSCR by assuming revenue is directly proportional to simulated property rents while operating expenses are assumed to grow at the inflation rate. Although expense ratios vary by location, property class, type of lease, services, etc., we assume the conservative initial expense ratios for the various property categories shown in Exhibit 1.

Finally, simulated revenue cash flows must be adjusted to account for the average lease term for a given property type. For example, a change in rents today will immediately impact hotel revenues since "leases" are typically for one night only. In contrast, a change in office rents today will have a lagged effect on reve-

---

[1] To replicate the serial correlation observed in the data, each sample iteration selects 3-year sequences rather than a single data point.

nues since the average office lease is approximately five years. In our simulation process, we account for this relationship by assuming the average lease terms and average roll times for each property category in Exhibit 2.

Simulating Loan-to-Value Ratios

LTV is another important measure used to assess the likelihood of default as well as the potential loss severity after foreclosure and liquidation. LTV is the current loan amount divided by the market value of the property. Highly leveraged transactions (high LTV ratios) provide less equity cushion against default and tend to increase loss severity when a default occurs. Simulated property values are calibrated to the volatility observed in actual property values for a given region and property type. The second condition of our default trigger is met when the LTV ratio exceeds 1.0 at any point in the simulation process.

CONSERVATIVE ASSUMPTIONS

We view the results from this statistical framework as conservative for the following reasons:

1. If trigger conditions are met, we assume a ruthless and immediate default occurs. In reality, if the DSCR falls below 1, owners will sometimes carry the property in an effort to resolve a temporary shortfall in revenue.

Exhibit 1: Expense Ratios by Property Category

	Expense Ratios (Operating Expenses/Revenues)
Industrial	10%
Retail	20%
Multifamily	35%
Office	45%
Hotel	70%

Exhibit 2: Assumed Average Lease Term and Time to Roll by Property Category

Property Category	Average Term of Lease	Average Time to Roll
Industrial	3.0 years	1.5 years
Apartments	1.0 years	0.5 years
Office	5.0 years	2.5 years
Retail	4.0 years	2.0 years
Hotels	Overnight	Instantaneous

Exhibit 3: Long-Term Growth Rates by Property Type

Property Type		Growth Rate
Apartment	Price	3.7%
	Rent	2.9%
Industrial	Price	1.8%
	Rent	1.9%
Office	Price	1.0%
	Rent	0.7%
Retail	Price	1.3%
	Rent	1.9%
Aggregate		1.9%

Source: CB Commercial 1984-1998

2. In general, to derive our baseline "expected" default curves, we center the simulation process around a 1% long-term growth rate in property values and rents. Historical data from the 15-year period 1984-1998 suggest that over long periods of time, rents and property values increase by an average of about 1.9% per year. Exhibit 3 provides observed price and rent long-term growth rates for each property category.

3. The highly leveraged transactions of the 1980s amplified the correction in commercial real estate values seen in the late 1980s and early 1990s beyond what would be expected in a "normal" real estate cycle. Nevertheless, our simulation framework includes unadjusted data from this entire period despite the fact that a similar scenario seems highly unlikely in the near future.

APPLICATION OF THE CMBS DEFAULT MODEL

Our simulation-based default model is particularly useful in comparing the relative default risk of multiple commercial deals with diverse loan characteristics. For example, Exhibit 4 provides projected cumulative defaults in basis points for six representative CMBS deals. The projections were generated assuming actual property value and rent volatilities derived from the property type and location of each loan backing the deals. We also calibrated the model to a long-term growth rate in property values and rents of 1%. It is important to note that although a change in the long-term growth rate assumption changes the absolute level of projected defaults, it does not affect the relative performance of the deals. The projected cumulative defaults shown in Exhibit 4 are consistent with the risk profile of the loans backing each deal. For example, projected defaults are highest in GMAC 97-C1 reflecting the large percentage of loans with DSCRs < 1.25. In contrast, BSCMS 98-C1 has the lowest projected cumulative defaults at 168 basis points, which is consistent with the absence of loans with DSCRs < 1.25 and the very low percentage of loans with LTVs > 75%.

Exhibit 4: Projected Defaults for Representative CMBS Deals

Deal	Projected Cumulative Defaults (in basis points)	Actual CMBS Data			
		% of Loans DSCR< 1.25x	% of Loan LTV > 75%	% of Loan Office	% of Loan CA
Chase 98-1	321	9.70%	25.60%	21.30%	15.70%
FULB 98-C2	305	7.70%	36.60%	20.40%	11.80%
BSCMS 98-C1	168	0.00%	7.50%	17.20%	27.40%
GMAC 97-C1	613	28.12%	27.16%	18.07%	17.30%
GMAC 98-C1	394	8.00%	38.30%	11.00%	9.00%
MCFI 98-MC2	553	21.00%	52.00%	34.00%	12.00%

Exhibit 5: Expected and Worst Case Defaults from Model Simulation: MSCI 1998 - HF2

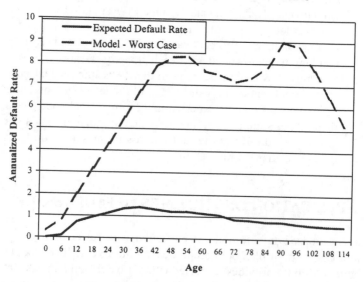

The simulation approach also provides a framework for analyzing the impact of defaults on individual tranches within a structure. For example, Exhibit 5 shows our expected default curve for a representative CMBS deal — MSCI 1998-HF2. If the losses implied by the expected curve shown in Exhibit 5 are applied to the deal structure, we find that all of the tranches down to the B-rated bond remain intact.[2] However, the unrated and CCC rated tranches are completely wiped out while 17% of the principal of the B-rated tranche is eroded (see Exhibit 6).

---

[2] We assume a loss severity of 30%.

Exhibit 6: Projected Cumulative Losses by Tranche for MSCI 1998 - HF2 Using Expected Defaults Curve

Tranche	Size of Tranche ($ mill)	Cumulative Loss ($ mill)	Cumulative Loss As a %of Original Bal.
AAA (10yr)	547.80	0.0	0
AA	52.90	0.0	0
A	52.90	0.0	0
BBB	58.20	0.0	0
BBB–	21.20	0.0	0
BB	18.50	0.0	0
B	10.60	0.0	0
B–	15.90	2.7	17
CCC	10.60	10.6	100
Unrated	10.60	10.6	100

Assumptions: 30% severity; 18 month lag to recovery

Exhibit 7: Projected Cumulative Losses by Tranche for MSCI 1998 - HF2 Using Worse Case Scenario

Tranche	Size of Tranche ($ mill)	Cumulative Loss ($ mill)	Cumulative Loss As a %of Original Bal.
AAA (10yr)	547.80	0.0	0
AA	52.90	0.0	0
A	52.90	0.0	0
BBB	58.20	0.0	0
BBB–	21.20	9.1	43
BB	18.50	18.5	100
B	10.60	10.6	100
B–	15.90	15.9	17
CCC	10.60	10.6	100
Unrated	10.60	10.6	100

Assumptions: 30% severity; 18 month lag to recovery

We can further stress the deal by selecting the single worst case scenario from all of the random scenarios generated during the simulation. This vector, also shown in Exhibit 5, peaks at an 9.0% CDR, over six times the peak CDR of the expected case and well above the highest CDR registered by commercial loans held by insurance companies since 1990. If we apply losses from the worst case scenario we find that all of the investment grade tranches remain intact; 43% of the BBB– tranche is eroded; and all of the BB and lower rated tranches are completely wiped out (see Exhibit 7). Although not done here, we can further assess the risk profile of a particular deal by again using our simulation results to define confidence intervals around our expected default curve.

Chapter 11

Project-Loan Prepayments and Defaults

Steve Banerjee
First Vice President
Prudential Securities Inc.

Lisa Pendergast
Senior Vice President
Prudential Securities Inc.

Weisi Tan
Vice President
Prudential Securities Inc.

P roject-loan securities have a long history in the mortgage-backed securities marketplace. The emergence of commercial mortgage-backed securities (CMBSs) as a core fixed-income asset over the last several years has served to raise the profile of this market, with project-loan securitizations beginning to garner increased attention from fixed-income investors. Project loans are insured by the Federal Housing Administration (FHA), whose mandate is to foster the growth of the nation's multifamily-housing supply. In particular, the FHA assists private and public borrowers in constructing, purchasing, rehabilitating, and refinancing multifamily rental housing, condominiums, cooperatives, hospitals, nursing homes, and assisted-living facilities. In addition, project loans provide investors with prepayment protections not unlike those found in the CMBS market. The commercial properties securing project loans and the prepayment protections provided to investors make project-loan securities an excellent CMBS alternative — an issue made all the more pertinent by today's low-volume, private-label new-issue CMBS market.[1]

Our objective in this chapter is to quantify the factors that impact FHA project-loan performance. The current convention is to assume 15% CPJ (15% CPR after hard lockout), in conjunction with a default-seasoning curve that peaks in year three at 2.5% before trailing off to 1.26% in year seven and 0.25% in year 14.

---

[1] Information about the various project loan programs is provided in Chapter 4.

The lack of a robust quantitative-research study to date can be attributed to the difficulties associated with obtaining a sufficiently large and statistically consistent data set. Even though the FHA has been insuring these loans since 1934, the difficulties reflect in large part the changes in the FHA's policies and underwriting guidelines, as well as changes to the various project-loan sections, over the decades. To redress this deficiency, Prudential Securities Inc. (PSI) has compiled a statistically significant and consistent data sample, culled from a pool of over 5,000 GNMA-guaranteed project loans originated between 1971 and 2000.

Based on the historical information garnered on project-loan prepayments and defaults, PSI developed two separate benchmark seasoning curves, one for voluntary prepayments (or refinancings) and the other for involuntary prepayments (or defaults). The prepayment- and default-seasoning curves derived from the PSI data sample can be applied to current project loans or to pools of project loans, to model cash flows and thus to better gauge both the call risk that is inherent in these deals and the impact that such call risk would have on basic bond measures such as yield, average life, duration, and convexity.

A DETAILED EXAMINATION OF THE
PSI PROJECT-LOAN DATA SET

To optimally analyze the prepayment and default behavior of project loans, PSI compiled data on over 5,000 GNMA project loans originated between 1971 and 2000. This original PSI data sample comprises loan-specific information derived from prospectuses on 5,215 GNMA-guaranteed project loans. Once the data compilation was complete, the data-sample criteria were refined to reflect those loans originated under FHA insurance programs that are not only in effect today, but that also command sufficient origination volume. This exercise reduced the data sample from 5,215 loans to 3,557 loans. Within this refinement process, the key data-selection criterion was prepayment protection. Over the years, prepayment-protection provisions on FHA-endorsed project loans have varied by originator and by year of origination; it wasn't until the late 1980s that HUD began to inject some standardization into the types of call protections embedded in the loans that it endorses. The refined PSI data sample therefore includes a total of 4,088 loans originated beginning in 1986, a period when the prepayment-protection characteristics on project loans began to become more consistent.

The increased prepayment-protection consistency detected in 1984 through 1986 loans was initially a response to market demand. However, HUD Mortgagee Letter 87-9, published on February 20, 1987, specifically addressed the issue of creating more uniform mortgage-prepayment provisions for HUD-insured and co-insured multifamily projects. The letter clarified HUD's position with respect to the inclusion of provisions prohibiting partial or full prepayments (lock-outs) and prepayment penalties in fully insured and co-insured project mortgages.

HUD Mortgagee Letter 87-9 applied to all project mortgages endorsed for full insurance under Sections 207, 213, 220, 221(d)(3) or (d)(4), 223(f), 231, 232, 241, or 242 of the National Housing Act, or endorsed for co-insurance under Sections 221(d) or 223(F) of the National Housing Act. The basic policy for GNMA-guaranteed project loans stipulated that project loans may include: a lockout provision with a maximum term of ten years plus the construction period; or a prepayment penalty that would be no more than 1% at the end of the tenth year following the construction period (if the initial penalty is 3% or less); or a combination lockout/penalty provision with a lockout period of less than ten years, and a penalty that would be no more than 1% at the end of the tenth year following the construction period stated in the construction contract.

As was noted earlier, even prior to the publication of HUD Mortgagee Letter 87-9, there was an attempt by lenders and by HUD to originate mortgages with more consistent prepayment penalties. Therefore, in the PSI data sample, we include not only loans originated after the publication of Letter 87-9, but also loans originated beginning in 1986.

Loan size is an another important factor in prepayment estimation. When working with a relatively modest sample size, prepayment estimations at certain seasoning points may be unduly influenced by a small number of large-balance prepaid loans. In effect, the prepayments at these seasonings will appear exaggerated. Therefore, it makes sense not to include the whole spectrum of loan size. On the other hand, if loan size is truncated excessively, the data sample may lack the critical mass necessary to be meaningful. After careful consideration, the loans with balances in the upper 5% distribution in loan size were removed from both the prepayment and the default data samples. The removal of loans in the upper 5% distribution in loan size further reduced the data sample to 3,217 loans. The 3,217 project-loan data sample was used in full as the PSI default data sample. However, this sample was further refined in creating the prepayment data sample.

Since the PSI project-loan data sample comprises loans originated between 1986 and 2000, and since over 66% of the 10-year hard-lockout project loans in our data sample were originated after 1993, the data provide very little prepayment information on 10-year hard-lockout loans. (The distribution of prepayment penalty by origination year is shown in Exhibit 1.) In light of this, 1,008 10-year hard-lockout loans in the default sample are not considered in computing the prepayment-seasoning curves in this study. However, the default experience of 10-year hard-lockout loans is independent of lockout or penalty, and therefore is used in the development of PSI's default curves.

Thus, PSI's prepayment estimations are drawn from a data sample comprising 2,209 loans, while the project-loan default data sample comprises 3,217 loans. The project-loan data sample contains detailed information on current, prepaid, and defaulted loans. The information available includes:

- Prepayment-lockout/-penalty information.
- Loan coupon.

Exhibit 1: Project-Loan Origination Volume by Origination Year

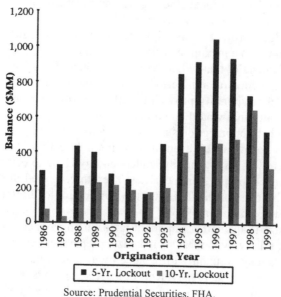

Source: Prudential Securities, FHA.

- Loan origination date.
- Loan term.
- Section of FHA Act.
- Loan balance at origination.
- Loan balance at termination, or latest balance.
- Loan exit category (defaulted, prepaid, or matured).
- Date of loan exit.

Exhibit 2 shows the loan-balance distribution in the prepayment and default data samples. The average loan sizes are $4.05 million and $4.03 million respectively for the prepayment and default data samples; the median loan balances are around $3.3 million for both sets of data.

The distribution of coupons for the data samples is presented in Exhibit 3, with coupons stratified in 50 basis point bands. The bulk of the loans appear to have coupons between 7.0% and 9.5%. The coupon distribution for the two data samples is very similar.

Most project loans have maturities of either 35 or 40 years, along with a minority of 30-year maturities (see Exhibit 4). The distributions are identical for the two data samples. Finally, the vintage distribution for the prepayment-penalty loans in the two data samples is depicted in Exhibit 5, which highlights the relative magnitudes of origination by vintage, within the 5-year lockout and 10-year lockout programs.

Exhibit 2: Project-Loan Original Loan-Balance Distribution for PSI Data Samples

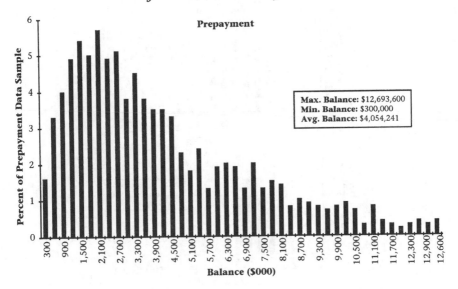

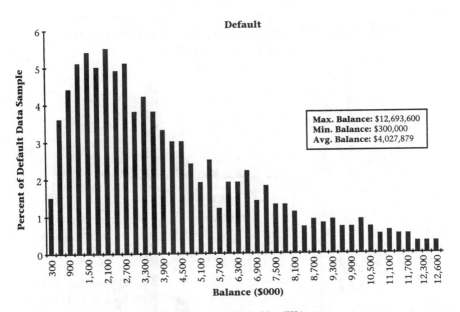

Source: Prudential Securities, FHA.

Exhibit 3: Project-Loan Coupon Distribution for PSI Data Samples

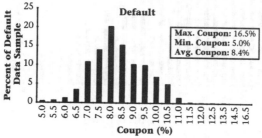

Source: Prudential Securities, FHA.

Exhibit 4: Project-Loan Term Distribution for PSI Data Samples

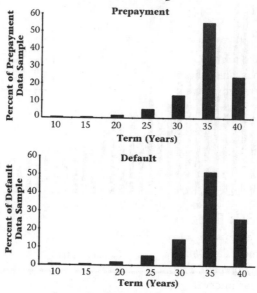

Source: Prudential Securities, FHA.

Exhibit 5: Project-Loan Originations by Vintage for PSI Data Samples

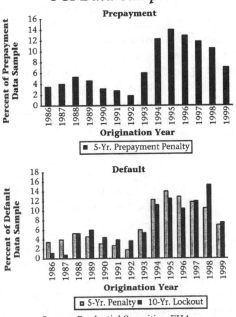

Source: Prudential Securities, FHA.

PROJECT-LOAN PREPAYMENTS

All FHA-insured project loans provide varying degrees of call protection to investors. Call protection in the form of a prepayment lockout and/or a penalty is specific to a particular project loan, and is negotiated at the time of loan origination. The two most common prepayment provisions extant today are 10-year lockouts and 5-year lockouts, followed by a fixed 5% penalty in year six that declines 1% annually to 1% in year ten (known as "5, 4, 3, 2, 1"). Prior to the mid-1980s, a number of project loans carried what was known as "24 down an eighth"; under this provision, the prepayment penalty, which would begin at 3%, would be phased out by one-eighth of one percent annually for 24 years. Additionally, there are loans that either have no prepayment penalties or are lacking specific prepayment-lockout/-penalty information.

PSI's Prepayment-Seasoning Curve

Since loan age is a key driver in project-loan prepayments, loan prepayments within the prepayment data sample were identified along with their age/seasoning at the time that they prepaid. Prepayment amounts were then aggregated by loan-age groups at 1-year intervals, and were compared to the total outstanding balance at the beginning of the seasoning period. This outstanding balance was adjusted downward by the scheduled amortization during a period to arrive at the scheduled balance at the end of the period. The prepayment rate during any seasoning period was then expressed as percentage ratio of the prepaid dollar amount in that period to the scheduled balance at period-end. Exhibit 6 shows project-loan prepayments in dollars expressed as a function of loan age.

For example, for loans in the 10-year seasoning category (with loan ages of 108 months through 119 months), $63.80 million of unscheduled principal prepayments were recorded. The outstanding balance at the beginning of the 10-year category was $432.70 million, while scheduled amortization during the 10-year period was $6.10 million. The prepayment rate (in % CPR) over this 1-year period is given by the following:

$$\text{Prepayment rate} = 100 \times \frac{\text{Prepaid Amount During the Period}}{\text{Scheduled Balance at End of Period}}$$

$$= 100 \times \frac{\$63.80}{\$432.60 - \$6.10}$$

$$= 15.0\% \text{ CPR}$$

The prepayment-seasoning curve, which is presented in Exhibit 7, is derived from ten years of historical prepayment observations. At year five, as the 5-year lockout period expires, prepayments begin to rise sharply for the next 12 months. This is followed by slower gains in prepayment speeds until year seven, when speeds start rising again, reaching 15% CPR at year ten.

Exhibit 6: Project-Loan Prepayments by Seasoning ($MM)

	Age (Years)									
	1	2	3	4	5	6	7	8	9	10
Outstanding Balance	8,466.4	7,405.1	6,285.0	4,966.3	3,429.4	2,290.4	1,414.3	983.0	717.5	432.7
Prepaid Balance	–	–	–	48.0	135.7	185.2	130.5	105.2	82.5	63.8

Source: Prudential Securities, FHA.

Exhibit 7: Project-Loan Prepayment-Seasoning Curve

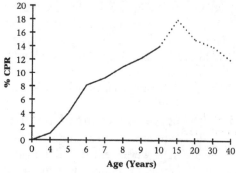

Note. Prepayments beyond year ten are projections based on PSI's estimate regarding growth in equity and burnout, among other parameters.

Source: Prudential Securities, FHA.

Projecting Prepayment Speeds Beyond Year Ten

There are only limited historical prepayment data on the project loans in the PSI prepayment data sample beyond the 10-year point. However, we can make reasonable projections on prepayment speeds beyond ten years based on the impact of seasoning, burnout, and changing loan-to-value (LTV) ratios. LTVs are generally impacted by scheduled amortizations and by changes in property values. Scheduled amortization plays an insignificant role in lowering LTV ratios in the early years, given the fact that scheduled principal paydowns become appreciable only after ten years of seasoning. Changes in property values, however, can have an immediate impact on loan LTVs. Specifically, rising property values lead to lower LTV ratios, and thus increase the incentive for borrowers to take cash out of the property through refinancing. Property values normally increase with the passage of time, although there have, of course, been periods when property values have declined. However, over a period of five years or more, valuations generally do increase.

We study this relationship between project-loan prepayments and LTVs for loans in the PSI prepayment data sample. For the purpose of this analysis, we assume that loans originated under sections 232 and 221 (d)(4) have initial LTVs of 90%; all other loans were assumed to have 80% LTVs at inception. Over the life of the loans, property values were adjusted using the National Council of Real Estate Investment Fiduciaries (NCREIF) property-index time series for stabilized multifamily properties.[2]

By applying the NCREIF appreciation index and factoring in the amortization to the prepayment data sample, we capture the change in LTV values over time for each loan. To calculate the impact of LTV on prepayments, we identify all prepaid loans in the prepayment data sample, as well as the LTV ratio on the prepayment date, based on our NCREIF appreciation index and standard amortization. Exhibit 8 shows the relationship between prepayments and LTVs, and clearly illustrates what intuitively makes sense — as LTVs decrease, property-owners refinance to tap into the built-up equity.

Note from Exhibit 8 that the 50%-to-60% LTV bucket has a CPR of 2.43%. The sharp decrease in LTV from 80% to 90% at origination to 60% or less is explained by the fact that these loans have seasoned by four to five years, and the lockout period has allowed equity to build. The 2.43% CPR in the 50%-to-60% LTV bucket reflects the first significant prepayment activity since origination. However, it is the middle 40%-to-50% LTV bucket that displays the highest prepayment-speed pickup, with speeds increasing to 9.39% CPR. This highlights the fact that the bulk of early prepayments occur after the 5-year penalty period expires, a point at which LTV values also have declined to 50% to 60% or lower. The jump in prepayment speeds in the 40%-to-50% LTV bucket reflects the combination of lower LTVs and the pent-up borrower demand to prepay that is caused by lockout.

---

[2] For more information on the NCREIF property index, see *NCREIF Briefs*, Spring 2000.

Exhibit 8: LTV Effect on Project-Loan Prepayments

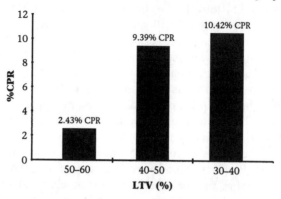

Source: Prudential Securities, FHA.

If our analysis were to stop here, one would conclude that prepayment speeds jump about 7% CPR for every 10% decrease in LTV. However, these results would be skewed by the pent-up demand of borrowers that is released after lockout expires. Therefore, a more reasonable analysis requires us to look beyond the period immediately after lockout, when pent-up demand has dissipated. In fact, upon further seasoning, the increase in speed moderates dramatically. Note in Exhibit 8 that moving from the 40%-to-50% LTV bucket to the 30%-to-40% LTV bucket triggers an increase of only about 1% CPR.

To summarize, the above analysis shows that, beyond year ten, as LTVs decline and equity builds up, borrowers have greater incentive to undertake equity-takeout refinancings, which results in higher prepayment rates. However, the proportion of readily refinanceable loans eventually declines as a result of burnout, and causes prepayments to decline.

Applying LTV Analysis to Prepayment Projections

Between the age of 10 and 15 years, we assume annual property-value appreciation of 7%.[3] This causes LTVs to decline at least 7% annually. Scheduled amortization would only decrease LTVs further, although this is ignored in our projections. Based on our projection of a 1% CPR increase for every 10% decline

---

[3] According to the NCREIF Property Index, multifamily property values appreciated at the rate of 10% per year during most of the 1990s. However, considering the slower growth period from 1978 to 1985, we estimate the longer-term annual property-value appreciation rate to be around 7% per year. Arguably, the NCREIF multifamily index may not be the optimal data series for this exercise, as the multifamily properties represented in the index are investment-grade only. How-ever, the fact that NCREIF affords access to a consistent and reliable multifamily data sample overwhelms the slightly higher appreciation rates of the Class A properties in the index versus the more mixed asset quality in project-loan pools. What's more, the fuller growth rates in property appreciation indicated by NCREIF are more likely than not offset by the fact that scheduled amortization is not applied to the future LTV growth-rate assumptions in our study.

in LTV, we estimate that prepayments will reach approximately 19% CPR in year 15. Beyond the 15-year point of seasoning, burnout effects will begin to dominate, and prepayments are expected to decline. This is depicted in Exhibits 7 and 9. Exhibit 9 presents, in tabular form, the entire prepayment-seasoning curve shown in Exhibit 7.

PROJECT-LOAN DEFAULTS

Properly projecting voluntary prepayment speeds is, of course, integral to the proper valuation of project-loan securities. However, as most project loans have some level of prepayment protection and therefore a modicum of predictability, project-loan defaults can often be the more volatile of the two metrics, thus making the accuracy of pricing projections all the more important. Accurate projections of future defaults are extremely important in structuring project-loan securitizations and in sizing individual tranches, as significant variances in actual versus projected defaults will have the greatest impact on the average lives of the shorter-dated tranches and on the performance of the IO.

PSI's analysis of project-loan defaults is similar in nature to the prepayment analysis. As with prepaid loans, defaulted loans are identified by seasoning buckets, and the default rate is expressed as a percentage of the outstanding balance within that seasoning stratification. Exhibit 10 presents the defaulted dollar balances as a function of seasoning, while Exhibit 11 gives the default rate as a percentage of the outstanding balance.

Exhibit 9: Project-Loan Prepayment-Seasoning Curve

Age (Years)	% CPR
0 to 4	0.0
4	1.0
5	4.0
6	8.2
7	9.3
8	11.3
9	12.3
10	15.0
15	19.0
20	15.0
30	14.0
40	12.0

Note. Prepayments beyond year ten are projections based on PSI's estimates regarding growth in equity and burnout, among other parameters.

Source: Prudential Securities, FHA.

Exhibit 10: Project-Loan Defaults by Seasoning ($MM)

	Age (Years)								
	1	2	3	4	5	6	7	8	9
Outstanding Balance	12,205.2	10,537.8	8,777.0	6,842.1	4,779.2	3,200.7	2,092.7	1,470.3	1,079.9
Defaulted Balance	67.4	132.1	193.3	152.1	143.4	38.0	36.1	17.2	15.0

Source: Prudential Securities, FHA.

Exhibit 11: PSI Project-Loan Default Curve

Age (Years)	Default (%)
1	0.52
2	1.26
3	2.20
4	2.22
5	3.00
6	1.19
7	1.72
8	1.17
9	1.39

Source: Prudential Securities, FHA.

Exhibit 12: Project-Loan Default Rates

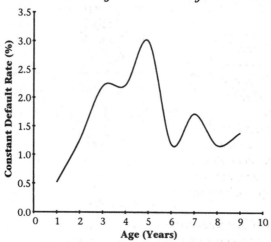

Source: Prudential Securities, FHA.

Exhibits 11 and 12 show that the default rate peaks during the fifth year at approximately 3.0% CDR; after that, it drops off sharply, stabilizing at around 1.25% CDR in the eighth year. As we mentioned earlier, we believe that the default rate will continue to decline gradually with increasing age, as the more default-prone borrowers leave the pool.

APPLYING PREPAYMENT AND DEFAULT CURVES TO 10-YEAR LOCKOUT LOANS

The project-loan prepayment analysis is based primarily on 5-year lockout/5-year penalty loans, while the default analysis is based on both 5-year lockout/penalty and 10-year lockout loans. When considering 10-year lockout loans, we recommend shifting the prepayment-seasoning curve forward, starting out at 1.0% CPR in the ninth year, then jumping to 4.0% CPR in year ten, and so on. This is a rather conservative approach, since the built-up LTV advantage at the expiration of the 10-year lockout is likely to result in higher actual prepayments. The default curve can be used without any modification, since it incorporates the default experience of 10-year lockout loans.

CONCLUSIONS

The PSI project-loan study reflects what intuitively makes sense — that the prepayment and default experience of these loans is dictated mainly by loan age. The results of the PSI study are as follows:

- The project-loan prepayment-seasoning curve is equivalent to a single flat lifetime-speed assumption of 15% CPR, assuming that no significant voluntary prepayments occur through the lockout period. At year five, as the 5-year lockout periods expire, prepayments begin to rise sharply for the next 12 months, rising to an approximate 8.2% constant prepayment rate (CPR) in year six. This is followed by slower gains in prepayment speeds until year seven, when speeds begin to rise again, reaching 15% CPR at year ten.
- The project-loan default-seasoning curve peaks in year five at a 3% constant default rate (CDR). The default rate drops off sharply beginning in year six, and stabilizes at around 1.25% in year eight. We believe that the default rate will keep declining gradually with increasing age, as the more default-prone borrowers leave the pool.

While the PSI prepayment-seasoning curve is generally in line with the prepayment-seasoning curve currently in use, there are slight differences between the PSI default-seasoning curve and current convention. PSI's default curve peaks later (at five years versus three years) and at a slightly higher rate (3% versus 2.5%). However, these differences have an insignificant impact on project-loan average life, such that we would advocate the continued application of the current default curve.

Chapter 12

Valuing the Prepayment and Credit Risks of Commercial Mortgage Securities

Michael Youngblood, Ph.D.
Managing Director
Banc of America Securities LLC

The market for multifamily and commercial mortgage securities has grown dramatically in the 1990s, from a meager $5.7 billion in 1990 to $170.7 billion in the first quarter of 1999. Such vigorous issuance has provided investors with a wide range of opportunities, spanning virtually all investment grades (from AAA rated to unrated), intermediate and long maturities, fixed and floating interest rates, and property types. In addition, it has enlarged the secondary market for multifamily and commercial mortgage securities. Nevertheless, the proliferation of multifamily and commercial mortgage securities should not obscure the risks to which they expose investors. Greater liquidity does not necessarily mean lower risk, as the markets for high-yield securities and syndicated bank loans attest. The primary risks facing investors are prepayment or default of one or more of the underlying mortgage loans. These events could result in reinvestment of principal at lower interest rates and or in outright loss of expected interest or principal, or both. Even if a subordinated class or cash reserve fund should absorb any loss, the elevated cash flow variability or the reduction in available credit enhancement could widen yield spreads and undermine performance. These are, obviously, the primary risks of single-family mortgage securities as well, although the much larger size of the underlying loans and the much smaller number of them magnify these risks for multifamily and commercial mortgage securities.

Consider the most salient examples of the risk of prepayment and default of these securities in recent years:

- One $122 million privately-placed floating-rate multifamily security, issued in June 1993 and maturing in August 1998, was refinanced two years later. Ironically, the borrower used the same collateral to support a new $125 million fixed-rate security, maturing in 2015, in July 1996.

189

- Cumulative losses have exhausted the $122.2 million reserve fund of Resolution Trust Corporation, Series 1991-M2, leaving a single $51.9 million subordinated class to protect $151.6 million of senior classes from future losses (as of the July 1996 remittance report). In light of the vulnerability of the senior classes, Moody's Investors Service and Standard & Poor's Rating Group have sliced the original ratings from Aa1/AA or Aa2/AA to Baa3/B.
- The first two non-RTC multifamily securities issued in the 1990s have effectively failed. The rating of very first security tumbled from AA in 1991 to D (Standard & Poor's) in July 1996, as the most senior class incurred losses of $1.7 million, or 3.1% of the unpaid principal balance, after the utter depletion of the subordinated classes. To forestall potentially huge investor losses, the issuer of the second non-agency security of 1991 repurchased all of its senior classes in 1994. The ratings on this security and one other, which was also repurchased, were withdrawn before they could be cut.

The poor performance of these landmark issues, three of which contributed prominently to re-establishing the non-agency multifamily market in 1991, after its virtual dissolution in the late 1980s, highlights the risks inherent in multifamily and commercial securities.

We can evaluate the risks of prepayment and default of multifamily mortgage loans and securities through the same option-theoretic approach that has evolved to evaluate them for single-family mortgage loans and securities. This approach has evolved from the seminal work of Black and Scholes,[1] Merton,[2] and Cox, Ingersoll, and Ross,[3] and from continuous refinements by Fabozzi and practitioners over the past decade. In this chapter, we focus exclusively on multifamily loans and securities to illustrate the approach. We focus here on prepayment and default of multifamily mortgage loans rather than securities because the former necessarily leads to the latter. And the operation of non-agency credit enhancement in absorbing losses on the loans underlying multifamily securities requires no explanation to institutional investors. While using a common option-theoretic approach, we need to adjust for certain fundamental differences between multifamily and residential loans, borrowers, and properties. By adjusting for these differences, we can specify the multifamily (and, without loss of generality, commercial) prepayment and default functions that allow optional valuation under Monte Carlo or binomial simulation of an interest rate process.

---

[1] Fischer Black and Myron Scholes, "The Pricing of Options and Corporate Liabilities," *Journal of Political Economy*, 81 (1972), pp. 637-54.

[2] Robert Merton, "Theory of Rational Option Pricing," *Bell Journal of Economics and Management Science*, 4 (1973), pp. 141-83.

[3] J.C. Cox, J.E. Ingersoll Jr., and S.A. Ross, "A Theory of the Term Structure of Interest Rates," *Econometrica*, 53 (1985), pp. 385-407.

CONSTRAINTS ON PREPAYMENT

Multifamily and residential mortgage loans differ fundamentally in their terms and conditions. Multifamily mortgage loans generally amortize over terms of 240 to 360 months, with a final balloon payment of principal due in 60 to 240 months. Some loans amortize fully over terms of 300 to 360 months, with no balloon payment. Some loans do not amortize at all, but pay only interest until the final maturity date. Most loans have significant constraints on prepayment before maturity, which can take many forms:

- lock-out periods, which absolutely prohibit prepayment and which may be succeeded by further constraints.
- yield maintenance premiums that require the borrower to pay the present value of the change in the yield of a specified Treasury note between closing date and prepayment date, depriving him or her of any pure interest-rate incentive to refinance; variations in calculating these premiums may reduce the borrower's disincentive.
- prepayment penalties, expressed as a percentage of the unpaid principal balance of the loan, which typically decline as the loan approaches maturity.
- defeasance provisions, which do not permit prepayment of the underlying mortgage loan until its scheduled balloon or maturity date, but which allow the borrower to substitute a portfolio of U.S. Treasuries which match the scheduled payments of principal and interest.

Loans that do allow the borrower to prepay, subject to constraints like these, usually require payment in full and explicitly prohibit partial payment. In contrast, the huge majority of single-family mortgage loans, whether fixed-rate or adjustable-rate, amortize over 15- or 30-year terms. (Of course, the comparatively small number of residential balloon loans amortize over 360 months, with final payments of principal due in five or seven years.) Single-family loans generally permit prepayment in full or in part at any time without penalty.

RATIONAL EXERCISE OF OPTIONS

The multifamily borrower has invested equity in and raised debt on the security of the apartment property solely to obtain the after-tax real financial returns that it generates, in the form of periodic income and ultimate proceeds from sale. In maximizing the return on equity, the borrower, who is rarely an individual and usually a partnership or corporation, will act rationally to prepay or to default on the mortgage loan. In contrast, residential borrowers usually derive housing services as well as financial returns from the equity and debt invested in a house; the physical or emotional value of housing services may outweigh the investment returns. Hence, the residential borrower may not act rationally to maximize return on investment. Moreover, individuals generally lack access to the full information about alternative returns from investment or costs of debt that institutional borrowers generally possess, which ignorance may contribute to evidently irrational actions.

The multifamily borrower will generally prepay the mortgage loan, subject to the constraints set forth in the related note or deed of trust, when the present value of the scheduled payments exceeds the present value of payments on a new loan under whatever terms may prevail in the future, plus transaction and other costs. If the borrower seeks to prepay when yield maintenance or prepayment penalties are required by the note, then these payments will effectively increase the present value of the alternative loan. Similarly, the borrower will incur substantial upfront costs in refinancing a multifamily mortgage loan, which will overtly increase the present value of the alternative loan. These expenses include:

- the fees to the commercial loan broker who located the lender of the new loan (1% to 3% of the new loan amount)
- commitment fees and other "inducements" to the lender (1% to 5%)
- the title insurance policy or its equivalent (1%)
- fees for a FFIEC-eligible appraisal, engineering report, and Phase I environment assessment
- legal fees, including those for recordation

The last two typically represent 0.50% of the new loan amount. It is estimated that borrowers incur transactions costs, on average, of 5% of the new loan amount. These average transaction costs are roughly equivalent to an additional 1% on the annual interest rate of a 10-year non-amortizing balloon mortgage loan. In sharp contrast, residential borrowers can obtain new loans for average points and fees of 1.50%, or less, of the loan amount.

Furthermore, the engineering report and Phase I environment assessment may reveal deferred maintenance, or violations of building codes, or environmental hazards. These may range from the innocuous, i.e., potholes in the parking lot, to the pathological, i.e., friable "popcorn" asbestos sprayed on a significant proportion of the interior surface of an apartment building. If these conditions impair the current or future value of the building, then the lender will routinely require the borrower to cure these conditions. The lender will always require cure of building code violations, without which the borrower cannot obtain a certificate of occupancy. The lender may not agree to advance any or all of the funds needed to cure these conditions, which would present the borrower with additional upfront expenditures, further inflating the present value of alternative credit. Together, prepayment penalties, transactions costs, and deferred maintenance expenditures set a high threshold on prepayment that can deter the borrower from prepayment.

Prepayment Function

In light of these considerations, we can define the *prepayment function* as the relationship between the present value of the existing loan under the terms set forth in the mortgage note, and the present value of an alternative mortgage loan under whatever terms lenders may offer in the future. The prepayment function discounts the principal and interest payments scheduled under the original loan by current interest rates, plus the average risk premium or yield spread that lenders currently charge for comparable loans as expressed mathematically below:

$$\Pi_0 = \sum_{i=0}^{T} (P_i + I_i)\left(1 + \frac{r_0 + s}{2}\right)^{-2t_i} \tag{1}$$

where

Π_0 = the original loan amount
P_i = the scheduled principal payment of period i
I_i = the scheduled interest payment of period i
T = the final period
r_0 = the base rate at origination (month 0)
t_i = the time to receive principal and inters payments of period i
s = the risk premium

It also discounts the principal and interest payments scheduled under the alternative loan by the interest rates that prevail in the future, plus the same risk premium, and then adds prepayment penalties, transaction costs, and deferred maintenance expenditures as expressed below:

$$\sum_{i=0}^{T} (P_i + I_i)\left(1 + \frac{r_{i_0} + s}{2}\right)^{-2\left(t_i - t_{i_0}\right)} = \Pi_{i_0} + PP_{i_0} + PTC_0 + DM_0 \tag{2}$$

where:

$T, t_i, s, P_i,$ and I_i are the same as above
r_i = the discount rate at i_0
     = the alternative loan amount at i_0
PP_{i_0} = the prepayment penalty at i_0
PTC_0 = the prepayment transaction cost
DM_0 = deferred maintenance expenditures

If the value of first term of the inequality, the existing loan, exceeds that of the second term, the alternative loan, then the borrower should prepay, presumably in the following month.

The rationality of the borrower simplifies this part of the valuation of multifamily loans relative to that of residential loans. One does not need to introduce an econometric model to estimate the likelihood or rate of non-rational prepayment as one does with residential loans. One needs only to solve the prepayment function in conjunction with an appropriate interest-rate process.

UNDERSTANDING THE BORROWER'S DECISION

Unlike the residential borrower who acquires a house as a shelter and as an investment, the multifamily borrower acquires an apartment property only as an investment. He or she acquires the property, with a mixture of equity and debt, in order to receive the monthly *net operating income* and the proceeds from eventual sale that it will generate. Net operating income is the cash that remains after deducting the opportunity cost of vacant units and the operating expenses of a property from its gross possible income.[4] It does not include deductions for accounting depreciation or debt service payments. Most real estate investors calculate the expected return on equity and debt from net operating income and sale proceeds, using one of the many forms of the *discounted cash flow approach*.

However, the borrower does not receive net operating income, but rather the residual cash that remains after payment of scheduled principal and interest and of escrows for property taxes, insurance premiums, replacement reserves, and other impounds. Indeed, multifamily loans sometimes require the apartment manager to remit all rents, late payment penalties, deposit forfeitures, and other collections directly to a lock box, which the lender controls. The lender will remit to the borrower only the residual amount that remains after payment of all amounts due. Similarly, the borrower does not receive all of the proceeds from the eventual sale of the property, but rather the residual cash after repaying the unamortized loan amount. No lender will release the title on sale of a property until payment of the remaining loan amount, any interest accrued but not yet paid, and any late payment penalties outstanding.

Therefore, the borrower should expect to receive the present values of the monthly net income from the property and the net proceeds from sale. The present values of the net income and the net proceeds will jointly determine the borrower's decision each month over the life of the mortgage loan either to make principal and interest payments, and other mandatory payments, or to default. Understanding this monthly decision is essential to the analysis that follows: the valuation of the borrower's option to default depends on both the net income and the net proceeds. Unless net income falls below zero (when net operating income is less than principal and interest payments), the borrower will not default, even if the present value of net proceeds is negative (when the market value of the property is less than the loan amount). Monthly net income must fall below zero *and* the market value of the property must fall below that of the loan balance.

---

[4] See Charles Wurtzebach and Mike Miles, *Modern Real Estate*, 4th ed. (New York: John Wiley, 1991), pp. 206-211.

Furthermore, the borrower will include transaction costs in the monthly decision to pay or to default on the loan. Whereas one can quantify the transaction costs incurred in prepayment, one cannot precisely quantify those incurred in default because they include three components that vary widely among borrowers:

• decreased availability and increased cost of future debt and equity
• lender recourse to the borrower
• federal income tax liability

First, some lenders do not extend credit to real estate borrowers with a history of uncured defaults. Those who do extend credit to such borrowers routinely impose more stringent terms; these terms may become onerous for borrowers with a history of opportunistic default. Second, fewer loans originated in the 1990s than heretofore allow recourse to the borrower in the event of default. The declining popularity of recourse provisions belongs, in part, to fierce competition from conduits and other non-traditional lenders and, in part, to the legal form of many borrowers. If the borrower takes the legal form of a limited partnership or a special purpose corporation, the mortgaged property may be the only asset. Where recourse provisions exist, the borrower must weigh the likelihood of the loss of other assets in addition to those explicitly pledged in the mortgage note. One cannot measure the value of these assets, or the lender's ability to locate and attach them. Third, the borrower will incur a federal income tax liability equal to the difference between the loan amount and the property value. The value of this difference to the borrower depends upon his or her marginal income tax rate and other considerations, which one does not know.

Nevertheless, one can estimate the loss of operating funds, the forfeiture of property, and certain expenses:

• operating income from the property until definitive foreclosure
• working capital, accounts receivable, and escrows
• furniture, fixtures, and equipment used to furnish or manage the property
• management fees for operating the property
• legal fees, which increase if the borrower also files for bankruptcy

Offsetting these costs, the borrower may retain rents, late payment fees, and other miscellaneous income collected over several months, until the lender can accelerate the mortgage note and take control of the property. We estimate that these transaction costs average 7.0% of the loan amount.

Default Function

In light of these considerations, one can define the *default function* from two simultaneous relationships:

• monthly net operating income less scheduled principal and interest, and other payments over the term of the *loan*

- the present value of monthly net operating income over the life of the *property*, plus transaction costs, less the present value of scheduled principal (including the final balloon) and interest, and other payments over the term of the loan

As long as the first relationship remains positive, the borrower will not default. He or she has sufficient income to pay monthly debt service, and, bolstered by the endemic optimism of real estate investors, will continue to make scheduled payments even if the second relationship has turned negative. As long as the second relationship remains positive, the borrower will not default. He or she retains the excess of the property value over the loan amount, or positive equity. If the first relationship turns negative, then he or she can sell the property, repay the outstanding loan, thereby avoiding default, and realize the amount of positive equity. This relationship reveals an important aspect of the default option on mortgage loans: the loan amount represents the price at which the borrower can sell, in effect, the property to the lender at any time in the future, should equity become negative. When the first and second relationships turn negative, the borrower will default. He or she lacks the income to pay scheduled monthly principal and interest, while the future value of the property, plus transaction costs, has fallen below the loan amount, leaving negative equity.

Rents, Vacancies, and Operating Expenses

The default function of the first relationship compares net operating income to scheduled payments of principal and interest, and escrows. Hence, it requires projection of net operating income as the sum of gross possible rents, the opportunity cost of vacant units, and operating expenses, for each month over the term of the loan. We project future rents as a function of employment growth, income growth, population growth, household formation, housing affordability, net change in the stock of apartments, the natural vacancy rate — all from the housing sub-market in which the property is located — and future 10-year Treasury rates. We estimate the opportunity cost of vacant units from the *natural vacancy rate*, as developed by Rosen and Smith[5] as an equilibrium function of historical rents and operating expenses. Last, we project future operating expenses from their historical correlation with rents. Like the prepayment function, the default function discounts the scheduled principal and interest payments, and other payments, on the loan by the interest rates that prevail in the future, plus the initial risk premium or spread charged by the lender. Therefore, we can project both the net operating income from the property, over the life of the property, and the scheduled payments, over the term of the loan, given an interest rate process.

Similarly, the default function of the second relationship discounts monthly net operating income over the life of the property by the interest rates

---

[5] Kenneth Rosen and Lawrence B. Smith, "The Price-Adjustment Process for Rental Housing and the Natural Vacancy Rate," *American Economic Review*, vol. 73 (1983), pp. 779-786, and Lawrence B. Smith, "A Note on the Price Adjustment Mechanism for Rental Housing," *American Economic Review*, vol. 64 (1974), pp. 478-481.

that prevail in the future, plus the multifamily risk premium. We project net operating income as before over the expected *economic life* of the property, which we obtain the from the mandatory FFIEC-eligible appraisal or engineering report. A new apartment property has an expected economic life of 50 years, assuming that rehabilitation does not extend it, but most of the apartment properties underlying multifamily (and mixed-property commercial) securities are not new, which reduces the term over which they can generate net operating income.

The default function of the second relationship discounts the net operating income by the interest rates expected to prevail in the future, plus a multifamily risk premium. The multifamily risk premium is the entrepreneurial return that the borrower requires for investing equity and debt in the apartment property. We measure it by the spread between the *yield capitalization rate* of the property and the interest rates that prevailed at origination of the mortgage loan. The yield capitalization rate is the internal rate of return that equated the appraised or sales value of the apartment property, at the time of the origination of the mortgage loan, to the future net operating income that it may generate over its economic life, assuming no rehabilitation.[6]

Therefore, default occurs in any month i_0 over the term of the mortgage loan, if both of the following relationships are satisfied:

$$NOI_{i_0} < P_{i_0} + I_{i_0} + E_{i_0} \tag{3}$$

$$\sum_{i=i0}^{EL} NOI_i \left(1 + \frac{r_{i_0} + ycr}{2}\right)^{-2(t_i - t_0)} + DTC_0$$

$$- \sum_{i=i_0}^{T-1} (P_i + I_i + E_i)\left(1 + \frac{r_{i_0} + s}{2}\right)^{-2(t_i - t_0)} < 0 \tag{4}$$

where:

NOI_{i_0} = a (future) payment of net operating income, from the rent process, at period i

r_{i_0} = the discount rate at period i_0

ycr = the discount mortgage risk premium

P_i = the scheduled principal payment of period i

I_i = the scheduled interest payment of period i

T = the final period in the term of the mortgage loan

EL = the final period in the economic life of the property

r_0 = the base rate at origination (month 0)

t_i = the time to receive principal and inters payments of period i

s = the risk premium

DTC_i = default transactions costs at period i

---

[6] See Kenneth M. Lusht and Jeffrey D. Fisher, "Anticipated Growth and the Specification of Debt in Real Estate Value Models," *AREUEA Journal*, vol. 12 (1984), pp. 1-11.

Alternatively, we can re-write equation (4) such that default occurs if the following inequality obtains:

$$\frac{\sum_{i=i0}^{EL} NOI_i \left(1 + \dfrac{r_{i_0} + ycr}{2}\right)^{-2(t_i - t_0)} + DTC_0}{\sum_{i=i_0}^{T-1} (P_i + I_i + E_i) \left(1 + \dfrac{r_{i_0} + s}{2}\right)^{-2(t_i - t_0)}} < 1 \tag{5}$$

If the ratio of present value of the property, plus default transaction costs, to the present value of the mortgage loan falls below 1 and if the relationship in equation (3) is less than zero, then the borrower will default.

INTEGRATING PREPAYMENT AND DEFAULT EXPERIENCE

The default and prepayment functions assume the same interest rate process, which generates the future interest rates that discount both the principal and interest payments of the mortgage loan and the net operating income of the apartment property. For the interest rate process, we employ a proprietary multifactor model of the term structure. We begin with the discount rate of the on-the-run 1-month Treasury bill and generate a series of 1-month arbitrage-free forward rates that extend over the entire Treasury yield curve, i.e., over 360 months. We calibrate these rates so that they recover, or produce the exact prices of, the on-the-run Treasury coupon curve. These are the future interest rates described in the two previous sections. Generating these rates requires the on-the-run Treasury yield curve and a measure of interest-rate volatility for each of the 360 months. To provide the monthly volatilities, we interpolate the term structure of volatility from the series of average implied volatilities of puts and calls on (U.S. dollar) interest rate swaps, which range from one week to 10 years in term. Furthermore, we can generate a full path of 360 arbitrage-free riskless discount rates for any sequence of 360 monthly volatilities that we may produce with Monte Carlo or other methods.[7]

By applying the default and prepayment functions simultaneously to the path of forward discount rates generated by this process, we can simulate the borrower's decision to default on or prepay any multifamily loan in the present or any future month. Indeed, we can value the borrower's options to default and to prepay by simulating these decisions over all possible paths of forward discount rates. While this comprehensive simulation would require infinite calculations, we can achieve equivalent valuation of the borrower's options by simulating a finite set of paths of forward discount rates that achieves a normal distribution, using established tests with appropriate size and power for the normal distribution.

---

[7] See Frank J. Fabozzi, *Valuation of Fixed Income Securities and Derivatives* (New Hope, PA: Frank J. Fabozzi Associates, 1995), pp. 131-154.

To value the options to default and to prepay, we simulate the borrower's rational decisions over a sufficiently large set of discount rate paths in the following sequence:

- Decompose the loan amount into its scheduled monthly payments of principal and interest over months (t) of its remaining term, and its balloon payment, if any, at term (T).
- Re-price the loan, using the appropriate on-the-run Treasury note, plus a risk premium, which is the average yield spread charged by lenders on comparable loans for the same term.
- Solve for the Z-spread of the loan, using current forward discount rates.
- Calculate the present value of the loan over every month in its term with the associated forward discount rate plus the Z-spread.
- Over every path, calculate the present value of the loan over every month with the associated forward discount rate plus the Z-spread.
- Compare the present value of the loan, obtained using current rates, with the present value of the loan (plus prepayment penalties, prepayment transaction costs, and deferred maintenance expenditures) in each path, using path-specific rates; if the conditions of equation (1) obtain in any month in any path, prepay the unamortized principal balance.
- Decompose the property value into its projected net operating income over months (t) of its expected economic life (EL).
- Solve for the yield capitalization rate and the related Z-spread of the mortgaged property, using the contemporary appraised value or sales price, and current forward discount rates.
- Calculate the present value of the property over every month with the associated forward discount rate plus the Z-spread.
- Compare the present value of the property, obtained using current rates (plus default transaction costs) with the present value of the loan in each path, using path-specific rates; if the conditions of equations (3) and (4) or (3) and (5) obtain in any month in any path, default the mortgage loan.
- Integrate the principal and interest payments over every month and every path; then solve for that risk-adjusted spread to the discount rates in every path that produces an average loan price equal to price of the loan.

CREDIT RISK OPTION-ADJUSTED SPREAD

This approach to the simultaneous valuation of the borrower's options to prepay and default enables us to solve for the option-adjusted spread (OAS) or, more precisely, the credit risk option-adjusted spread (CROAS) of a multifamily mortgage loan. Solution of CROAS requires only two steps, assuming the prior simulation of arbitrage-free forward discount rates along a sufficiently large number of paths. First, we integrate the principal and interest payments that result from allowing rational prepayment and default in every month over the term of the loan and over every path of forward discount rates. One series of payments, from origination to termination of the loan, corresponds to each path of discount rates. Second, we solve iteratively (by trial and error) for the spread, that added to the forward rates along each path, will discount each series of monthly payments to its present value, the average of which equals the current price of the loan (plus accrued interest). The semi-annual bond-equivalent of this spread is the CROAS in the equation below:

$$P + I = \sum_{i=0}^{N} \sum_{j=0}^{T} (PF_{i,j} + IF_{i,j}) \times D_i \times \prod_{i=d}^{i+d} \left(1 + \frac{r_{i,j} + s'}{12}\right)$$ (6)

$$s = 2 \times \left[\left(1 + \frac{y' + s'}{12}\right)^6 - \left(1 + \frac{y}{2}\right)\right]$$

where

P = the price
I = the accrued interest
N = the number of paths
T = the number of months to maturity
$PF_{i,j}$ = the principal cash flow in ith path and jth month
$IF_{i,j}$ = the interest cash flow in ith path and jth month
D_i = the extra discount factor in ith path due to fractional month of the cash flow's timing
$r_{i,j}$ = the 1-month Treasury rate (30/360) in ith path and jth month
y' = the mortgage-equivalent 10-year
s' = the CROAS expressed in mortgage equivalent term (12 month compounding)
y = the bond-equivalent 10-year Treasury yield
s = the CROAS expressed in bond equivalent term (semi-annual compounding)

This CROAS is directly comparable to the OAS of any mortgage or non-mortgage security evaluated using the same interest rate process.

Furthermore, we can calculate the first and second derivatives of the price and CROAS of the multifamily loan with respect to the term structures of interest rates and volatility: *effective duration, convexity, volatility sensitivity, volatility convexity*, and so on. We calculate these additional parameters of value by numerical methods, changing the term structures of interest rates or of (average implied swaption) volatility. For *effective duration*, we increase the term structure of discount rates by any arbitrary magnitude, for example, 25 basis points, for all paths and solve for the average price that results. We then decrease the term structure by the same magnitude for all paths and solve for the average price that results. The difference between the two average prices that result, scaled by the change in basis points and the current price, is the effective duration of the mortgage loan as shown in equation (7).

$$D = \frac{\Delta P}{2P\Delta y} = \frac{P_+ - P_-}{2P\Delta y} \tag{7}$$

where

D = the duration
C = the convexity
P = the current price
P_+ = the projected price when the yield curve is up by Δy
P_- = the projected price when the yield curve is down by Δy

Equation (7) measures the sensitivity of the price of the loan to a change in the term structure of interest rates, unlike the modified duration of an option-free securities, which measures the sensitivity of the price to a change in yield. The second derivative of price with respect to the term structure of interest rates, *convexity*, follows directly from this calculation. It is the effective duration scaled by the current price multiplied by the square of the same change in interest rates as shown in equation (8).[8]

$$C = \frac{\Delta^2 P}{100P\Delta y^2} = \frac{P_+ - 2P + P_-}{100P\Delta y^2} \tag{8}$$

We calculate the volatility sensitivity and the volatility convexity of the mortgage loan in the same way.

A MULTIFAMILY EXAMPLE

Consider the example of a representative multifamily mortgage loan, which was underwritten to FNMA DUS standards and originated in August 1996. FNMA's underwriting standards for the DUS program are representative of those employed by most institutional lenders; indeed, most conduit lenders have openly embraced these standards for their multifamily programs for the expedient reason that the rating agencies and institutional investors generally accept them. The lender furnished the following limited information about the loan and the related property:

---

[8] Andrew Kalotay, George Williams, and Frank J. Fabozzi, "A Model for Valuing Bonds and Embedded Options," *Financial Analysts Journal* (May-June 1993), pp. 35-46, and Fabozzi, *Valuation of Fixed Income Securities and Derivatives*, pp. 93-130.

Property city, state, and zip code:	Houston, TX 77077
Principal balance amount:	$8,000,000
Mortgage interest rate:	8.42%
Maturity date:	8/1/2006
Original amortization term:	30 years
Prepayment premium option:	Yield maintenance
Yield maintenance period:	7.0 years
U.S. Treasury yield rate:	5.625%
Security due date:	2/1/2006
Total number of units:	436
Annual net operating income:	$951,904
Loan-to-value ratio:	79.21%
Appraised value:	$10,100,000
Occupancy:	92%
Debt service coverage ratio:	1.29×

From our own analysis of the Briar Forest sub-market, in which this property is located, and our econometric models of the apartment market in metropolitan Houston, we add the following to FNMA's information:

Risk premium of DUS Tier II loans:	1.67%
Yield capitalization rate:	13.00
Long-term rent growth rate:	3.26
Long-term rent volatility:	6.86
Natural vacancy rate:	11.20
Prepayment transaction costs:	5.00
Default transaction costs:	7.00

From this information and our projections of rent growth, rent volatility, and the natural vacancy rate for the apartment property, we calculate the following parameters of risk and value:

Frequency of prepayments:	11.3%
Average months to prepayment:	83
Average prepayment price:	107-04 (32s)
Option Cost:	9 b.p.
Frequency of defaults:	20.7%
Average months to default:	82
Average loss severity:	27.1%
Option cost:	45 b.p.
Z-spread:	166 b.p.
Prepayment and default option cost:	54 b.p.
CROAS:	112 b.p.
Effective duration:	6.08 years
Convexity:	0.30

This multifamily mortgage loan has an 11.3% probability of prepaying and a 20.7% probability of defaulting over its 10-year term. The probabilities of prepayment and default combine to reduce the nominal and Z-spreads of this mortgage loan by 54 basis points to a CROAS of 112 basis points. Similarly, the effective duration of the loan, which reflects the combined risks, is 6.08 years, whereas the modified duration of the loan, which assumes neither prepayment nor default, is somewhat longer, 6.25 years.

It is striking that the frequency of default and the average severity of loss projected on this multifamily loan, which was underwritten to common institutional standards, fall within the ranges of default and loss experienced historically by mainstream institutional lenders. From his most recent study of the historical performance of commercial mortgage loans originated by life insurance companies in the years 1972-1991, Synderman finds an aggregate lifetime rate of default of 13.8%.[9] However, Synderman concedes that the historical default rate is artificially low, because many of the loans in the insurance company sample remain outstanding — they have yet to default or mature. After adjustment, he projects an 18.3% lifetime default rate. Similarly, on reviewing Synderman's first two studies, Fitch Investors Service noticed that the widespread restructuring of loans by life companies reduced the frequency of default.[10] Based on this review and a separate study of the commercial mortgage portfolios of 11 life companies, Fitch projects a much higher lifetime default rate of 30%. This level forms the baseline for its rating of commercial mortgage securities. It is also consistent with the default rate projected on the representative multifamily mortgage loan.

In addition, Synderman finds that the severity of loss of commercial mortgage loans (measured as a percentage of the unpaid principal balance) varies widely by the origination year, from a low of −7% in 1972 to a high of 96% in 1984. He concludes that the severity of loss averaged 33% in the 1970s and 45% in the 1980s; the average yield cost of default was 50 basis points. Fitch adopts the average loss severity of the 1980s, projecting a loss factor of 40% to 50% for defaulted commercial mortgage loans. As with default frequency, the loss severity projected on the representative multifamily loan is consistent with the historical experience of mainstream commercial lenders. Indeed, Synderman's estimate of the yield cost of default of 50 basis points is virtually the same as the yield cost of default of 45 basis points on this multifamily loan.

MODEL SENSITIVITIES

We can explore the risks of this multifamily mortgage loan in greater depth by calculating the sensitivity of the CROAS to its salient parameters: *loan-to-value ratio, debt service coverage ratio, term to maturity of the loan, long-term rent growth rate, long-term rent volatility,* and *natural vacancy rate.* By exploring the partial derivatives of these parameters to CROAS, we expose the influence on the likelihood of prepayment and default of the underwriting criteria, the terms and conditions of the loan itself, and the local property market (see Exhibit 1). Accordingly, we vary each parameter across a wide, but arbitrary range of values

---

[9] Mark Synderman, "Update on Commercial Mortgage Defaults," *Real Estate Finance Journal* (Summer 1994), pp. 22-32.
[10] Fitch Investors Service, Inc., "Commercial Mortgage Stress Test," *Structured Finance* (June 8, 1992), pp. 1-12.

and record the CROAS that results, in the form of basis points and price; we hold all other parameters and the price of the loan constant.

- Increases in the loan-to-value ratio (LTV), by diminishing the borrower's equity and increasing his or her leverage, decrease CROAS modestly. A decline in LTV from 79.8% to 55% increases CROAS from 112 basis points to 136 basis points. Decreases in LTV increase CROAS symmetrically.
- Increases in the debt service coverage ratio (DSCR) increase CROAS slightly less than the given changes in LTV. An increase from 1.29× to 2.5× DSCR would increase CROAS from 112 basis points to 131 basis points. Decreases in DSCR also affect CROAS symmetrically.
- Term to maturity affects CROAS inversely: the longer the term of the loan, the lower CROAS. This inverse relationship reflects the operation of volatility; the longer a loan remains outstanding, the broader the range of rental growth rates, including negative rates, that may occur. Term to maturity affects most options in this fashion, especially the short-term exchange-traded financial options that the Black-Scholes or Black futures models evaluate accurately. Indeed, given the unambiguously positive influence that shorter terms have on CROAS, it is paradoxical that the four rating agencies penalize loans with them, requiring more credit enhancement than for otherwise identical loans with longer terms.

Exhibit 1: Sensitivity of Parameters and Terms of Multifamily Mortgage Loan Expressed as CROAS (in basis points and price in 32s)

The influence of these parameters on CROAS reveals its acute vulnerability to the initial equity and leverage of the borrower, and to the conditions of the local market. Investors will need to scrutinize carefully loans with LTVs above 85% or DSCRs below 1.2%, and loans with underlying properties located in volatile real estate markets.

LTV (%)	100	95	90	85	Base 79.8	75	70	65	60	55
CROAS (b.p.)	83	91	99	106	112	120	125	129	133	136
CROAS (32s)	4-24	4-10	3-27	3-15	3-05	2-21+	2-14	2-05	1-30+	1-25
DSCR	0.90	1.00	1.10	1.20	1.29	1.40	1.50	1.75	2.00	2.50
CROAS (b.p.)	94	102	109	110	112	116	117	122	126	131
CROAS (32s)	4-02+	3-21	3-09	3-07	3-05	2-30	2-27	2-19	2-12	2-03+
Term (Years)	30	25	20	15	10	7	5	3	2	1
CROAS (b.p.)	52	54	59	76	112	128	130	143	184	229
CROAS (32s)	5-24+	5-21+	5-11	4-18+	3-05	2-17+	2-11	1-19	0-23+	0-08+
Rent Growth (%)	−1.0	0.0	1.0	2.0	3.3	4.0	4.5	5.0	5.5	6.0
CROAS (b.p.)	42	64	81	98	112	123	127	131	134	137
CROAS (32s)	15-28+	5-20+	4-25+	3-28	3-05	2-16	2-08+	2-02	1-29	1-22+
Rent Vol (%)	25.0	20.0	15.0	10.0	6.9	5.9	4.9	3.9	2.9	1.9
CROAS (b.p.)	−83	−35	11	77	112	128	137	144	150	154
CROAS (32s)	12-21	10-14	8-08	5-00	3-05	2-07+	1-23+	1-10+	0-29+	0-23+

Exhibit 2: Structure of Evans Withycombe Finance Trust, August 1994 (Dollars in Millions)

Class	Amount	Coupon (%)	Maturity	Call Date
A-1 (Senior)	102.0	7.98	8/1/2001	3/1/2001
A-2 (Sub.)	15.0	7.98	8/1/2001	3/1/2001
A-3 (Sub.)	9.0	7.98	8/1/2001	3/1/2001
A-4 (Sub.)	5.0	7.98	8/1/2001	3/1/2001

- The long-term rent growth rate affects CROAS strongly and asymmetrically. An increase from 3.26% to 6.0% increases CROAS from 112 basis points to 137 basis points, but a decrease to −1% drops CROAS to 42 basis points. It is noteworthy that the rent growth rate crosses a threshold of sensitivity below 2%. From 2% to 0%, the rent growth rate cannot overcome the influence of the projected 6.9% volatility, which propagates enough simulated negative growth rates to render CROAS consistently negative. Of course, below 0%, negative growth rates predominate with commensurate effects on CROAS.
- Long-term rent volatility affects CROAS even more strongly than the rent growth rate. It governs the range of potential growth rates associated with the simulated forward discount rates, in effect, raising or lowering the influence of interest rates on rents. High levels of volatility will propagate over time broader ranges of rent growth rates, including negative rates, that ultimately turn CROAS negative.
- The natural vacancy rate acts asymmetrically on CROAS. Increasing vacancy rates diminish CROAS more than increasing ones inflate CROAS. It is particularly striking that CROAS declines very rapidly once the vacancy rate exceed 25%.

APPLYING THE MODEL: AN EXAMPLE

The analysis of this representative multifamily mortgage loan leads directly to that of non-agency multifamily and, by extension, commercial mortgage securities. It enables one to quantify the risks of prepayment and default of the underlying mortgage loans, and to measure the adequacy of the credit enhancement provided by the security. Consider a truly exemplary multifamily mortgage security, the Evans Withycombe Finance Trust, which was issued in August 1994 by a special purpose Delaware limited partnership, which is, in turn, wholly-owned by a publicly-held real estate investment trust. The multifamily security consists of four classes, one senior (A-1) and three subordinate (A-2, A-3, and A-4), all totaling $131 million (see Exhibit 2). The three subordinated classes, which total $29 million and represent 22.1% of the principal balance, protect the senior class against loss from default on the underlying mortgage notes. Each class receives payment of interest sequentially at a 7.98% annualized rate; class A-1 receives interest, then A-2, and so on. The securities do not amortize and mature in August 2001; they cannot be prepaid in whole or in part until March 2001. Unusually, the servicer has no obligation to advance interest in the event that the borrower fails to pay on any due date.

The underlying collateral consists of 22 apartment properties, which are located in the Phoenix and Tucson metropolitan areas. They incorporate 5,380 apartments units, with 4.88 million square feet of rentable space; the average apartment size is roughly 907 square feet. The borrower describes the properties as "oriented to upscale residents seeking high levels of amenities, such as clubhouses, exercise rooms, tennis courts, swimming pools, therapy pools, and covered parking." The units rented for an average of $606 a month in the 12 months ending May 31, 1994, subject to a 92% economic occupancy rate. The apartments units were constructed between 1984 and 1990, leaving little scope for economic or functional obsolescence. A subsidiary of the public REIT manages the properties on behalf of the special purpose partnership. The underwriters estimated a debt service coverage ratio of 1.68× and a loan-to-value ratio of 54% at issuance of the security. After updating this information for current apartment market conditions in Phoenix and Tucson, we project a long-term rental growth rate of 2.3% on these properties, a long-term volatility of the rental growth rate of 4.3%, and a natural vacancy rate of 10%.

Assuming that dealers would offer the senior class A-1 at a nominal spread of 75 basis points over an interpolated Treasury note with a 4.7-year maturity, we calculate a CROAS of 74 basis points (see Exhibit 3). We estimate a zero probability of prepayment, given the absolute prohibition against it until March 2001, and a zero probability of default, given the high DSCR, low LTV, and favorable rental growth and volatility rates of the properties. Arbitrarily reducing the initial DSCR to 1.20× and raising the initial LTV to 80% would produce a 17.7% probability of default, and an 11% expected loss rate; the CROAS of class A-1 falls by six basis points to 68 basis points. Under this scenario, losses of 1.95% of the principal balance of the mortgage notes, or $2.55 million, would result. Losses of this magnitude would eliminate 51% of the A-4 subordinated class, but leave classes A-2 and A-3 intact. Arbitrarily reducing the initial DSCR to 1.0× and raising the initial LTV to 100% would produce a 47.5% probability of default and a 12.3% expected loss rate; the CROAS of class A-1 would fall by 106 basis points to −32 basis points. Under this scenario, losses of 5.84% of the principal balance of the mortgage notes, or $7.65 million, would result. Losses of this magnitude would eliminate the A-4 subordinated class entirely, and 29.5% of the A-3 class, but leave the A-2 class intact. The senior class would not suffer actual loss, but rather an erosion of relative value such that it would yield substantially less than a comparable Treasury note. Since extreme conditions must occur to undermine the performance of class A-1 to such an extent, we conclude that the credit enhancement for class A-1 more than compensates for the likely risk of default and may render class A-1 a candidate for upgrading from AA by Standard and Poor's.

Exhibit 3: Scenario Performance of Evans Withycombe Finance Trust, Class A-1

Scenario (DSCR / LTV)	Nominal Spread	CROAS	Loss Frequency (%)	Loss Severity (%)
1.68/54	75	74	0.0	0.0
1.20/80	75	68	17.7	11.0
1.00/100	75	-32	45.7	12.3

ADVANTAGES OF THE MODEL

The approach to joint valuation of the prepayment and default options of multi-family loans that we developed in this chapter offers the following important advantages over other approaches:

- It unifies the valuation of multifamily and commercial mortgage loans and securities with that of single-family mortgage loans and securities, by means of a common interest rate process. The simulation of arbitrage-free forward discount rates using the term structure of (average implied swaption) volatility along a sufficiently large number of paths by Monte Carlo methods provides the framework for discounting all monthly (or other periodic) future cash flows, whatever their source, commercial or residential, by appropriate risk premia. Hence, one can directly compare the usual first and second derivatives of price, rate, and volatility across the various types of loans and securities.

- It unifies the valuation of the mortgage loan and the related apartment property, by a more complex application of the common interest rate process. It discounts all future monthly cash flows, from loan or from property, by the same set of forward discount rates, plus respective risk premia. It offers thereby a framework capable of valuing a wide variety of financial instruments, not only mortgage loans and securities. Furthermore, it simulates the future net operating income from an apartment property as a function of economic and demographic variables, drawn from the local real estate sub-market, and the yield of the 10-year Treasury note. It thereby creates a direct link to forward 10-year discount rates and an indirect link through dynamic covariance coefficients for each economic and demographic variable to the 10-year rate. These coefficients will vary in size, sign, and lag. Hence, we can simulate the future net operating income for a property consistently with the simulation of future interest payments on alternative mortgage loans, which could lead to prepayment. In contrast, most other approaches simulate the value of the loan separately from the value of the property, using distinct stochastic processes. Accordingly, they may randomly associate future states of the property with future discount rates, propagating potentially aberrant relationships; one could find a very high growth rate or high variability of property price inflation associated with a very low discount rate.

- It estimates the value of the property by the function described above for each month of the term of the related loan, including the final balloon payment. Thus, it avoids recourse to an externally specified value of the property at maturity of the loan. The continuous internal determination of property value overcomes a critical weakness in the discounted cash flow approach that many lenders, borrowers, and appraisers use to value multifamily loans and properties: the arbitrary choice of the value of the property at maturity of the loan. Amid its countless variations, the discounted cash flow approach generally applies a constant discount rate, usually the yield of a comparable Treasury note plus a risk premium, to the projected annual net operating income and to the final sale price or market value of property, as of the maturity of the loan. This value is determined by capitalizing the projected net operating income in the last year at a projected rate. The projected capitalization rate is seldom derived by any methodology; rather, appraisers and others often use a rule of thumb, adding 1% or more to the initial capitalization rate, which is itself an average of capitalization rates sampled from recent sales or loans. Thus, the discounted cash flow method, thus, founders at a critical point in any valuation by arbitrary, if not randomly, selecting terminal property value.

- The continuous internal determination of the value of a specific property overcomes another critical weakness in the valuation of multifamily properties: the arbitrary choice of the rate of return or "building-payout rate." Those who evaluate the property by a pure stochastic process often assume that it will offer the same rate of return as did equity real estate investment trusts (REITs), i.e., 8%, over some arbitrary period of time such as 1980-1987. This choice of rate of return invites numerous objections. REITs provide investors with valuable liquidity, which permits a higher valuation and lower rate of return on the properties that they own. REITs represent many different property types, so that any average return will not reflect a return specific to apartment properties. REITs own different types of properties in different markets, allowing a smoothing of return by the natural covariance of returns across property types and markets, which again leads to imprecision in valuing an individual apartment property. REITs typically use much less debt than other real estate investors; lower leverage implies lower risk and, appropriately, lower returns to investors. Also, REITS provide professional management of income-producing properties that small apartment properties (36 units or less) may not, which would motivate investors generally to require higher returns and expect higher variance of returns from them. In contrast, our approach infers the yield capitalization rate of a specific property and the risk premium to current interest rates implied by this rate. It then adds the property-specific risk premium to the forward discount rates across all paths, which produces a different series of capitalization rates for each path. Therefore, our approach provides greater specificity as well as greater flexibility in the valuation of mortgaged properties.

- It estimates the incidence of default and loss on foreclosure by the same function. Default occurs when the two conditions of the default function occur simultaneously. The number of paths on which default occurs automatically furnishes the frequency of default. The delay between default and final foreclosure and sale, which we obtain by random draws from a normal distribution that assumes an average of 24 months and variance of five months, permits calculation of the accrued interest foregone. (To the accrued interest, we add additional foreclosure costs of 5% the loan balance, and deduct net operating income received from the property over the foreclosure period.) The loss on foreclosure of the property derives from the difference between the property value, 24 months or so after default, and the unpaid principal balance of the loan. Hence, the magnitude of loss arises from the internal operation of our approach to value. Of course, one can compare the incidence of default and severity of loss projected on any loan to the historical experience of comparable loans originated by life insurance companies, RTC-administered financial institutions, or agency multifamily portfolios.

- Finally, our approach offers a compromise in the persistent debate on the subject of *ruthless* versus *non-ruthless* default. Some contend that a borrower will rationally default on a property whenever its present value falls below that of the related mortgage loan, without consideration of transaction costs; hence, ruthless default. Any delay by the borrower in defaulting on the loan arises from his or her unwillingness to forego the persistent value of the option to default in the future, since the property value may continue to decline. (This decline magnifies the borrower's implicit gain and the lender's loss, because the loan amount fixes the strike price or tacit sales price of the property to the lender.) However, others contend that a borrower will rationally default on a property whenever its present value falls below that of the related loan, but will include transaction costs in assessing its value; hence, non-ruthless default. The borrower will not default as soon as the present value of the property falls bellow that of the loan, eliminating equity, but waits until negative equity should accumulate to the amount of observable and unobservable transaction costs.

- While our approach clearly incorporates transaction costs in anticipating the borrower's rational decision, it also tenders a compromise to the opponents in the debate. We contend that the borrower should default in any month when two conditions occur: when net operating income falls below scheduled debt payments and when property value falls below loan amount, eliminating the borrower's equity. In practice, the second condition occurs before the first. The present value of expected net operating income falls below the present value of scheduled mortgage payments before income falls below scheduled payments. Property value declines faster than loan value, in part, because net operating income is discounted with a much higher risk premium than is the mortgage payment. Accordingly, the borrower may have sufficient cash flow to make scheduled payments even though the property value has fallen below the loan amount, plus transactions costs. He or she will rationally delay default as long as net operating income continues to exceed scheduled monthly payments, even though equity is negative. Therefore, the future option to default consists only of the option to default before these cash flows decline to zero. Our approach conflates the value of the present and future options to default.

- Furthermore, those who conclude that the borrower has an option to default in the present and in the future must ignore the presence of the lender, who should act as rationally as the borrower. While few mortgage notes give the lender the ability to act unilaterally when the borrower's equity turns negative, all lenders have the legal right to accelerate the note and begin foreclosure as soon as the borrower fails to pay. The separate assignment of rents enhances the lender's ability to collect rents as soon as default occurs. Indeed, the lender will attempt to take possession of the property in order to forestall the borrower from optimizing the value of the option to default! The lender endeavors to obtain the property before its value falls below that of the loan, minimizing the value of default to the borrower. In most states, within three months of the first failure to pay scheduled principal and interest, the lender can obtain possession of, if not title to, the property and begin to receive net operating income. In conclusion, if a value to default in the future does exist, it consists either of the option to receive cash flow until it turns negative, or an option on property value from the month that cash flow turns negative until the lender assumes control of the property. These options have little time or intrinsic value, and we already incorporate them within our approach to valuation.

Chapter 13

The CMBS Market, Swap Spreads, and Relative Value

Brian P. Lancaster
Managing Director
Bear Stearns & Co. Inc.

The linkage between the CMBS market and interest rate swaps has grown dramatically over the past few years. This chapter clarifies the relationship between the CMBS and swap markets. We first cover the basics of the swap market. We then discuss the impact of the swaps market on the CMBS market. Finally we provide a quantitative analysis which shows that the 10-year swap has been the best predictor of 10-year triple-A CMBS spreads versus Treasuries since January 1998.

INTEREST RATE SWAPS

A standard or vanilla interest rate swap is merely a contractual agreement between two parties to exchange two sets of cash flows usually based on a fixed rate the other based on a floating rate (usually LIBOR). The cash flows are typically interest-only based upon a notional amount of principal from which the payments are calculated. To illustrate, in Exhibit 1, counterparty A agrees to pay counterparty B a fixed rate cash flow stream of the 10-year Treasury yield plus 106.5 bps (the spread one typically hears quoted when asked "where are swaps?") based on $1 million of notional principal in exchange for receiving 3-month LIBOR flat. So with a 10-year Treasury yield of 6.02% and a 3-month LIBOR rate of 5.00%, counterparty A would have an annual liability of $70,850 or $35,425 semi-annually.[1] In exchange, counterparty B would have a liability for that quarter of $50,000/4 = $12,500.

Exhibit 1: Fixed for Floating 10-Year Interest Rate Swap

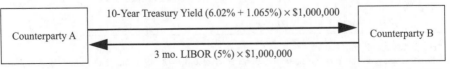

[1] Day count, compounding, etc. have been ignored to simplify the example.

WHY SWAP SPREADS INFLUENCE CMBS SPREADS

The primary reason swap spreads influence CMBS spreads is the increasingly prevalent use of swaps to hedge CMBS positions by all market players. In addition, the movement in swap spreads is viewed as a benchmark for the movement of AA/A "credit spreads" in general. The average credit rating of the counterparties exchanging the cash flows is about AA/A. Since a number of investors cross between CMBS and corporates, 10-year triple-A CMBS spreads tend to move with 10-year single-A spreads. Thus as swap spreads widen and tighten versus Treasuries, so too do 10-year triple-A CMBS spreads. As supply, credit, or liquidity events push out these corporate bond spreads, swap and CMBS spreads widen as well.

The link between swap spreads and the corporate bond market is one reason why during the fall of 1998 as the bond markets "panicked" about a possible global financial meltdown and liquidity dropped, swap spreads widened to such historically wide levels. Ironically, during this period, 10-year triple-A CMBS spreads decoupled from the swap market and became incredibly cheap versus swaps. This was due to technical factors specific to the CMBS market including the forced liquidation of CMBS holdings due to the large dominance of leveraged hedge funds in the CMBS market. In addition, a number of Street firm's CMBS traders were constrained from making liquid markets in CMBS, since their conduits already had large positions of commercial mortgages waiting to be securitized.

THE RELATIONSHIP BETWEEN SWAP SPREADS AND CMBS: THE PROOF

There is compelling evidence that since January 1998,[2] 10-year swap spreads have been the dominant factor in determining the spread between 10-year triple-A CMBS and the 10-year Treasury. The R-squared was 92% and the fits shown in Exhibit 2 are quite striking. While over time the exact values of the regression multipliers will somewhat vary and significant movements of other variables may have an impact, swap spreads will continue to play a central role in explaining the 10-year triple-A CMBS spreads.

Using weekly data from January 1998 to September 3, 1999,[3] with the 10-year swap spread as the only explanatory variable, our estimated regression equations are:

$$\text{CMBS Spread}(t) = 11.74 + 1.356 \times \text{SW10}(t) + e(t)$$

and

$$e(t) = 0.645 \times e(t-1) + u(t)$$

---

[2] For further details see Chapter 1.

[3] For this analysis the nine week period between September 18, 1998 and November 16, 1998 was excluded due to the unusual market conditions during this period such as forced liquidations, the exit of important market players, etc.

Exhibit 2: Predicted versus Actual 10-Year Triple-A CMBS Spreads

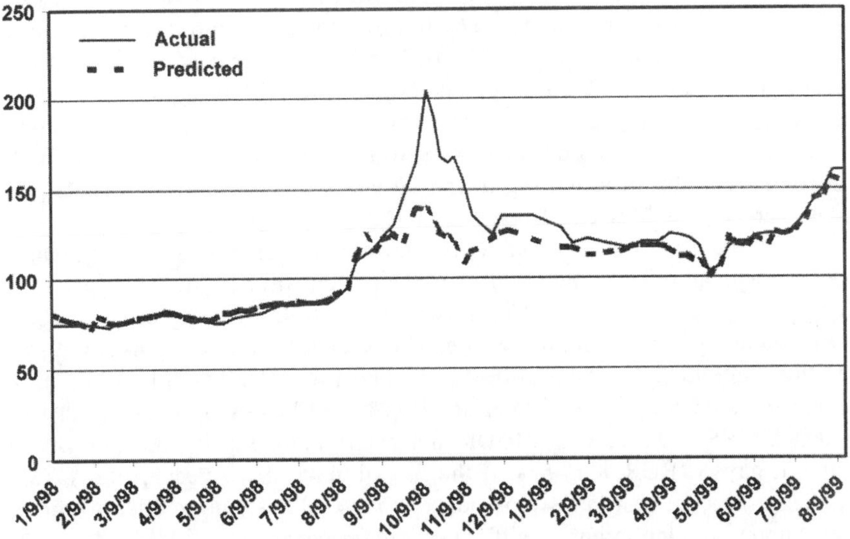

where the week is indexed by t, SW10 is the 10-year swap spread and $e(t)$ is the residual. According to this equation, if the 10-year swap spread widens 10 bps, the basis is predicted to widen, on average, 13.56 basis points. For example, if on August 13, the 10-year swap spread is 105 bps, then the model predicts that 10-year AAA CMBS on August 13 should be 154.15 bps [= 11.74 + 1.356(105)]. If the actual 10-year triple-A CMBS spread is 160 bps, then the model says that 10 year triple-A CMBS are 5.85 bps cheap. In terms of timing, the model is also saying that if the swap spread remains unchanged at 105 bps, about 35% of this cheapness should "go away" in one week (i.e., in one week, 10-year AAA CMBS should tighten about 2 bps. (35% × 5.85 bps).

When we revisited and updated our original analysis through May 2000, we found the relationship stronger than ever with 10-year AAA CMBS moving 1 bps for every 1 bp in swaps. Given the potentially greater spread stability of AAA security (AAA CMBS) versus AA/A ones (the swap) we would not be surprised if over time 10-year AAA CMBS spreads move less than 1 bp for every 1 bp of swap spread movement.

THE IMPORTANCE OF SWAPS TO THE CMBS MARKET

Because swap spreads and CMBS spreads are highly correlated, CMBS market participants (conduits, investors, traders, etc.) can use them to hedge positions and determine relative value. Swaps can be an effective hedging tool. Because their spread tends to change along with CMBS spreads, an investor or conduit who owns or is "long" CMBS (i.e. receiving fixed-rate cash flows)[4] can go "short" swaps (i.e. paying fixed-rate cash flows) to hedge both interest rate movements and spread movements.[5] If CMBS and swap spreads widen, the CMBS investor loses money on CMBS and makes money on the swap and vice versa. If done with the correct ratio one can substantially mitigate losses due to spread volatility. For example, based on the CMBS-swap relationship estimated, we expect that for every 1 bp of widening in the 10-year swap spread, 10-year triple-A CMBS spreads would widen 1 bp.

If the fixed-rate spread received from the CMBS is greater than the fixed-rate spread paid on the swap, then the participant has "net net" locked in a profitable spread over LIBOR (see Exhibit 3) while hedging himself against spread widening. Of course, if the spread between CMBS and swaps is not stable then this can reduce the profitability of this position. For example, in Exhibit 3, we have created a synthetic floater at LIBOR + 55 bps by purchasing a 10-year triple-A CMBS and receiving LIBOR in a swap. As long as the position is maintained, it pays LIBOR + 55 bps. If the spread between 10-year triple-A CMBS and the 10-year interest rate swap widened to say 70 bps, our position would lose money upon liquidation but gain if the spread tightened.

The above portfolio is hedged against changes in the overall level of interest rates. That's because the participant has through the above transaction in effect created a synthetic floater (see Exhibit 3). Since uncapped floating rate instruments tend to have negligible durations, the value of the transaction will be less sensitive to changes in interest rates.

Because swaps can help hedge against spread widening as well as rising rates, they have become a valuable tool for CMBS conduits to remain profitable or at least to minimize losses under current volatile market conditions. Indeed, for those conduits that currently use them effectively they can be an effective competitive weapon as market volatility shakes out those less sophisticated players who do not.

Exhibit 3: 10-Year Triple-A CMBS Hedged with 10-Year Interest Rate Swap Creates Synthetic Floater

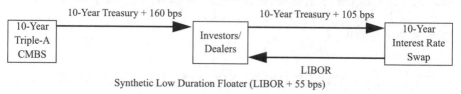

Synthetic Low Duration Floater (LIBOR + 55 bps)

---

[4] Technically this is referred to as "going long spreads" in swap market jargon.
[5] The cost of this option depends on bid/offer spreads in the swap market.

FACTORS INFLUENCING SWAPS

While factors such as Treasury financing rates, credit spreads, and liquidity play a major role in determining swap spreads, during the first half of 2000, "rising interest rates" and the inverted yield curve have also been factors. The inversion of both the Treasury and swap rate curves is the result of the Federal Reserve's tight monetary policy.[6] As inverted curves are typically a harbinger of an economic slowdown or cooling, this has caused swap spreads, which are sensitive to credit risk, to widen.

In addition, since swaps can change the duration of one's assets and liabilities, the market's overall "demand for duration" is increasingly being reflected in swap spreads. Given the bearish tone of the market during the first half of 2000 and the market's expectation that the Fed might raise rates, more market participants want to pay fixed and receive floating, thereby contributing to wider swap spreads. Because CMBS and swaps are linked, swap spreads have taken CMBS spreads with them even though little has changed in the real estate markets.

In 1999, the situation of too many market participants wanting to pay fixed was exacerbated by two factors. First, the "Street" — including corporate bond traders, residential mortgage traders, CMBS, and ABS traders — as well as CMBS conduits not to mention many investors, learned the lessons of the fall of 1998 and the strong relationship between swaps and bond spreads. As a result they are to a greater extent than ever before using swaps (i.e., paying fixed) to neutralize the price volatility of their inventories. Second, many corporate Treasurers were concerned about a potential rate hike and the possibility that Y2K issues could disrupt capital markets in the fourth quarter of 1999, pushed their corporate, ABS, and CMBS issuance forward to earlier in the year. This increased the need of the Street to pay fixed to hedge these underwritings, while at the same time forcing out spreads on A/AA credits which also pushes out swap spreads.

The growth and use of swaps in recent years has been positive for the CMBS sector in that it has given the market a way to partially hedge against spread volatility. This gives broker/dealers a better ability to provide liquidity in difficult market environments. However, this increased usage may have the negative side effect of partially causing increased short term swap spreads (and therefore CMBS spread) volatility.

Increased usage may have also created problems for the institutions and dealers on the other sides of these transactions. For example, in 1999, 10-year swap spreads increased 8 bps and swaption volatility soared 1.7% reportedly due to "trouble" at one or more major players in the swaps markets.[7] "Problems" in the swaps market have also caused risk management groups at financial institutions to curtail positions of swap traders and players in the hedge fund market with the unfortunate side effect that spreads can move more abruptly than in the past.

---

[6] Another factor has been the Treasury department's buy back of long dated Treasuries due to the declining deficit of the U.S. government; however this is more of a technical than fundamental issue.

[7] Extensive buying of interest rate caps was also a factor.

CONCLUSION

It is readily apparent that swaps will continue to play an important role in both hedging and determining relative value in the CMBS market. Swaps have also linked the CMBS market more tightly than ever before to the capital markets. Given that about 25% of the financing in the commercial real estate market now comes from CMBS, changes in swap spreads reflecting the market's changing credit and liquidity perception may help dampen real estate market volatility as the CMBS market increasingly serves as a governor of commercial real estate financing flows.

Chapter 14

The Effect of the Real Estate Cycle on Commercial Mortgage and CMBS Spreads

David P. Jacob
Managing Director
Nomura Securities International, Inc.

C.H. Ted Hong*
President
Beyondbond, Inc.

In this chapter we address how the real estate cycle should affect CMBS spreads, and how investors should alter the required yield on their CMBS as a function of what stage the real estate cycle is in. In answering this question, we make use of the options approach and option-adjusted spreads (OAS) to examine the effects of the real estate cycle. We conclude that the effects of the real estate cycle on the value of CMBS can be substantial. The timing and the length of the cycle makes a difference especially for default sensitive classes such as IOs and B-rated classes.

THE ANALYTICAL FRAMEWORK

The basic principle underlying the option approach is that the investor/lender in a CMBS/commercial mortgage is receiving a higher nominal yield than Treasury securities in return for giving the property owner the right to default on the mortgage payments, and thereby terminate his obligations under the mortgage, by giving up his property. The property owner will, loosely speaking, exercise his default option when (1) he can no longer pay his debt service and (2) the expected value of his property is less than the expected market value of his future obligations. The expected value of his future obligations equals the expected present value of his debt service less the value of his default option. Since most commercial mortgages have strong prepayment protection we assume here that they are noncallable. At maturity, the value of the default option is the greater of zero and

* C.H. Ted Hong was a Director at Nomura Securities International when this chapter was written.

the final payment due less the property value. Prior to maturity, the calculation of the value of the default option requires an option pricing model.[1]

For those unfamiliar with the option approach, one can think of the analysis as a large scale simulation (with associated probabilities) of future possible income scenarios. The computed OAS is the expected spread over Treasuries (or swaps) that is achievable after taking into account the probability of defaults including their timing and the resulting losses. OAS enables the investor to look at an adjustment to the nominal yield, which is based on no defaults and no losses. Our basic idea is that as the peak in the real estate cycle approaches, the probability of default during the life of the loan obviously increases. The default probabilities are larger because the mortgage does not have a chance to deleverage, and the property has less of a chance to appreciate in value early in the life of the mortgage. For an equivalently leveraged commercial mortgage or CMBS with equivalent subordination levels, this should lead to an adjustment to required nominal spreads based on the current stage in the cycle. The OAS is a quantification of the adjustment to the yield of the CMBS classes and commercial mortgages.

Our approach is to first structure a CMBS from a pool of ten loans with a range of loan-to-values (LTVs) and debt service coverage ratios (DSCRs). The CMBS and loan spreads reflect the pricing conditions of the market in December 1998. We then compute OAS for each of the CMBS classes as well as the loan pool, assuming no trend in net operating income (NOI) or property value. This corresponds to the case where investors make the assumption that there is no real estate cycle, so that the volatility in NOI causes property income to fluctuate around the current level of NOI. This case is then compared to various trend scenarios in NOI. In addition, alternative CMBS structures are examined, and the effects on OAS of more or less leveraged loan portfolios are shown.

DATA AND INFORMATION FOR ILLUSTRATION

We begin with laying out the details of the example that we are going to use.

Loan Pool Description

The sample pool consists of ten loans, each $20 million in size. They are 10-year balloon loans, all with 7.00%[2] coupons and follow a 30-year amortization schedule. We assumed that the loans are non-prepayable. The average life of each loan

---

[1] For a full explanation of the OAS approach see David P. Jacob, C.H. Ted Hong, and Laurence H. Lee, "An Options Approach to Commercial Mortgages and CMBS Valuation and Risk Analysis," Chapter 17 in Frank J. Fabozzi and David P. Jacob (eds.) *The Handbook of Commercial Mortgage-Backed Securities* (New Hope, PA: Frank J. Fabozzi Associates, 1997).

[2] In a more realistic example we would have varied the loan rate or spread based on the risk level of each loan, i.e. as a function of its respective LTV, DSCR, and NOI. To avoid weighted average coupon effects, we chose to use the same coupon. However, the basic results obtained here would be the same regardless of the choice of coupons.

is 9.4 years. We assume that the NOIs of each of the underlying properties are not correlated and have the same volatility. In addition, the loans have the following credit characteristics:

Loan	LTV	DSCR
1	61.6%	1.48×
2	63.3%	1.44×
3	65.1%	1.40×
4	67.0%	1.36×
5	69.0%	1.32×
6	71.1%	1.28×
7	73.3%	1.24×
8	75.7%	1.20×
9	78.3%	1.16×
10	81.1%	1.12×

The pool's loan-to-value is 70% and its weighted average debt service coverage ratio (WADSCR) is 1.30×.

Market Environment

The U.S. Treasury curve was assumed to be:

Term:	3 mo.	6 mo.	1yr.	2yr.	5yr.	10yr	30yr
Yield:	4.42%	4.48%	4.50%	4.61%	4.61%	4.76%	5.52%

The spread on the loans is 226 bp (to the curve).

Deal Structure

The loans are structured into the following CMBS classes shown in Exhibit 1.

For this deal structure, we first computed option-adjusted spreads based on a no-trend in NOI assumption, at various levels of NOI volatility ranging from 6% to 30% on an annual basis. In Exhibit 2 below, we compare the OAS for each class to the nominal yield spread at each level of NOI volatility. We also show the expected (probability weighted) principal loss to each class under each volatility scenario.

In order to understand this exhibit, we first focus on the collateral pool which is shown in the first row. The nominal spread on the pool was +226 bp, which is what the lender would achieve under a zero-default scenario. At higher levels of NOI volatility, the OAS is below the nominal spread to reflect the adjustment to the spread due to increasing probability of defaults and losses. For example, at a 12% NOI volatility, the OAS is 179 bp. This represents a 47 bp loss in expected spread due to expected losses of principal of 4.7%. The way to visualize this is to imagine many scenarios with NOI changing up and down with a 12% volatility.[3] Under some of these paths, where NOI is declining, defaults and

---

[3] The interest rate also varies corresponding to its volatility. The property value changes as a function of the interest rates and NOI levels. Note that we need the entire probability space to determine the timing and loss severity of the loan defaults; however, because of the path dependence for CMBS classes, a Monte Carlo simulation is used to obtain OAS and other relevant measures for each bond.

losses occur in some time periods. The average loss of principal on this pool of loans across all these paths and time periods is 4.7%. At a 30% NOI volatility level the OAS is computed to be −18bp due to the 17.6% expected loss of principal. (We expect that NOI volatility between 9% and 20% will capture most properties. Cross collateralized pools will tend to have lower NOI volatilities due to the less than 100% correlation between the incomes of the underlying properties.

As one scans down to the AAA securities, one can see that even at the highest level of NOI volatility there are barely any losses to principal under any scenarios. This is by the design of the senior-subordination structure, which allocates losses to the lowest outstanding class. The variation in the OAS of the AAA securities is a function of the allocation of principal recoveries from foreclosures causing the bonds to shorten in average life. The OAS drops because the investor receives principal back early at par, while he paid a premium price of 101.5.[4]

Exhibit 1: Deal Structure

Class	Amount mil.	Sub	Coupon %	Price %	Treasury %	Spread bp	WAL yr	Duration yr
Collateral	$200.00		7.00	100.00	4.74	226	9.4	6.7
AAA Short	$24.50	28.00	6.35	101.50	4.61	138	5.1	4.2
AAA Long	$119.50	28.00	6.42	101.50	4.76	146	10.0	7.3
AA	$12.00	22.00	6.52	100.00	4.76	176	10.0	7.3
A	$11.00	16.50	6.77	100.00	4.76	201	10.0	7.2
BBB	$9.00	12.00	7.00	96.05	4.76	281	10.0	7.0
BBB−	$3.00	10.50	7.00	89.60	4.76	381	10.0	6.9
BB+	$8.50	6.25	7.00	77.31	4.76	600	10.0	6.6
BB	$2.00	5.25	7.00	76.05	4.76	625	10.0	6.6
BB−	$2.00	4.25	7.00	67.96	4.76	800	10.0	6.3
B+	$3.50	2.50	7.00	63.86	4.76	900	10.0	6.2
B	$1.00	2.00	7.00	61.93	4.76	950	10.0	6.1
B−	$1.50	1.25	7.00	56.61	4.76	1100	10.0	5.9
UR	$2.50	0.00	7.00	29.20	4.76	2424	10.0	4.2
CS1 (short IO)	$10.00		0.60	1.28	4.58	500	1.8cf	1.6
PS1 (long IO)	$190.00		0.46	2.83	4.61	500	5.1cf	4.2

Notes on the structure:
1. The two AAAs are structured to be sequential for principal payments and pro-rata for allocation of losses.
2. The first IO class, CS1, was created by stripping 60bp from the first $10 million of principal of the short AAA class. The second IO class, PS1, has interest stripped from the AAAs, AA, and single A class.
3. The average life for the IO classes is noted with a "cf" to indicate cash flow average life.
4. The duration calculated here, is the modified duration.
5. The spreads and subordination levels are reasonably representative of the time period corresponding to the end of 1998
6. While the second IO class is usually priced at a tighter spread than the first IO, we left them the same in our example so that the relative OAS adjustment is easily observed.

---

[4] There is another effect, which is noticeable in the second AAA class. The OAS is higher than the nominal spread due to the positive slope of the yield curve. At very high levels of volatility this effect is outweighed by the early principal payments.

Exhibit 2: OAS at Specified Level of Volatility/Expected Loss of Principal (Assumes No Trend in NOI)

Class	Nominal Spread	OAS in bp/Expected Loss in percent											
		6%		9%		12%		16%		20%		30%	
Collateral	226	217	1.5	202	2.9	179	4.7	140	7.4	96	10.3	−18	17.6
AAA Short	138	134	0.0	131	0.0	125	0.0	117	0.0	112	0.0	105	0.0
AAA Long	146	150	0.0	150	0.0	149	0.0	149	0.0	149	0.0	141	0.6
AA	176	179	0.1	176	0.4	169	1.6	165	1.9	165	1.8	10	17.4
A	201	203	0.3	192	2.0	176	3.9	160	5.6	121	9.5	−286	42.2
BBB	281	275	1.5	253	4.6	224	7.8	166	13.4	31	25.5	−744	67.3
BBB−	381	364	3.4	330	7.6	286	11.8	170	22.3	−75	40.6	−1147	80.5
BB+	600	566	5.9	514	11.7	428	19.1	205	36.0	−224	59.5	−1495	88.3
BB	625	567	9.2	488	16.9	339	28.4	−71	53.1	−715	75.8	−2009	93.1
BB−	800	724	11.4	621	20.1	426	34.6	−60	60.3	−782	80.7	−2050	94.2
B+	900	789	14.7	648	25.6	368	43.5	−294	70.4	−1125	86.8	−2263	95.1
B	950	799	18.7	599	32.7	225	52.5	−617	78.7	−1604	91.5	−2324	95.5
B−	1100	925	21.0	641	39.5	204	59.5	−772	83.4	−1692	92.8	−2220	95.6
UR	2424	2201	30.2	1767	50.6	1096	71.4	−18	88.4	−677	93.4	−1181	95.8
CS1 (short IO)	500	258	N/A	−253	N/A	−982	N/A	−1489	N/A	−1816	N/A	−2319	N/A
PS1 (long IO)	500	436	N/A	355	N/A	270	N/A	206	N/A	182	N/A	164	N/A

At the other end of the credit spectrum, the BB−, which is priced at a nominal spread of +800 bp, has an OAS of +426 at a 12% NOI volatility (which is not bad considering the 34.6% expected loss of principal), but an OAS of −60 bp at a 16% NOI volatility and −782 bp OAS at a 20% NOI volatility.

This kind of exhibit can be very useful for a relative value investor. For example, one can see why one might prefer the long AAA bond to the collateral, since its yield holds up better than the collateral under high levels of expected default even though it has a lower yield than the collateral under less stressful volatility assumptions. Similarly a less risk adverse investor might find the BB− attractive relative to the collateral, because of the high relative yield even under the 12% NOI volatility assumption. However, it is less clear why an investor would prefer the A rated bond to the collateral, since it has a lower OAS at low levels of NOI volatility and at very high levels of NOI volatility! It would appear that the A rated bond at a +201bp nominal spread does not provide much extra value relative to the collateral.[5] Perhaps, investors are willing to give up some yield relative to the collateral for the benefits of owning a security instead of a whole loan.

Similarly, the BB− class appears to offer more value than the B rated class. Unless NOI volatility is 9% or below, the BB has higher OAS, and the expected principal loss is always less. In the marketplace the buyer of the single B rated class is often the same as the buyer of the unrated class. As we discuss in the next paragraph, the unrated class in our example could be an attractive secu-

---

[5] A similar result is found in Chapter 6.

rity for some investors, but part of the price they have to pay to get it may include purchasing the single B class.

The unrated class presents an interesting opportunity at the nominal spread of +2,424 bp or 29% nominal yield. It appears superior to everything rated BB and below. While this is one way of interpreting the results, and on average under the above assumptions it will outperform the BB and below, the unrated class still has greater risk unless one is able to rely on the "Law of Large Numbers" from probability theory. In layman's terms, if one could purchase many of these classes, the result would be true on average. However, for small portfolios one cannot achieve the average performance. There are many more scenarios under which the unrated class will be wiped out resulting in negative yields for the investor, whereas the BB rated bonds remain untouched. One way of observing this is the higher expected principal losses for the unrated class, no matter what the volatility of NOI is (unless it is zero). Thus, for investors who are not able to purchase many unrated classes over various different time periods and who are unable to tolerate instances of severely poor performance, the class may not be an appropriate purchase regardless of how high the nominal yield and OAS are.

The exhibit also clearly illustrates the leverage created by the senior-subordinated structure. For example, using the 12% NOI volatility assumption, the single B– rated classes which has less than a tenth of the subordination of AAA classes, has a little more than ten times the expected loss of principal of the collateral.

The IO classes sometimes defy intuition. The first thing to keep in mind about the IO classes is that they are hurt by erosion of their notional principal, however it occurs. Assuming that no voluntary prepayment is permitted, erosion of principal can occur either from scheduled principal paydowns such as amortization, recoveries from foreclosures, or the allocation of losses. The second thing to understand about IO classes is that their cash flow is very front loaded. Thus, more so than with other classes, they are very sensitive to the timing of defaults. Early defaults, regardless of the recovery rate, are very damaging to the yield of the IO classes. High recovery rates translate into prepayments without penalty, and low recoveries result in the lowering of balances through the allocation of losses. At the other extreme, balloon defaults have no effect on the IO classes yield, regardless of the recovery.

In the current deal structure we have two IO classes. The first one, CS1, is created by stripping 60bp from the first AAA class. As a result, the impact of the first unscheduled $10 million of principal to come in from recoveries is absorbed by this class. To understand the vulnerability of this class, consider that if any one loan were to default during the time when the first AAA bond was outstanding and experience a recovery rate of more than 50%, it would wipe out the notional principal on which this IO is receiving income. The argument for purchasing this class by some investors is that early defaults are unlikely for newly underwritten loans. While this is generally true, the class is vulnerable if this turns out not to be the case. Moreover, the OAS model, by design incorporates the lower default rate into the early years of newly underwritten loans. So the first IO, would be a good buy in our example, only if one expected a relatively low NOI volatility. (As we will see in some later examples, when lower LTV loans were used, the results dramatically improve, and the first IO outperforms the second IO.) The second IO class, PS1, performs extremely well in our example. On an OAS basis, it outperforms every class above the BBB– rated bonds.[6] The result is not too surprising considering that the IO is carved from the interest cash flows of the single A– rated class and above. However, even in deals where some of the IO comes from the lower rated classes as well, the performance of this IO class tends to stand up well, since again its cash flow are front loaded, and the large majority of its cash flows generally come from the most senior bond classes.

Most current deals do not use the two IO structure, but rather combine the two into one class. In Exhibit 3, we show the OAS for the two IO structure compared to the combined IO class.

The results of the combined IO fall, as expected, between the two individual IO classes. They are closer to the PS1 performance, because it is so much larger in size (38 times larger). It is quite clear from Exhibit 3 why most deals today use the one IO structure. Nevertheless, as we noted above and will show in a later example, when the LTV on the loans is lower, a case could be made for the two IO structure. The results also would show CS1 in a better light if it were carved off of more than just $10 million in notional principal.

The pattern of defaults produced by the OAS model is worth looking at for a moment because it demonstrates the richness and depth of the OAS framework. Exhibit 4 shows the cumulative probability of default for the collateral. For the first year the probability of default is shown to be zero, even under the 30% NOI volatility assumption. The probability begins to increase, with a jump occurring between years 5 and 6. Defaults then begin to level off. This is followed by another jump at the balloon date. This is consistent with empirical studies. With newly underwritten loans with DSCRs greater than one, it takes time for income to drop. Gradually the lower quality loans experience problems under certain paths. After they default, they are no longer part of the pool. On the other hand, along some paths, income improves, which provides a cushion against future declines. This combined with the benefits of amortization causes the leveling off in defaults. The balloon date causes additional stress, as the borrower has to come up with the balloon payment.

Exhibit 3: OAS in bp at Specified Level of Volatility (Assumes No Trend in NOI)

Class	Nominal Spread	OAS (in bp)					
		6%	9%	12%	16%	20%	30%
CS1 (short IO)	500	258	–253	–982	–1489	–1816	–2319
PS1 (long IO)	500	436	355	270	206	182	164
IO (Combined)	500	434	350	261	194	168	148

[6] This result is corroborated in Chapter 6.

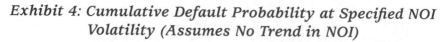

Exhibit 4: Cumulative Default Probability at Specified NOI Volatility (Assumes No Trend in NOI)

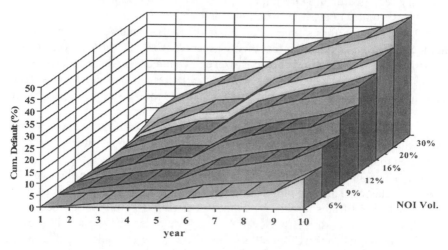

We now turn to the central topic of this chapter, namely the impact of the real estate cycle on CMBS spreads. We use the same example as before, but instead of assuming that there is no trend in NOI, and that any change in NOI is due to volatility, we assume that there is a real estate cycle and that we are at the peak in the cycle. We assume that NOI will actually trend down over the next ten years.[7] The property markets, at least in the past, have exhibited cycles, driven by imbalances between the supply and demand for space. Most real estate market participants would likely agree that we are, today, in a significantly more advanced stage in the real estate cycle than we were seven years ago, when the CMBS market was in its nascent stage.

Exhibit 5 shows the OAS results for the collateral and CMBS classes of our sample deal. Looking across the top row and comparing it to the results of Exhibit 2, it is clear that the downward trend in NOI causes the OAS to be lower. For example, at a 12% NOI volatility the OAS for the collateral is 153 bp compared to 179 bp where there was no trend in NOI. The result should not be surprising, since the declining trend in NOI leads to, on average, lower coverage and value over time. Thus, the cumulative defaults will be higher, and the losses will be higher. The model enables us to quantify the effect. In our example, the downward trend in NOI causes the expected losses to be about 1.6 times larger.

In general, all the results in Exhibit 5 are worse when compared to those in Exhibit 2. The AAA bonds are still largely untouched even with the imposition of the cycle. This further demonstrates how well these classes are protected, and

---

[7] A 20-year real estate cycle is assumed. The downward trend in NOI varies with respect to the volatility level. It ranges from 8% to 34%, corresponding to the volatility scenarios, 6-30%.

the value that they offer. While the other senior classes are also reasonably well protected, they breakdown at the higher levels of NOI volatility. The biggest impact to the spread among the regular classes is felt by the single B rated classes. For example, the drop in the OAS (at a 12% NOI volatility) of the B–rated class from an OAS of 204 bp to –366 bp, is a 279% drop in spread! For the buyer of this class, it would seem that he better be right about the trend in NOI not just the volatility. These lower rated classes are generally small in size, and they are highly leveraged with respect to defaults, as a result small differences in the default rate can make a tremendous difference in the realized yields.

Once again the IO classes defy intuition. As before, the second IO class, PS1, stands up well under all scenarios, and appears to offer significant value. However, there are some unusual results which show up, particularly in the case of the first IO, CS1. If we compare the OAS for CS1 shown in Exhibit 6 to the results in Exhibit 2, we find that the OAS is higher in all cases when there is a downward trend in NOI. This is counter-intuitive! How can it be that when the expected losses are higher that the OAS can be higher? Recall what we said earlier about IO classes. They are particularly sensitive to the timing of the defaults. The only way that the IO can be better off under the higher default scenarios, is if the defaults are occurring later (or default with zero recoveries which can lead to an extension of the average life of the notional principal due to reduced amortization cash flow from the defaulted loans). As we examined the details of our results, we, in fact, did find that the defaults although higher were occurring later. We show the cumulative default in Exhibit 6.

Exhibit 5: OAS at Specified Level of Volatility/Expected Loss of Principal (Assumes Downward Trend in NOI)

| Class | Nominal Spread | OAS in bp/Expected Loss of Principal in % | | | | | | | | | | | |
		6%		9%		12%		16%		20%		30%	
Collateral	226	209	2.4	185	4.6	153	7.4	101	11.4	45	15.5	–101	25.0
AAA Short	138	136	0.0	135	0.0	134	0.0	129	0.0	125	0.0	117	0.0
AAA Long	146	150	0.0	151	0.0	151	0.0	150	0.0	148	0.2	123	2.8
AA	176	178	0.1	174	0.9	170	1.5	157	3.2	107	9.1	–455	54.8
A	201	196	1.4	179	3.9	161	6.1	93	13.5	–91	31.0	–1109	81.6
BBB	281	259	4.1	223	8.5	162	15.0	–35	33.2	–396	57.7	–1594	91.1
BBB–	381	345	6.2	285	13.1	176	23.7	–147	48.9	–647	73.0	–1849	94.2
BB+	600	535	10.1	439	19.7	244	36.1	–222	64.0	–837	83.8	–2028	95.3
BB	625	518	15.2	360	29.1	31	51.8	–618	78.2	–1298	91.0	–2144	95.3
BB–	800	669	17.7	471	34.3	76	58.8	–616	82.4	–1274	92.4	–2207	95.4
B+	900	719	22.1	432	43.3	–54	67.9	–874	87.8	–1580	93.9	–2304	95.8
B	950	700	27.9	313	52.4	–307	75.8	–1238	91.2	–1873	94.9	–2393	96.6
B–	1100	797	31.4	333	58.5	–366	80.4	–1270	92.5	–1809	95.3	–2390	97.3
UR	2424	1960	45.2	1440	68.9	620	87.4	–82	93.8	–509	96.0	–1208	97.8
CS1 (short IO)	500	274	0.0	–150	0.0	–299	0.0	–590	0.0	–707	0.0	–1117	0.0
PS1 (long IO)	500	413	0.0	334	0.0	280	0.0	237	0.0	223	0.0	187	0.0

Exhibit 6: Comparison of Cumulative Default Between No-Trend and a Downtrend (Assumes NOI Volatility of 16%)

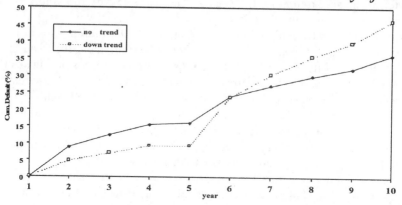

Comparison of Cumulative Defaults

One can see that while the defaults are ultimately greater for the downward NOI case, they are lower in the earlier years. The borrower is postponing the exercising of his default option until later. While this may seem counter-intuitive, it is actually very rational and correct from the option stand point. Because of the downward trend, the owner of the property is able to maximize the value of this option by *waiting*. The default option allows the borrower to extinguish the obligations under his debt agreement by defaulting and turning over his property. His option value is maximized by exercising his option later when the property is worth the least. Thus, when NOI is trending down, under some scenarios his default option value can outweigh the drop in property value and delay the timing of default. Of course, the declining NOI trend will lead to more defaults, but the defaults occur later. Bonds which are most sensitive to the timing of defaults are most affected. This is why CS1 performs better as shown in Exhibit 6. Similar results show up for the UR class under the higher NOI volatility assumptions for the same reason. For example, at a 20% NOI volatility assumption the OAS of the UR class is −509 bp assuming a downward trend in NOI, compared to −677 bp with no-trend. This is even with the larger expected principal losses.[8]

While we do not show the results here, the model is consistent in that if we do our analysis under the assumption that NOI is trending up (i.e., that we are at the beginning of the cycle) things look better. If we assume that we are somewhere in the middle the results are somewhere in the middle. The point is that the timing of the cycle should impact the spread at which you purchase the CMBS class particularly the lower rated classes. This is true even if the loans are underwritten for the expected average NOI.

---

[8] The result is also evident in the first AAA class at higher levels of volatility. This is because the class is priced at 101.5, which in essence means it has a bit of IO embedded in it.

Exhibit 7: OAS at Specified Level of Loan Pool LTV
(Assumes NOI Volatility of 16% and No Trend Imposed)

Class	Nominal Spread	OAS in bp			Expected Loss in %		
		50%	70%	90%	50%	70%	90%
Collateral	226	209	140	−98	2.1	7.4	17.2
AAA Short	138	134	117	73	0.0	0.0	0.0
AAA Long	146	149	149	115	0.0	0.0	1.7
AA	176	179	165	−59	0.1	1.9	21.6
A	201	203	160	−279	0.2	5.6	37.1
BBB	281	279	166	−598	0.7	13.4	55.8
BBB−	381	373	170	−822	1.6	22.3	66.9
BB+	600	577	205	−1103	3.6	36.0	78.6
BB	625	559	−71	−1793	9.0	53.1	89.3
BB−	800	698	−60	−1971	12.9	60.3	92.2
B+	900	694	−294	−2558	22.9	70.4	96.1
B	950	582	−617	−3265	36.4	78.7	98.3
B−	1100	586	−772	−3698	46.6	83.4	99.1
UR	2424	1853	−18	−3067	55.1	88.4	99.4
CS1 (short IO)	500	450	−1489	−4191	N/A	N/A	N/A
PS1 (long IO)	500	453	206	−543	N/A	N/A	N/A

Effects of Leverage

The last subject we cover in this chapter is the effects of leverage. One of the trends that has been observed is that as real estate markets recover and particularly at the peaks lenders tend to provide more leverage, whereas at the beginning of the recoveries leverage is low reflecting conservative underwriting due to the recent memory of poor performance. Based on what we have seen here, the reverse ought to be true, higher leverage at the beginning of the cycle and lower as the cycle peaks.

Exhibit 7 compares the results for 50%, 70% and 90% LTV, and DSCR of 1.82×, 1.30×, and 1.01× (assuming the same subordination levels).[9] Obviously, the lower leverage levels dramatically reduce the probability of defaults and result in higher OAS for all classes. It is interesting to note how much better the first IO class performs. This is because defaults occur later on so when most if not all of the cash flow of the IO has been received. The two IO structure was more prevalent in the earlier CMBS deals, particularly those deals with large low leverage loans. As before if we applied a downward trend to the NOI, the OAS numbers are generally lower.

For CMBS deals that are backed by loans that are more highly leveraged, and for which the rating agencies have not adequately increased the required subordination, the investor needs to be very optimistic about the stability of NOI.

---

[9] While it is likely that the different levels of leverage would result in different levels of subordination from the rating agencies, we left the subordination levels unchanged for comparative purposes.

Clearly the results for the high leverage scenario are terrible. What is also clear is that there are high levels of defaults, even early on causing the first IO to be wiped out, yet the AAA survives. The results clearly demonstrate how careful investors have to be in assessing the correct leverage and coverage. In 1998, there were certainly deals that were getting done with leverage close to the 90% level. The widening in spreads in the fall of 1998 probably resulted in many marginal deals not getting done. However, investors/lenders have short memories and often try to convince themselves that the leverage is not too much. The OAS results show how bad things can be with the higher leverage. This is without any assumed peak in NOI. The combination of high leverage at the peak of the cycle should certainly cause investors/lenders to be cautious.

CONCLUSION

We have shown how the real estate cycle can have a significant effects on the value of commercial mortgages and CMBS, particularly those classes that are most sensitive to the timing of defaults. Investors need to adjust their targeted nominal spreads as a function of the timing of the real estate cycle. They also need to understand the risk profile of the lower rated CMBS even when the default adjusted spreads show these securities to have fundamental value. And, finally, rising leverage at a time when NOI is no longer rising should make investors especially cautious.

Chapter 15

CMBS in Japan

Patrick Corcoran, Ph.D.
Vice President
J.P. Morgan Securities Inc.

Joshua Phillips*
Vice President
Nomura Securities International

T he emergence of a burgeoning CMBS market at the bottom of the commercial property cycle in Japan in some ways parallels the earlier 1990s U.S. experience. This chapter compares the growth of CMBS and recovery of commercial property markets in Japan with the early 1990s U.S. experience. Over 1999-2000, it is the differences between Japan and the U.S. in both CMBS and property markets that are most striking. However, the comparison of the two country markets, in our view, continues to provide an illuminating perspective on the future of CMBS in Japan.

THE EXPANDING CMBS MARKET

There are both parallels and differences between Japan's emerging CMBS market and conditions in the United States in the early 1990s. One important difference is that the United States had a much more extensive experience with public markets and securitization. In the United States early 1990s episode, the Resolution Trust Corporation (RTC) built on the foundation of earlier securitization in residential mortgages and other assets. The RTC pioneered securitization of commercial mortgage collateral by selling off the seasoned performing and non-performing loans of failed banks and thrifts in the form of CMBS. This early effort paved the way for the securitization of newly originated performing loans, which only came several years later.

By contrast, Japan's market in non-performing loans (NPLs) has been relatively unimportant for the development of the CMBS market. In part, this reflects government policy to support ailing banks with infusions of public money rather than selling off the bad assets RTC-style. It also reflects an absence of

---

* Mr. Phillips was employed at J.P. Morgan Securities when this chapter was written.

property cash flow in the real estate collateral underlying many NPLs. Taking note of such differences, we believe that the new loan CMBS market may play an even more important role in Japan than it has in the United States.

Beginning in February 1999 up to the end of March 2000, we counted 26 CMBS transactions with total value of ¥370.8 billion. This compares with just under $5 billion of RTC CMBS deals (about ¥550 billion) done in the United States in 1990 (Exhibit 1). Moreover, we expect that Japan's expanding CMBS market will continue to keep pace with the United States early 1990s track record. This implies issuance of about ¥600 billion between April 2000 and the end of March 2001.

WHAT IS DRIVING THE EXPANSION IN CMBS DEALS?

Weakness of the Portfolio Lender Model

To see CMBS issuance about 70% that of the United States in the early 1990s is quite striking and suggests that Japan is following a similar path. Measured by its GDP, Japan is about half the size of the United States. On the other hand, debt held by banks in Japan is substantially larger than in the United States. The same is the case for total real-estate-related debt outstanding.

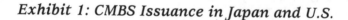

Exhibit 1: CMBS Issuance in Japan and U.S.

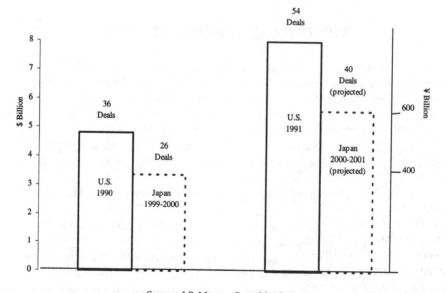

Source: J.P. Morgan Securities Inc.

Similar to the United States early 1990s experience, a major part of Japanese borrower demand for non-recourse commercial mortgage loans arises from the inherent weakness of the "portfolio lender model." U.S. bank and life company lenders traditionally made mortgage loans on their own balance sheets as "portfolio lenders," thereby earning a spread over their liability cost of funds. However, the late 1980s/early 1990s sharp downturn in real estate underscored overly aggressive lending and an inadequate return on capital earned by these lenders. As a result, traditional U.S. lenders at that time scaled back lending activity and the CMBS market accounted for a major new share of loans to borrowers.

The beginning of the U.S. CMBS in the 1990s market might also be contrasted with its "false start" in the late 1980s. In the earlier period, there were a few CMBS deals done in the United States. However, because of overly aggressive lending by life companies and banks, securitizers won very little of the lending business. Moreover, to win business, portfolio lenders made new loans at very tight spreads. Since capital market skepticism about real estate in the late 1980s resulted in relatively wide CMBS spreads, very little securitization profit was left on the deals done.

In contrast with the approach of traditional portfolio lenders, the CMBS market allows the capital markets to judge the adequacy of the risk/return profile in commercial mortgage loans. In the United States early 1990s experience, the growth of the CMBS market was aided by a credit crunch, as traditional portfolio lenders ceased lending altogether. However, as these lenders gradually returned to the lending markets, CMBS pricing provided explicit signals about how the underlying loans should be priced. This pricing provided a capital market "discipline" to lenders that had been absent previously in the private U.S. markets.

Parallel to the U.S. experience, Japan also experienced an initial credit crunch, which is less severe as of this writing than several years ago. However, the policy of providing capital infusions to ailing banks rather than RTC-type asset sales seems likely to extend the weak position of financial intermediaries. Banks still have large NPL positions, which should limit their competitiveness as portfolio lenders for some time to come. In addition, Japanese banks must repay government loans of ¥8.8 trillion. Thus, both the large initial scale of financial system problems as well as their likely protraction suggest that demand by borrowers for non-recourse commercial mortgages will have to be met by loans that are securitized in the capital markets.

Exhibit 2 shows our count of 1999-2000 CMBS deals. This information may not cover every deal, but represents our best efforts to monitor activity in the market. (An appendix at the end of this chapter summarizes our deal information in somewhat more detail.) As shown in Exhibit 3, almost half of the deals (41% of issuance by volume or seven out of 26 deals) were sale-leaseback transactions. Many corporations have experienced reduced ability to obtain debt or equity funding. For these entities, the ability to sell and lease back real estate assets is an attractive alternative funding source. Most Japanese financial institutions and corporations are under pressure to focus on core business operations and improve earnings. Sale-leasebacks of owner-occupied real estate can help accomplish this goal. Looking at the sale-leaseback transactions in Exhibit 2, a wide variety of companies have used the technique including banks and financial companies, industrial concerns, and retailers.

Among the non sale-leaseback transactions in Exhibit 2, four deals (21% by volume) represented mortgages to finance property acquisitions while 11 deals (31% by volume) helped meet the "leveraged finance" needs of existing property owners.

Looking at underlying property collateral (Exhibit 4), there are 14 transactions (56% by volume) involving the financing of office properties. Of these, four transactions involve real estate companies and six life companies. In a macro environment where many companies have weakened balance sheets, companies with valuable real estate assets can use them to obtain scarce new financing.

Some of the 1999-2000 transactions benefited from off-balance-sheet treatment to originators for loans, as long as senior CMBS tranches were sold. This is likely to change soon. The Japanese Institute of Certified Public Accountants is likely to recommend on-balance sheet treatment for loans in which B-pieces are retained. This obviously increases the importance of the B-piece market. As discussed in the Rating Agency section, the supply of B-piece investments has been quite limited. We expect modest growth in the supply of B-piece investments to be matched by increased investor demand for B-pieces to take up some of the slack (see Demand for CMBS section below).

A striking feature of Japan's emerging CMBS market is several deals focused on new development (Exhibit 2). In the early 1990s U.S. market, this did not occur at all. Partly, the U.S. experience reflected low demand for development financing at the bottom of the real estate cycle and partly significant supply of development financing by banks. By contrast, replacement demand for real estate is far higher in Japan, even at the bottom of the property cycle. In turn, this reflects fundamental differences in the property markets (see property market section below). A recent development CMBS deal is also discussed in more detail below.

Demand for CMBS

The emergence of a new market in structured product, including CMBS, in Japan clearly required that investors become more familiar with these new structures. In 1999-2000, the strong initial reception by investors for CMBS has been striking. From a U.S. perspective, Japan's financial system is at an earlier point with relatively few capital market instruments available to investors. In the bond market, there is relatively little competition from other capital market instuments for investors' ¥1,430 trillion ($13 trillion) in savings. Reflecting a scarcity of spread product, many institutional investors have recently begun to allocate part of their funds to "alternative" investments, a category that includes mezzanine or subordinate CMBS.

Exhibit 2: March 1999 - March 2000 CMBS deals

Deal No.	Issuer	Property Type	Transaction type	Arranger	Arranger type	Rating	Amt (JPY bn)	Closing
1	Kilimanjaro Limited	Office	Leveraged Finance	NSSB	Foreign	Mdy/S&P	6.60	Mar-00
2	Red Lions Capital	Office	Leveraged Finance	JP Morgan	Foreign	Mdy	10.80	Mar-00
3	Millenium Capital	Office	Leveraged Finance	IBJ Sec.	Group	Mdy	11.50	Mar-00
4	Forester SPC	Retail	Sale Leaseback	N/A	Unknown	R&I	28.50	Mar-00
5	Prime Quest	Office	Leveraged Finance	Daiwa SBCM	Group	Mdy/JCR	5.15	Mar-00
6	M's Fort Co., Ltd.	Apartment	Leveraged Finance	IBJ Sec.	Non-Group	S&P	24.00	Mar-00
7	NEST Funding Corp.	Office	Sale Leaseback	Daiwa SBCM	Group	Mdy	51.40	Mar-00
8	Urbanity Capital TMK	Office	Leveraged Finance	Daiwa SBCM	Non-Group	Mdy	9.30	Mar-00
9	Millenium Residential SPC Co., Ltd.	Apartment	Development	Sakura Securities	Group	Mdy	11.70	Mar-00
10	Kyodo Jutaku Securitization SPC	Apartment	Leveraged Finance	Starts Co.	Group	N/A	0.25	Mar-00
11	Amco Ventures Corp.	Office	Acquisition Finance	JP Morgan	Foreign	Mdy	30.70	Feb-00
12	MM Property Funding	Office	Sale Leaseback	DKB Sec.	Non-Group	R&I	13.50	Feb-00
13	Ohmori Kaigan SPC	Factory	Development	Daiwa SBCM	Group	JCR	12.00	Feb-00
14	Feris K.K.	Office	Sale Leaseback	N/A	Unknown	N/A	N/A	Feb-00
15	NeopasTMK	Office	Development	DKB Sec	Group	N/A	2.60	Jan-00
16	International Credit Recovery Japan One Ltd.	NPL	Acquisition Finance	MSDW	Foreign	Mdy/S&P/Fitch	21.00	Nov-99
17	Pacific Century Residential One	Apartment	Leveraged Finance	Jardine Fleming Sec.	Foreign	N/A	6.63	Oct-99
18	Star Capital	Office	Leveraged Finance	Nomura Sec	Non-Group	Mdy	9.60	Sep-99
19	New Shopping Center Funding Corp	Retail	Sale Leaseback	Paribas	Foreign	Mdy	41.00	Sep-99
20	N/A	Warehouse	Sale Leaseback	Sakura Bank	Group	JCR	3.60	Aug-99
21	Azuchi Estate Funding Limited	Office	Acquisition Finance	N/A	Group	Mdy	18.35	Aug-99
22	Takanawa Apartment SPC	Apartment	Leveraged Finance	Fuji Bank	Group	S&P	3.00	Jun-99
23	Sumquest Co. Limited	Office	Leveraged Finance	Daiwa SBCM/IBJ Sec.	Group	Mdy	24.50	Jun-99
24	Network Capital	Office	Sale Leaseback	Daiwa SBCM	Group	JCR	13.50	Apr-99
25	Someino S.C.	Retail	Leveraged Finance	Wako Securities	Non-Group	R&I	5.10	Mar-99
26	LM Capital	Apartment	Acquisition Finance	JP Morgan	Foreign	Mdy	6.50	Mar-99
						Total	370.8	

Source: J.P. Morgan Securities Inc.

Exhibit 3: Japanese CMBS by Transaction Type

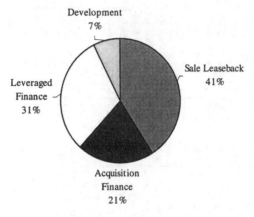

Source: J.P. Morgan Securities Inc.

Exhibit 4: Japanese CMBS by Collateral Type

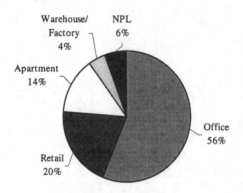

Source: J.P. Morgan Securities Inc.

Investors' appetite for CMBS has also been bolstered by increasing recognition of Japan's solid "bottom of the market" real estate fundamentals (see property markets section below) and by progress in legal reform that is necessary to accommodate structured bonds (see section on Special Purpose Corporations (SPCs) below).

DEAL OVERVIEW

Growth in Japan's CMBS market in 1999-2000 has paralleled that in the early 1990s U.S. experience in a number of ways. First, like the U.S. market, Japanese

CMBS deals have been primarily fixed-rate borrowings with prohibition against prepayment prior to the balloon date. There have been a few Japanese floating-rate deals. One was the LM Capital Ltd. Deal in March 1999, an interim financing deal permitting the purchaser of a group of condominium properties to sell the properties as the market allowed. More recently in the spring of 2000, there were several floating-rate deals in the pipeline, reflecting an increased demand by borrowers for interim financing. With real estate rents and prices in higher-quality properties showing the firmness of an inearly recoveryl• stage, we expect more properties to be sold and repositioned. The demand for interim financing is likely to increase.

The CMBS market in Japan has been entirely a large loan market with single borrower deals, either single property or multi-property, the norm. This parallels the early U.S. experience in new loans, beginning in 1994, with its emphasis on large loan deals. However, the difference in Japan so far is that there has been no pooling of borrowers' large loans into what the early U. S. market called megadeals, or pools of large loan borrowers.

Why the difference? In our view, the primary reason is that Japanese investors have a larger ialearning curveln to climb than U.S. investors in the early 1990s. In part, this is so because the United States had a richer capital markets history that witnessed residential loans and other assets securitized beginning in the 1970s. Secondly, and even more importantly, U.S. non-recourse real estate finance was already well established by life companies, banks, and thrifts in the private commercial mortgage market in the 1950s and 1960s.

In Japan, by contrast, real estate loans were made corporate-style with little meaningful reference to real estate underwriting criteria. In the early 1990s U.S. experience, investors had to learn the differences in rating agency approaches to underwriting real estate loans compared to previous insurance company underwriting. The rating agencies' heavy emphasis on current property cash flow was a new development at that time.

In Japan, by contrast, it is fair to say that there was no real-estate-based lending market in commercial properties prior to 1998-1999. In the past, Japanese banks made loans corporate-style to industrial and real estate companies secured by real estate but with recourse. CMBS investors in Japan have to learn structural and other issues related to securitization. In addition, they also have to learn genuine real-estate-based underwriting itself, which is a new development.

The hallmark of real-estate-based lending is that the loans made are non-recourse to the borrower. In the event that such a non-recourse loan (NRL) defaults, the lender or investors have recourse to the property but not to the borrower's other assets. In 1999-2000, most of the non-recourse loans made were done with securitization as the intended exit strategy. In some cases, however, such loans were made and not intended for securitization. A number of these transactions, parallel to non-recourse whole loans in the U.S. market, are shown in Exhibit 5.

Exhibit 5: Non-Securitized Real-Estate Loans

Deal No.	Original RE Owner	Underlying Assets	Transaction type	Arranger	Arranger type	Rating	Amount (JPY bn)	Closing or Announcement
1	Daiichi Life	4 office Bldgs.	Office	IBJ	Group	MDYS	10	Feb-99
2	Tokyu Land	Akasaka Tokyu Bldg.	Office	IBJ	Non-Group	NA	18.1	Sep-99
3	Mazda	Research facilities etc.	Sale Leaseback	Citi Bank	Foreign	NA	38.2	Sep-99
4	Sumitomo Light Metal Inds.	Factory	Sale Leaseback	NA	Group	NA	16	Sep-99
5	Nippon Tochi Tatemono	Kawasaki Branch office of DKB	Development	DKB Sec.	Group	NA	0.5	Jan-00
6	Izumiya	2 exsisting properties in Osaka-fu	Sale Leaseback	Sumitomo Trust	Non-Group	NA	NA	NA
						Total	82.8	

Source: J.P. Morgan Securities Inc.

Exhibit 6: Types of CMBS Arrangers

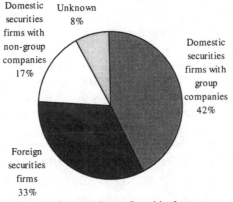

Source: J.P. Morgan Securities Inc.

These non-securitized loans add materially to the volume of non-recourse loans. If we add the Exhibit 5 transactions (¥82.8 billion) to the Exhibit 2 securitized transactions (¥370.8 billion), we get a total non-recourse loan figure of about ¥453.6 billion. The point to emphasize beside this impressive total is that this is a market that did not previously exist. In two of the Exhibit 5 transactions, the loans are not strictly non-recourse because the lender looked either to the borrower's broader credit (the Mazda deal) or to other additional collateral (the Daii-chi Life deal). In addition, some of the sales-leaseback transactions (Exhibit 5) provided off-balance-sheet treatment to originators. As discussed above, this benefit is likely to change.

The historical absence of a real estate finance market in Japan might also be expected to slow the evolution of CMBS in other areas. For example, in the U.S. early 1990s experience, large loans were the "trail blazers" in the early CMBS market. However, they were soon eclipsed by the growing market in conduit, or small loan securitization. In the latter development, mortgage bankers and mortgage brokers helped to bring together borrowers and lenders just as they had previously in the old private loan market. In Japan, this type of infrastructure has naturally been absent and there has essentially been no conduit-style lending so far.

WHO IS DOING THE DEALS?

A variety of domestic and foreign firms have completed CMBS deals. As indicated in Exhibit 2, many CMBS transactions were completed in Keiretsu (related group company) transactions, where the borrower and the securities firm are closely related. These transactions are labeled "Group" under the column "Arranger type." About half of the transactions involve non-related borrower and security firm entities (Exhibit 6). Of these latter transactions, the largest share

(33%) have been arranged by foreign securities firms with a smaller portion arranged by domestic securities firms (17%).

For example, as shown in Exhibit 7, Daiwa SBCM has done the largest amount of CMBS in Japan. These deals primarily involve Sumitomo group companies. In these transactions, CMBS was utilized as a new restructuring method under the leadership of Sumitomo Bank and Daiwa Securities. If the Keiretsu transactions are removed from the totals, the revised league table result, with much stronger showing by the foreign securities firms, is shown in Exhibit 8. In addition to the foreign securities firms shown in Exhibit 8, other firms are gearing up to do business.

Exhibit 7: Top 10 Underwriters of Japanese CMBS Including Keiretsu Transactions

Rank	Bank	JPY Billion	Number of deals
1	Daiwa SBCM	115.9	6
2	JP Morgan	48.0	3
3	Paribas	41.0	1
4	IBJ Sec.	35.5	2
5	MSDW	21.0	1
6	DKB Sec.	16.1	2
7	SakuraSecurities	15.3	1
8	NomuraSec	9.6	1
9	JardineFlemingSec.	6.6	1
10	NSSB	6.6	1
	Total	315.5	

Source: J.P. Morgan Securities Inc.

Exhibit 8: Underwriters of Japanese CMBS excluding Keiretsu transactions

Rank	Bank	JPY Billion	Number of deals
1	JP Morgan	48.0	3
2	Paribas	41.0	1
3	IBJ	24.0	1
4	MSDW	21.0	1
5	DKB	13.5	1
6	NomuraSecurities	9.6	1
7	Daiwa SBCM	9.3	1
8	JardineFleming	6.6	1
9	Nikko Salomon Smith Barney	6.6	1
10	Wako	5.1	1
		184.7	12

Source: J.P. Morgsn Securities Inc.

Exhibit 9: Rating Agency Activity in Japanese CMBS

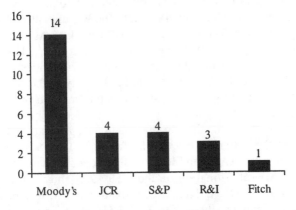

Source: J.P. Morgan Securities Inc.

Exhibit 10: Moody's Calculated LTV and DSCR Levels in the LM Capital Deal

Series	LTV %	DSCR*
A	39.8%	2.24
B	54.7%	1.63
C	69.6%	1.28
D	80.7%	1.11

* DSCR based on an assumed loan constant of 6.5%
Source: J.P. Morgan Securities Inc.

RATING AGENCY APPROACH TO CMBS

Of the 26 deals counted in Exhibit 2, Moody's has taken a preeminent role (Exhibit 9), rating 11 deals by itself and three deals jointly with other agencies. The domestic Japanese rating agencies, R&I and JCR, have rated three and four deals, respectively. Moody's has largely adopted the approach honed in the earlier U.S. experience with a tight focus on sustainable property cash flows, debt service coverage ratios (DSCR), and loan-to value ratio (LTV) measures to monitor balloon risk. Their approach also takes account of some differences in Japanese property markets, particularly the uncertainty surrounding valuation in a market with relatively few transactions (as of early 1999).

Exhibit 10 shows Moody's calculated DSCR and LTV ratios in the LM Capital Ltd. deal. The DSCR calculation employs an assumed debt service or irloan constantls of 6.5%. While the LM Capital deal is a floating-rate interim financing, Moody's gave no credit for cash flow generated through planned property sales. Thus, the deal was effectively rated as a permanent financing. Recently, in May 2000, as the borrower successfully sold condominiums as planned, the deal's pool balance was reduced by 48% and Moody's upgraded classes B (to Aaa from A2), C (to A2 from Baa3), and D (to Baa3 from B2). As a result of the property sales, the rating agency DSCR measure improved from 1.13x to 1.30x while Moody's stressed LTV measure improved from about 79% to 65%. The borrower's ability to sell the properties also testifies to the stability of the condominium market more generally. The LM Capital Ltd. deal is the first Japanese CMBS transaction to be upgraded by Moody's.

In general, it appears thus far that loan leverage has been conservative by the standards of the better-developed U.S. market. The 39.8% LTV (February 1999) calculated at the AAA bond level was achieved with a Moody's loan LTV of 80.7% and AAA subordination of about 50%. As shown in Exhibit 11 for a sample of deals, the AAA-equivalent LTV exhibited in LM Capital is generally representative of deals in 1999-2000. Both LTV and rating agency DSCR look conservative at the level of the bond classes, compared to U.S. standards, as well.

One result of the cautious leverage evident in Japan's CMBS market has been that the supply of below-investment-grade CMBS has been very limited. This has been the case because the rating agencies assign relatively few lower-rated bonds in deals where leverage in the underlying loan pool is prudent. In general, we expect the rating agencies to continue to require borrowers to supply substantial equity in their properties in order to qualify for lower-leverage securitizablecommercialmortgageloans. This will mean that, at least by U.S. standards, the supply of lower-rated bonds is likely to remain small. At the same time, there has been increased activity in the market for B-pieces in early 2000, reflecting marginal increases in both demand and supply (see discussion above).

EVOLUTION OF SPECIAL PURPOSE CORPORATIONS

The early CMBS transactions done in Japan employed an offshore special purpose corporation (SPC) structure. This structure is shown in Exhibit 12.[1] Following the passage of the September 1998 SPC Law, there has been increasing use of domestic SPCs in CMBS deals. The major problems cited with the 1998 law are (1) taxes on transfer profits are imposed on sellers when assets are transferred to the SPC, (2) limitations on the use of loans as a funding source, (3) an absence of bankruptcy remoteness, and (4) a lack of flexibility in managing and disposing of the underlying assets. A number of amendments to the 1998 law addressing these issues passed the Diet in Spring 2000.

---

[1] Japanese legal issues are discussed in International Structured Finance Special Report, "Japanese CMBS: 2000 Outlook," Moody's Investor Service (June 29, 2000).

Exhibit 11: Rating Agency Approach to CMBS

Settlement Date	Issuer	Underlying Assets	Rating Agency	AAA Rating Agency	AAA Other	AA Rating Agency	AA Other	A Rating Agency	A Other	BBB Rating Agency	BBB Other	Appraisal Corporation
03/26/1999	LM Capital	1,090 primarily residential units of Lions Mansion condominiums	Mdy	38.9%	37.0%	53.6%	50.9%	68.3%	64.9%	79.2%	75.3%	Mitsui Fudosan Investment Advisors, Inc.
03/30/1999	Someino S.C.	Itoyokado in Chiba	R&I	13.0%		29.6%		49.8%		65.0%		
04/27/1999	Network Capital	Sumitomo Bk's 20 branch office building	JCR			25.8%						REAC
06/30/1999	Sumquest Co. Limited	5 office bldgs. Located in central Tokyo and Kawasaki	Mdy			43.2%	35.4%	52.2%	42.8%	65.0%	53.3%	
08/01/1999	Azuchi Estate Funding Limited	Single Prperty	Mdy			48.1%		54.0%		61.0%		
09/26/1999	Star Capital	5 office building	Mdy			40.6%		56.3%				
09/30/1999	New Shopping Center Funding Corp.	10 General Marchandising Store	Mdy	35.8%	29.8%	42.9%	35.7%	49.9%	41.5%			Blake & Sanyu
02/25/2000	Amco Ventures Corp.	Japan Energy HQ Building	Mdy			44.5%	43.5%	56.8%	56.0%	66.0%	65.0%	JREI (Fudoken)
03/24/2000	Millenium Capital	5 properties(office building in Tokyo, Nagoya, Osaka)	Mdy									
03/28/2000	Red Lions Caital	12 properties	Mdy	36.6%		47.2%	46.2%	56.9%	55.8%	58.5%	57.4%	JREI (Fudoken)
03/29/2000	Kilimanjaro Limited	5 office buidings in Tokyo	Mdy, S&P			44.3%		53.9%		63.5%		
3/2000	NEST Funding Corp.	NEC Headquaters Building	Mdy	38.0%		46.0%		56.0%		67.0%		

Source: J.P. Morgan Securities Inc.

Exhibit 12: Offshore SPC Structure (LM Capital Deal)

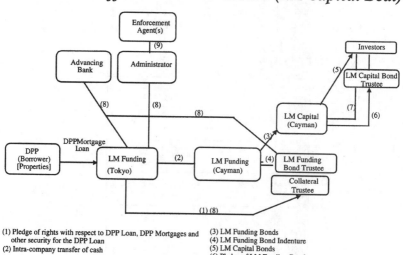

(1) Pledge of rights with respect to DPP Loan, DPP Mortgages and other security for the DPP Loan
(2) Intra-company transfer of cash
(3) LM Funding Bonds
(4) LM Funding Bond Indenture
(5) LM Capital Bonds
(6) Pledge of LM Funding Bonds
(7) LM Capital Bond Indenture
(8) Administration Agreement
(9) To be appointed in accordance with Administration Agreement

Source: J.P. Morgan Securities

Of our 26 CMBS deals, we had SPC information on 25 deals (see Appendix). Of these, 13 deals employed the domestic Japanese SPC (TMK) structure while 11 deals employed the offshore SPC structure. One deal employed a domestic stock corporation (Kabushiki Kaisha) and did not use an SPC. In addition, many deals utilizing the domestic SPC structure also employed an offshore SPC to further improve the bankruptcy remoteness. An example of this latter type of structure is shown in Exhibit 13 for the Red Lions Capital deal.

The point of bankruptcy remoteness is to ensure separation between the assets being securitized and the bankruptcy risk of the issuer or borrower. To ensure a perfected security interest, it is important to preclude the borrower or issuer SPC from filing voluntarily for "corporate reorganization." In this case, the enforceability of the perfected security interest will be controlled by the bankruptcy trustee. However, as noted in a Moody's report,[2] only a Kabushiki Kaisha (KK), a stock corporation, can file for a corporate reorganization. This risk is not so great for a Yugen Kaisha (YK) or the new domestic SPC (TMK).

In the Red Lions structure (Exhibit 13), the offshore bankruptcy-remote SPC is the sole shareholder of the common equity in the domestic SPC (Red Lions Capital TMK). Since it is difficult to limit shareholders' right to change directors in Japan and any director may petition a corporation into bankruptcy, the structure helps to mitigate bankruptcy-related risk.

---

[2] "Japanese CMBS: 2000 Outlook."

Exhibit 13: Domestic SPC Structure (TMK) with Offshore SPC (Red Lions Capital)

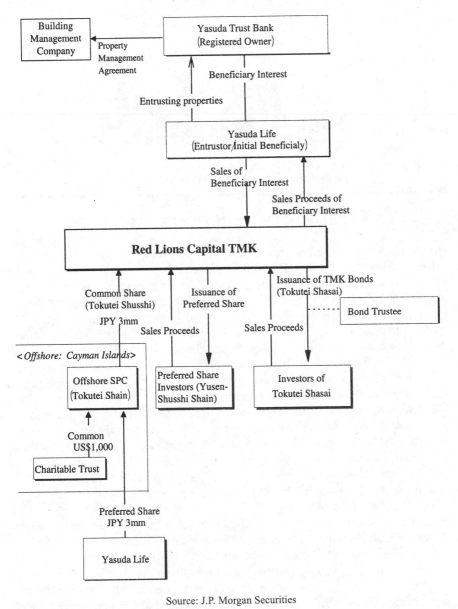

Source: J.P. Morgan Securities

Exhibit 14: Supply of New Office Space in Tokyo CBD Million Sq. Ft.

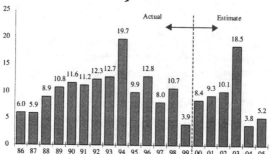

Note: New buildings with more than 107,642 ft sq for office usage in Tokyo CBD
Source: Mori Building, Mitsui Fudosan

PROPERTY MARKETS IN JAPAN

High-quality property markets in every major segment continue to see rents and prices stabilize or increase. By contrast, raw land prices remain weak and are hugely below peak levels in the late 1980s. In our view, modern properties in each property segment enjoy a bullish outlook for rent and property price stability or modest appreciation. However, older, poorly positioned properties configured on inadequate floor plates or with outdated designs face the prospect of more competition from newly constructed modern properties.

To some extent, the difference in performance between modern and older properties was also present in the early recovery U.S. real estate experience. In the U.S. case, the sharp depression in property rents at the cyclical bottom increased obsolescence and property irretirementslc out of the older stock of properties. As a result, the nominal vacancy rate overstated the amount of total space available. In Japan's case, we believe that differentials (in quality and cash flow) between class A and class C properties are somewhat sharper than in the U.S. In Japan, new construction has resurfaced, following depressed building activity in 1993-1997 (Exhibit 14). This construction activity reflects higher replacement demand for older properties than in the U.S. experience. Steady increases in the demand for space are being matched by newly developed properties rather than reductions in vacancies on the oldest real estate.

Japan has had a legacy of highly inefficient land use patterns. This has been encouraged by policies favoring agricultural land uses as well as a variety of restrictions and penalties on the transfer of land ownership. All of this contributed to an artificial scarcity of undeveloped land that helped to drive up its price during the ihbubblele years. Low land prices in mid-2000 combined with the prospect of more "laissez faire" land use policies point to many opportunities to develop lower cost property locations. These include faster growth in property markets at the edge of Tokyo and movement from higher cost to lower cost urban centers. While these types of directions for new development will be familiar to U.S. investors, they are very new for Japan. Nonetheless, they are directions that are greatly encouraged by the dramatic decline and continuing softness in undeveloped land values.

In our view, this suggests that properties in each of the major segments with modern amenities are comparable in risk to class A properties in the United States (or perhaps even lower risk) while older inefficient class C properties are more risky. In each of the major property segments, we favor more modern properties as well as locations that may benefit from possible shifts in land use patterns driven by the low price of undeveloped land. Put somewhat differently, we think commercial mortgage underwriting guidelines should be more stringent for what we are calling class B and class C properties. With genuine real estate underwriting at such an early point in Japan, we are in effect highlighting some of the risk criteria underwriters and investors need to consider. The new J-REIT legislation before the Diet offers the prospect that newly organized public real estate companies will be leaders (and mortgage borrowers) in what is potentially a new phase for Japanese real estate.

PROPERTY MARKETS AND CMBS DEVELOPMENT FINANCING

In the U.S. real estate market bottom of the early 1990s, demand for development financing was minimal and bank willingness to supply development lending easily supplied the limited demand. In Japan, the situation is the opposite. With the balance sheets of large financial intermediaries generally weak and demand for development financing strong, development financing has spilled over into the CMBS market. Three of the deals listed in Exhibit 2 involve development.

In one recent deal, Mitsui Fudosan Co., the largest real estate company in Japan, is securitizing eight condominium properties through Millennium Residential TMK, an SPC registered under the domestic SPC law. Like the Red Lions deal discussed above, the ordinary shares of the domestic SPC are solely owned by a bankruptcy-remote Cayman Island SPC.

In one sense, the Mitsui deal is similar to the LM Capital Ltd. deal in that it provides interim financing to a condominium developer while the individual units are being sold to households. However, the uniqueness of the deal is that it securitizes development projects both before and after construction authorization. In order to avoid project completion risk, Mitsui Fudosan is teaming up with Tokio Marine and Fire Insurance Corporation (Aa1/AAA), which will provide a performance bond. Tokio Marine's guarantee relates solely to project completion risk. The guarantee does not iowrapl? the principal and interest cash flows of the CMBS. If completed properties are sold at prices representing a revenue shortfall, CMBS investors bear this risk.

Moodys' analysis of the deal utilizes a stress scenario under which 40% of the properties are assumed to be sold at an early point prior to completion of construction but at a discount of 15%. Of the remaining property sales, 30% are assumed to take place at the end of construction at a 30% discount. The final 30% of the properties are assumed to be sold at the CMBS legal maturity date at a 50% discount. Additional protection for investors comes in the form of required property sales at severe discounts if Mitsui's property sales revenues fall below critical targets in mid-2001.

We expect continued evolution in development financing within CMBS. The presence of such financing within CMBS reflects some important differences in Japan's bottoming property markets and financing markets, relative to the U.S. early1990sexperience.

RELATIVE VALUE AND OUTLOOK

The cyclical parallels in property markets and financial systems in the 1990s U.S. and Japan in 2000 are striking. Rebounding property markets combined with important changes to the legal system and financial markets have all been stimulants to the rapidly expanding market in CMBS.

The growth of a CMBS market is all the more impressive, given the historical absence of real-estate-based finance and less developed capital markets. But things are changing fast and we look for the rapid expansion of CMBS to continue.

Property market fundamentals on more modern properties look very solid at the bottom of Japan's real estate cycle, just as they did several years earlier in the U.S. Compared to the huge savings pool of Japanese investors, CMBS face only limited competition from other capital markets instruments. CMBS deals in mid-2000 have seen AAA bonds priced at about 30 bps over the yen swap curve. This represents a significant tightening from pricing in the LM Capital Ltd. deal in February 1999. The AAA bonds in the latter floating-rate deal priced at a spread 60 bps over yen-Libor. CMBS spreads as of mid-2000 offer significant premiums to both ABS and corporate bond spreads, which are shown on a swap-adjusted basis in Exhibit 15. The combination of wide spreads and solid fundamentals is compelling.

Sharp declines in land values point to incentives for redirecting future development in lower cost directions and possibly repositioning much of Japan's older property markets. If land is not nearly as scarce as it appeared in the inbubblels real estate years, but is in fact much cheaper, it points to possible development of modern office properties in the suburban areas at the fringe of urban centers. If prohibitive transfer taxes no longer force tiny urban land parcels to remain uneconomically subdivided, such land parcels can possibly be assembled for the construction of larger modern office and other properties. Assuming that land-use policy continues to move in the laissez-faire direction, there is a case for rebuilding a much more modern Japan. It's an exciting thought and one in which CMBS is poised to play a major role.

Exhibit 15: Recent 5-Year Japanese CMBS versus 2-Year AAA ABS and Aa2 Corporates (All Swapped to Yen LIBOR)

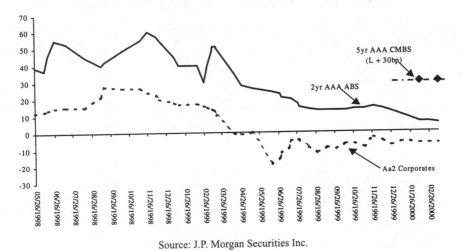

Source: J.P. Morgan Securities Inc.

APPENDIX A

JAPANESE CMBS MARKET PARTICIPANTS

Deal No.	Issuer	Original RE Owner	New RE owner
1	Kilimanjaro Limited	Itochu Corp	Itochu Corp
2	Red Lions Capital	Yasuda Life	Yasuda Life
3	Millenium Capital	Daiichi Life	Daiichi Life
4	Forester SPC	Jusco	Century Leasing system
5	Prime Quest	Sumitomo Realty	N/A
6	M's Fort Co., Ltd.	Mori Building Co.	Mori Bldg
7	NEST Funding Corp.	NEC	N/A
8	Urbanity Capital TMK	Nippon Life	N/A
9	Millenium Residential SPC Co., Ltd.	Mitsui Fudosan	
10	Kyodo Jutaku Securitization SPC	Starts Securities	Stars
11	Amco Ventures Corp.	Mitsui Fudosa IG	AIG&Mitsui Fudosan
12	MM Property Funding	Morinaga & Co.	Morinaga Milk Inds.
13	Ohmori Kaigan SPC	Asahi Brewery	
14	Feris K.K.	Hankyu Realty	N/A
15	Neopas TMK	Nippon Tochi Tatemono	
16	International Credit Recovery Japan One Ltd.	Morgan Stanley REF	Morgan Stanley REF
17	Pacific Century Residential One	11 companies	N/A
18	Star Capital	Nippon Life	Nippon Life Insurance
19	New Shopping Center Funding Corp	Mycal Corp.	Unknown Investor
20	N/A	Mitsui Zosen	Mitsui Zasen
21	Azuchi Estate Funding Limited	Unitika Ltd.	N/A
22	Takanawa Apartment SPC	Tokyo Tatemono Co., Ltd.	Tokyo Tatemono
23	Sumquest Co. Limited	Sumitomo Realty	Sumitomo Realty
24	Network Capital	Sumitomo Bank	N/A
25	Someino S.C.	Tokyu Land	Tokyu Land
26	LM Capital	Daikyo	Morgan Stanley REF

APPENDIX A (CONTINUED)

Deal No.	Underlying Assets	Arranger
1	5 office buildings in Tokyo	NSSB
2	12 properties	JP Morgan
3	5 office building in Tokyo, Nagoya, Osaka	IBJ Sec.
4	5 shopping centers to be completed by Jan,2001	N/A
5	Shinjuku Sumitomo Bldg.	Daiwa SBCM
6	2 of 3 Ark Hills residential buildings	IBJ Securities
7	NEC Headquarters Building	Daiwa SBCM
8	5 office buildings in Tokyo and Osaka	Daiwa SBCM
9	8 condominiums in Tokyo before construction	Sakura Securities
10	One room apartments	Starts Co.
11	Japan Energy HQ Building	JP Morgan Sec.
12	Morinaga Headquarters Building.	DKB Sec.
13	Factory in Omori	Daiwa SBCM
14	Shin Hankyu Building and land for sales	N/A
15	DKB Kawasaki branch	DKB Sec
16	Bulk of NPL and hard asset	MSDW
17	Condominiums	Jardine Fleming Sec.
18	5 office buildings	Nomura Sec
19	10 General Marchandising Store	Paribas
20	Warehouse in Osaka	Sakura Bank
21	Office building in Osaka	N/A
22	Eight stroy single apartment	Fuji Bank
23	5 office buildings in Tokyo and Kawasaki	Daiwa SBCM/IBJ Sec.
24	Sumitomo Bk's 20 branch office	Daiwa SBCM
25	Itoyokado in Chiba	Wako Securities
26	1,090 residential units of condominiums	JP Morgan

Source: J.P. Morgan Securities Inc.

APPENDIX B

JAPANESE CMBS DEALS

Settlement Date	Issuer	Originator/ Owner	Lead Manager	Series	Size CCY (MM)	Scheduled Maturity	Maturity Type	Mdy (current)	S&P	Fitch	Japanese Rating R (R& I) J (JCR)
3/26/99	LM Capital	MSREF	JP Morgan	A	3,190	4	pass-through	Aaa			
				B	1,206	4	pass-through	A2 (Aaa)			
				C	1,206	4	pass-through	Baa3 (A2)			
				D	898	4	pass-through	B2 (Baa3)			
				X	6,500			N R			
3/30/99	Someino S. C.	Tokyu Land	Wako Securities	A	700	5	Amortization				AAA (R)
				B	900	5	Bullet				AA-(R)
				C	1,700	5	Bullet				
				D	1,000	5	Bullet				
				E	800	5	Bullet				
4/27/99	Network Capital	Sumitomo Bank	Daiwa SBCM	A	7,000	5	Bullet				AA-(J)
				B	6,500	5	Bullet				A-(J)
6/30/99	Sumquest Co. Limited	Sumitomo Realty	Daiwa SBCM/IBJ Sec.	A	16,300	5	Bullet	Aa2			
				B	3,400	5	Bullet	A2			
				C	4,800	5	Bullet	Baa3			
6/29/99	Takanawa Apartment SPC	Tokyo Tatemono Co., Ltd.	Fuji Bank (Arranger)/ Fuji Sec (UW)	A	500	5	Bullet	A			
				B	2,000	5	Bullet	A			
				C	500	5	Bullet	BBB			
8/16/99	Azuchi Estate Funding Limited			A	11,400		Bullet	A2			
				B	1,700		Bullet	Baa2			
				C	5,250		Bullet	NR			
Aug-99		Mitsui Zosen	Sakura Bank	A	2,500	5	Amortization				A (J)
				B	1,100	5	Bullet				
9/26/99	Star Capital	Nippon Life		A	8,200	7	Bullet	Aa2			
				B	1,400		Bullet	A2			
9/30/99	New Shopping Center Funding Corp	Mycal Corp.	Paribas		41,000	5	Bullet	Aa1			
10/29/99	Pacific Century Residential One	11 companies	Jardine Fleming Sec.	A	4,925		Bullet				
				B	1,700		Bullet				
				C							

APPENDIX B (CONTINUED)

Coupon Type	Coupon	Pmt. Freq.	LTV	Stressed DSCR (6.5%)	Form	Underlying Assets	Trust	Note Trustee	SPC	Transaction Type
Float	1mo YL +60bp	Month	38.9	2.24	Euro/144A	residential units of Lions Mansion condominiums		LaSalle National Bank	Cayman SPC	Acquisition Finance
	1mo YL +150 bp	Month	53.6	1.63		Apartment				
	1mo YL +300 bp	Month	68.3	1.28						
	1mo YL + 312.75	Month	79.2	1.11						
Fixed	1.80%		13.0		Domestic Private	Itoyokado in Chiba	Mitsui Trust	Sakura Bank	Japanese SPC law	Leveraged Finance
	2.50%		29.6			Retail				
Fixed	1.90%	Semi	25.8		Domestic Private	Sumitomo Bk's 20 branch office building	Sumitomo Trust	Sumitomo Trust	Japanese SPC law	Sale Leaseback
	2.50%		49.8							
Fixed	2.09%	Semi	43.2	2.18	Domestic Public	5 office buildings located in central Tokyo and Kawasaki	Sumitomo Trust	Sumitomo Bank	Cayman SPC	Leveraged Finance
	2.59%		52.2	1.81						
	3.54%		65	1.45						
Fixed	1.75%	Semi			Domestic Private	Eight stroy single apartment		Fuji Bank	Japanese SPC law	Leveraged Finance
	2.74%									
	3.69%									
Fixed	2.35%		54	1.78		Office building in Osaka	Toyo Trust	Sanwa Bank	Cayman SPC	Acquisition Finance
	3.15%		61	1.55						
						Warehouse in Osaka				Sale Leaseback
			48.1	2.11	Domestic Private	5 office buildings	Toyo Trust		Japanese SPC law	Leveraged Finance
			56.3	1.8	Domestic Private					
Fixed	2.00%		40.6	2.61	Domestic Public	10 Retail Stores	Yasuda Trust		Cayman SPC	Sale Leaseback
Fixed	3.55-3.8%	Semi			Domestic Private	Condominiums	Yasuda Trust	Yasude Trust	Japanese SPC Law	Leveraged Finance
	5.0 - 5.5%				Domestic Public	Apartment				

APPENDIX B (CONTINUED)

Settlement Date	Issuer	Originator/ Owner	Lead Manager	Series	Size CCY (MM)	Scheduled Maturity	Maturity Type	Mdy (current)	S&P	Fitch	Japanese Rating R (R& I) J (JCR)
12/9/99	International Credit Recovery Japan One Ltd.	Morgan Stanley REF	MSDW	A	13,500	1	fast pay	Aaa	AAA	AAA	
				B	3,500	1		Aa2	AA	AA	
				C	2,200	1.5		A2	A	A	
				D	1,800	1.5		Baa2	BBB	BBB	
Jan-00	Neopas TMK	Nippon Tochi Tatemono	DKB Sec (Sales Agent)	A	500						
				B	1,050						
				C	1,050						
2/10/00	Ohmori Kaigan SPC	Asahi Brewery	Daiwa SBCM	A	5,500		Bullet				AA (J)
				B	3,000		Bullet				A (J)
				C	3,500		Bullet				BBB (J)
2/21/00	MM Property Funding	Morinaga & Co.	DKB Sec.(Lead)/ BOTM/MTB /Nikko Salomon Sec.	A	3,500	5	Amortization				AA+ (R)
				B	5,000	5	Bullet				AA (R)
				C	2,500	5	Bullet				A (R)
				D	2,500	5	Bullet				BBB (R)
2/25/00	Amco Ventures Corp.	Mitsui Fudosan & AIG	JP Morgan Sec.	A	22,000	5	Bullet	Aaa			
				B	4,400	5	Bullet	Aa2			
				C	4,300	5	Bullet	A2			
2/25/00	NEST Funding Corp.	NEC	Daiwa SBCM (Lead)/ MSDW/ NSSB	A	29,200	5	Bullet	Aaa			
				B	6,100	5	Bullet	Aa2			
				C	7,700	5	Bullet	A2			
				D	8,400	5	Bullet	Baa2			
Feb-00	Feris K. K.	Hankyu Realty									
3/1/00	Prime Quest	Sumitomo Realty	Daiwa SBCM	A	5,148			(P) Aa			AA(J)
				B				(P) A			A(J)
				C				(P) Baa3			BBB(J)
3/7/00	Kyodo Jutaku Securitization SPC	Starts Securities	Starts Co.	A	190		Bullet				
				Pref. Share	61						
3/17/00	Millenium Residential Special Purpose Company Co., Ltd.	Mitsui Fudosan	Sakura Sec.	A	9,500	1.25	Bullet	Aaa			
				B	1,000	1.25	Bullet	Aa2			
				C	1,200			NR			

APPENDIX B (CONTINUED)

Coupon Type	Coupon	Pmt. Freq.	LTV	Stressed DSCR (6.5%)	Form	Underlying Assets	Trust	Note Trustee	SPC	Transaction Type
Float	L+ 35	Quart.				356 NPLs collateralized by 605 real estate assets and 95 fee assets.			Cayman SPC	Acquisition Finance
	L+ 45	Quart.								
	L+ 90	Quart.								
	L+ 200	Quart.			Domestic Private	DKB Kawasaki branch Office			Japanese SPC law	Development
		Semi			Domestic Private	Factory in Omori	Sumitomo Trust	Sumitomo Bank	Japanese SPC law	Development
Fixed	1.75%	Semi			Domestic Private	Morinaga Headquarters Building. More than 20 tenants. Major ones are Morinaga & NEC	Mitsubishi Trust	DKB	Cayman SPC	Sale Leaseback
	1.97%									
	2.73%					Office				
	3.07%									
Fixed	1.63%	Semi	35.8	2.39	Domestic Private	Japan Energy HQ Building	Credit Suisse Trust	Chase Manhattan Bank	Cayman SPC	Acquisition Finance
	1.83%		42.9	1.99		Office				
	2.13%		49.9	1.71						
Fixed	1.64%		38	2.35	Domestic Private	NEC Headquarters Building (JPY 90bio)	Sumitomo Trust		Cayman SPC	Sale Leaseback
	1.84%		46	1.94						
	2.19%		56	1.59						
	2.84%		67	1.33		Office				
					Domestic Private	Shin Hankyu Building(8.4bio) and land for sales(2bio)			K. K.	Sale Leaseback
						Office				
					Domestic Private	Shinjuku Sumitomo Bldg.	Sumitomo Trust		Cayman SPC	Leveraged Finance
						Office				
Fixed	3.50%	Semi			Domestic Public	one room apartments in Chiba	Daiwa Bank	Daiwa Bank	Japanese SPC law	Leveraged Finance
						Apartment				
Fixed	0.56%				Domestic Private	8 condominiums (480 rooms) in Tokyo area before construction	Sakura Bank		Japanese SPC law	Development
	0.74%					Apartment				

APPENDIX B (CONTINUED)

Settlement Date	Issuer	Originator/ Owner	Lead Manager	Series	Size CCY (MM)	Scheduled Maturity	Maturity Type	Mdy (current)	S&P	Fitch	Japanese Rating R (R& I) J (JCR)
3/17/00	Urbanity Capital TMK	Nippon Life	Daiwa SBCM	A	7,800	5		Aa2			
				B	1,500	5		A2			
3/24/00	Millenium Capital	Daiichi Life	IBJ Sec.	A	7,700	5		Aa2			
				B	2,200	5		A2			
				C	1,600	5		Baa2			
3/28/00	Red Lions Capital	Yasuda Life	JP Morgan (Sales Agent)	A	8,700	5	Amortization	Aa2			
				B	1,800	5	Bullet	A2			
				C	300	5	Bullet	Baa1			
3/28/00	M's Fort Co., Ltd.	Mori Building Co.	IBJ Sec.	A	2,400	7	Amortization		AAA		
				B	12,100	7	Bullet		AAA		
				C	3,100	7	Bullet		AA		
				D	3,200	7	Bullet		A		
				E	3,200	7	Bullet		BBB		
3/29/00	Kilimanjaro Limited	Itochu Corp	NSSB	A	3,800	5		Aaa	AAA		
				B	800	5		Aa2	AA		
				C	1,000	5		A2	A		
				D	1,000	5		Baa2	BBB		
Mar-00	Forester SPC	Jusco			up to 28.5 billion						a-1(R)

APPENDIX B (CONTINUED)

Coupon Type	Coupon	Pmt. Freq.	LTV	Stressed DSCR (6.5%)	Form	Underlying Assets	Trust	Note Trustee	SPC	Transaction Type
			47.0	2.07	Domestic Private	5 office buildings in Tokyo and Osaka	Toyo Trust		Japanese SPC law	Leveraged Finance
			56.0	1.74		17.694bln				
Fixed			44.5	2.08	Domestic Private	5 properties (office building in Tokyo, Nagoya, Osaka)	Sumitomo Trust	IBJ	Japanese SPC law	Leveraged Finance
			56.8	1.69		60 tenants (top 3 34.5%, top 10 55.5%)				
			66.0	1.45		Office				
Fixed	2.15%	Semi	47.2	2.24	Domestic Private	12 properties	Yasuda Trust	Fuji Bank	Japanese SPC law	Leveraged Finance
	2.45%		56.9	1.85						
	2.95%		58.5	1.79		Office				
Fixed	1.48%	Semi			Domestic Public	2 of 3 Ark Hills residential buildings	Sumitomo Trust	Sakura Bank	Cayman SPC	Leveraged Finance
	2.06%									
	2.28%					Apartment				
	2.63%									
	3.28%									
Fixed	1.94%		36.6	2.63	Domestic Private	5 office buildings in Tokyo	Citi Trust		Cayman SPC	Leveraged Finance
	2.14%		44.3	2.12						
	2.54%		53.9	1.77		Office				
	3.94%		63.5	1.53						
						5 shopping centers in Miyagi, Yamagata, Mie and Hokkaido to be completed by Jan, 2001			Japanese SPC law	Sale Leaseback

Appendix B lists all CMBS transactions known to us that have been completed to date. As in any new market, the availability of information on new deals is generally poor due to the private nature of the transactions. This table represents our best effort at synthesizing this information into a usable form. While we have made every attempt to ensure its accuracy, we cannot guarantee this.

Certain terms have definitions that differ from their use in the U.S. securities market. In the column "Maturity Type," "pass-though" is used to describe a deal whose paydowns come from the sale of the underlying assets, not a pro-rata interest in those assets, as the term is used in the residential MBS market in the United States. "Amortization" in the same column describes a class of the deal that has its principal balance decrease over time from the amortization of the underlying pool.

Index